Laura Ahonen

Constructing Authorship in Popular Music

Laura Ahonen

Constructing Authorship in Popular Music

Artists, Media and Stardom

VDM Verlag Dr. Müller

Impressum/Imprint (nur für Deutschland/ only for Germany)

Bibliografische Information der Deutschen Nationalbibliothek: Die Deutsche Nationalbibliothek verzeichnet diese Publikation in der Deutschen Nationalbibliografie; detaillierte bibliografische Daten sind im Internet über http://dnb.d-nb.de abrufbar.

Coverbild: www.purestockx.com

Verlag: VDM Verlag Dr. Müller Aktiengesellschaft & Co. KG
Dudweiler Landstr. 125 a, 66123 Saarbrücken, Deutschland
Telefon +49 681 9100-698, Telefax +49 681 9100-988, Email: info@vdm-verlag.de
Zugl.: Helsinki, University of Helsinki, Diss., 2007

Herstellung in Deutschland:
Schaltungsdienst Lange o.H.G., Zehrensdorfer Str. 11, D-12277 Berlin
Books on Demand GmbH, Gutenbergring 53, D-22848 Norderstedt
Reha GmbH, Dudweiler Landstr. 99, D- 66123 Saarbrücken
ISBN: 978-3-639-09038-3

Imprint (only for USA, GB)

Bibliographic information published by the Deutsche Nationalbibliothek: The Deutsche Nationalbibliothek lists this publication in the Deutsche Nationalbibliografie; detailed bibliographic data are available in the Internet at http://dnb.d-nb.de.

Cover image: www.purestockx.com

Publisher:
VDM Verlag Dr. Müller Aktiengesellschaft & Co. KG
Dudweiler Landstr. 125 a, 66123 Saarbrücken, Germany
Phone +49 681 9100-698, Fax +49 681 9100-988, Email: info@vdm-verlag.de

Produced in USA and UK by:
Lightning Source Inc., 1246 Heil Quaker Blvd., La Vergne, TN 37086, USA
Lightning Source UK Ltd., Chapter House, Pitfield, Kiln Farm, Milton Keynes, MK11 3LW, GB
BookSurge, 7290 B. Investment Drive, North Charleston, SC 29418, USA
ISBN: 978-3-639-09038-3

Contents

Acknowledgements

In the same way as musical authors are dependent on the help of other music makers, I am no less indebted to many people, without whose assistance and support this work would never have been completed.

This book was written as a part of my doctoral studies of musicology undertaken at the University of Helsinki, Finland, between 2004 and 2007. The project was started in 2004 as I got the opportunity to work as a member of the Music and Media Project funded by the Academy of Finland (project No. 1206444).

Professor Erkki Pekkilä, Dr Janne Mäkelä, Proferssor Eero Tarasti and Alfonso Padilla deserve acknowledgements for their advice and support. I should also express my gratitude to Professors Anahid Kassabian and Helmi Järviluoma-Mäkelä for their willingness to get involved with my work. I also want to thank Dr Richard Littlefield for revising the language of my manuscript and Mrs Tiina Kaarela for the help with the layout.

In addition to the Academy of Finland, I am grateful to The Finnish Cultural Foundation and the Niilo Helander Foundation for providing me with financial assistance. At the time of my dissertation in November 2007, my PhD was published by the Finnish Society for Ethnomusicology. It was then known by the title: *Mediated music makers. Constructing author images in popular music.* I am also deeply thankful for VDM Verlag for publishing my work in their publication series.

It may be stating the obvious, but it is the support of my family and friends that has kept the whole process alive. Warm and special thanks go to my sister Hanna, with whom I have shared many soundtracks of my life. The person whose name I have saved for last, is Juuso – my tower of strength – who has given me love, hope and support through every stage of this project.

In the heart of Helsinki, Finland
October 2008

Laura Ahonen
(laura.e.ahonen@gmail.com)

INTRODUCTION –
UNRAVELLING MUSICAL AUTHORSHIP

Background –
On authorship in popular music

All musical works have something in common: they are all made by someone. There-fore, it should be possible to locate at least one author for all musical texts. When thinking back on the history of popular music, we may notice that musical works are typically personified with their performers (see e.g. Brackett 2000: 14–15; Frith 1983: 134–135). Even today, authors are used as categories through which musical works are evaluated, marketed and classified. In addition to the link between authors and their works, the notion of authorship has also affected the ways in which musical practices have been shaped and developed (Straw 1999: 201; Wall 2003: 153). The issue of authorship is also essential in explaining the hierarchical and evaluative man-ner of categorizing artists and their works. In fact, authorship and notions connected with it, such as authenticity, creativity and originality, are often used in justifying one tradition of music at the expense of some other (Keightley 2001: 134; Shuker 1994: 111–114). Against this background, we may understand that the functioning of popu-lar music culture, too, is largely based on authors and their works. In order to shed light on practices of popular music, this study approaches the question of musical au-thorship by examining the author images of a selected group of popular music artists, their areas of authorial responsibility and practices of music making – not forgetting the roles of the media and other parties operating within the field.

The issue of authorship as a subject of research may, at first, seem hard to grasp. In my view, authorship has such a central role in every single area of popular music – be it making, marketing or evaluating artists and their works – that the underlying question, i.e. that of authorship, is quite often regarded as a self-explanatory fact. Until recently, popular music studies have typically treated authorship as just that: authorship is something that exists, but it receives no special attention, at least not from a theoretical or philosophical point of view. By contrast, in literary theory and film studies the question of authorship has been a relevant subject of examination for a longer period of time (see e.g. Eagleton 1983: 127–151; Heat 1981; Lapsley et al. 1988: 105–128; Phillips 1999). As stated by musicologist Alastair Williams (2001: 36–37), music may not be as dependent on the author's signature as are some other forms of art, but the issue of authorship still affects the ways in which music is valued and examined. It seems peculiar, then, to assume that authorship within the context of popular music would be any less interesting or any less relevant a subject of research than it is in the aforementioned fields.

Along with the academic study of popular music and the widespread understanding of the cultural significance of popular culture in general, there also seems to be a growing demand for studies centered on the question of authorship in the context of popular-music culture. Certain of such musicological writings have served as important points of departure for my own study; namely, those by Simon Frith (esp. the chapter "Technology and Authority" in *Performing Rites* 1996: 226–245), Jason Toynbee (*Making Popular Music: Musicians, Creativity and Institutions* 2000), Will Straw (esp. the chapter "Authorship" in *Key Terms in Popular Music and Culture* 1999: 199–208), and Roy Shuker (*Understanding Popular Music* 1994). Besides having widened the field of musicological research in general (see e.g. Houni et al. 2005: 11, 13–14; Kärjä 2005: 54), feminist criticism has also penetrated into traditional, masculine constructions of authorship, which leave no creative role for women (Herman 2006: 24). Recent writings from the side of cultural studies do not limit themselves just to describing the actual process of music making; rather, they go on to question some earlier readings of (Western art) music history, such as the aesthetics of autonomy (with its separation of musical works from their social and cultural surroundings) and the "great composer history", with its patriarchal, ethnocentric and otherwise biased and constricted interpretations (see e.g. Leppänen et al. 2003; Middleton 2003: 2–3; Scott 1998: 137–139).

In line with such writings, my study is directed toward critical enquiry of ideas about musical authorship and their origins, not toward ideas surrounding a single, originating author. It is the refusal not to view works of popular music as bounded, originary texts created by a single *auteur* (but rather in terms of their intertextual connections, production processes and reception contexts) which Richard Middleton (2000: 8–9) calls "one of the strongest contributions of the cultural studies tradition" to popular music research. Another challenge for popular music studies is to come up with definitions of authorship that would apply especially to ways of making popular music, in contrast to other traditions of authoring cultural works. While acknowledging the fact that each art form has its typical structures of authorship, we should at the same time take note of the similarities that exist between different modes of cultural production. In this respect, theories of cinematic and literary authorship (see e.g. Eagleton 1983: 127–151; Lapsley et al. 1988: 105–128; Phillips 1999) offer interesting points of departure for my own enquiries in this study.

Another, more practical explanation for the growing interest in musical authorship is the fact that the making of popular music has become more professionalized (Toynbee 2000: 93; see also Negus 2001: 33–49; Shuker 1994: 99–111; Wall 2003).

The increased availability of music technology and new channels of mu
tion, including websites like MySpace and YouTube as well as file-shari
such as Napster, Kazaa and Limewire, have also raised new questions relating to
musical authorship (Bennett et al. 2006: 4; Connell et al. 2003: 263–267; McLeod
2005: 83). The idea of authorship of course plays a central role in copyright law, such
that the musical text is understood as the property of its author (Théberge 2004). As a
result, the creative input of each artist is put into a form that is quantifiable and that is
separable from the contributions of other writers, performers and musicians. Also, the
authorial roles of music makers have become more specified (Brackett 1999: 127; Des
Pres et al. 2000: 87–149; Shuker 1994: 99–100). Then again, it may be assumed that
the centering of attention on practical aspects of music making might detract from the
glamour that is traditionally linked with popular music culture and stardom. Similarly,
revelation of the different stages of author-image construction may take something
away from the initial mystique or allure of popular music practices. In a way, one goal
of this study is to build up an alternative image of musical authorship, though my aim
is to make it as diverse as possible. The purpose of the study is, therefore, to present
a versatile look at the construction of author images as it occurs in practices of music
making, while also taking into account the role of media, the music industry, and other
parties operating within the sphere of popular music culture.

Underlying themes and leading ideas – The author and the work

One reason for the limited amount of attention paid to musical authorship lies in the
problem of defining the term. Typically, the idea of authorship is understood through
the notions of *author* and *work*. That is, the creation of a work is thought to require
an author, while the notion of author suggests that there exists a work that the author
has created (Murray 1989: 6–7). According to Martha Woodmansee (1994a: 35) who
has studied issues of authorship and copyright law, the idea of author traditionally
refers to "an individual who is solely responsible – and thus deserving of credit – for
the production of a unique, original work". A similar definition has been given by
literary theorist Nancy Spivey (1997: 213): "An author is known for his or her work,
and texts can be attributed to a particular author". It is the permanency of the author's
work what also makes it possible to study the author's creations in different times and
places (Bosma 1996). The sense of stability produced by the work makes the author
appear a permanent figure also in popular music.

Even though there are similarities between the various modes of cultural production, the definitions given above seem more applicable to the visual arts than to popu-

lar music.[1] In the context of popular music, to understand authorship as a one-to-one relation between the author and his/her work often comes across as too simplistic, since there are no specific guidelines for making popular music in the first place, and since the musical backgrounds of popular music artists vary a great deal (Brackett 1999: 127; Des Pres et al. 2000: 87–149). Another essential point here is the fact that popular music is usually produced by the joint effort of a group, not by individuals (Brackett 2000: 14–17; Shuker 1994: 99–111). The making of popular music could in this sense be compared to the making of cinema: both art forms – cinema and popular music – are typically authored by several people who together share authorial responsibility for the work in progress (Gracyk 1996: 95; Livingston 1997: 132). That is to say, popular music, like film, is usually made *collectively*. That does not mean, however, that belief in single authorship might not still exist.

Besides linking the notion of authorship to a group of exceptional individuals with creative capabilities, it is a question of an ideological product and a social system (Foucault 1979, 159; Hartley 2002: 14). In this respect, it is impossible to separate authorship from the available resources and the ability to use them (Hartley 2002: 14–15; see also Toynbee 2003). Both the author and the work are, as Tim Anderson (2006: 298) puts it, "involved in political formations, economic strategies, social programs, moments of history, aesthetic movements, and individual desires". Whether or not an author can be found, the meanings given to each work are, thus, dependent on its circulation and uses, which vary in different times and places. This fluidity of meanings also applies for authors and their public personas. However, while a work can be separated from its author's signature (Barthes 1979: 78; see also Bennett 2005: 11), authors are still often treated as narrative ploys incorporated into the process of constructing meaning (Barthes 1990: 142–143; Foucault 1979: 147–148; Hartley 2002: 15). Although the author's status as the owner of his/her work may be put in question, it by no means follows that the author – be it a functional principle, a social space or an ideological notion – would not play a significant role in the various modes of cultural production, including popular music. Instead, by taking into account the poststructuralist critique[2] of authorship and by recognizing the historical and social conditions of music making, we may extend our ways of defining musical authorship (see also Houni et al. 2005: 11–12). In this study, then, popular music authorship is defined as a socially and historically constructed category; this definition urges us to

[1]   The idea of individual authorship applies to visual arts in the case of traditional painting, such as portraits. Nonetheless, when thinking of the modern works of visual arts, including media and video installations, there seems to be more similarities with the collective process of making popular music and film. Sculptors, too, may carry out their visions with the help of craftsmen, though credit for the resulting artifact(s) is still given to the public artist. The same may be said of literary authorship: it is worth remembering that, as a rule, editors, illustrators and publishers have their own share in the final outcome.

[2]   Poststructuralist theories on the "death of the author", as advanced by Roland Barthes and Michel Foucault, are discussed in chapter 7.

construe authorship as more than a relation between an author and his/her work. expanded definition of authorship allows for more precision in discussions of who (or who should be) referred to when one speaks of musical authors. Is the songwriter the only author in popular music? Or should the term "author" also be used in reference to producers, engineers, studio musicians, music video directors and other people working within popular music culture? Finally, in view of the fact that reception of musical works is an active process, the study also pays attention to the listener and his/her role as another producer – or author – of meaning.

Theoretical framework – Constructing the image

Another typical aspect of authorship in popular music is its *mediated*[3] nature. Today's popular music is seldom received in a non-mediated form, since it is produced for and through various technological media (Wall 2003: 108). The focus of the study does not, however, lie in the actual processes of music making, but rather in the *author images*[4] of artists and in the ways in which these images are produced, distributed and consumed. The mediated nature of author images does not, then, refer only to a means of technological transmission or to the intermediary practices of all the people who intervene in the making, distributing and consuming of popular music, but also to social relationships (of power and influence) "that occur *between* and *across* these activities" (Negus 1996: 65–71). As a result, the constructed author images communicate only a limited range of specific meanings, and thus, present a specified, while at the same time constructed, image of a particular artist. As Hannah Bosma (2000), in her study of gender in electronic avant-garde music, concludes: "Issues of authorship do not only relate to 'who did what', but also to who is represented as an author, and in what way." The starting point for this study of the author images of popular music artists lies, then, in the notion of *image*. As argued by Gunther Kress and Theo van Leeuwen (1999: 379), in the course of explaining the communicative structure of visual representations[5], the receiver's idea of the author or a contributor to the production process is only an image, and thus, a double of the real author. However, as Kress and van Leeuwen claim further, the image-based viewpoint should not make us set aside the social context in which the images are constructed and interpreted:

3   According to Grossberg et al. (1998: 14), the modern sense of mediation produces a notion of the space between the individual subject and reality as a space of experience, interpretation, and meaning. For more on mediation, see also Danesi 2002: 2–3; Keightley 2001: 133–134; Thwaites et al. 1994: 136–137.
4   My notion of *author image* is meant to emphasize my approach to the construction of images related to the question of (musical) authorship. This term also stands in contrast to the notion of "star image", since the making of popular music normally involves persons who are not necessarily celebrities or "stars".
5   Also in this study, the notion of representation is used when focusing on the visual aspects of the analysed author images. For more about the idea of representation, see Danesi 2002: 3–5; Wall 2003: 152–153.

Real authors and real readers we cannot ultimately know. This bracketing out of real authors and real readers carries the risk of forgetting that texts, literary and artistic texts as much as mass-media texts, are produced in the context of real social institutions, in order to play a very real role in social life. (Kress et al. 1999: 378–379.)

In the same way, the present examination of author-image construction of popular music artists does not focus on the actual, material or biological authors as such, but on their socially constructed images.

The purpose of the following section is to illustrate the process through which author images of popular music artists are constructed. There does not, however, exist a theoretical framework that would be applicable to all authors involved in music making, since artists' areas of responsibility vary a great deal. For example, there are singer-songwriters who perform only self-written material, as well as singers whose creative input is restricted to the public performing of music that someone else has written for them (Abbate 1993: 234–235; Des Pres et al. 2000: 87–149). In addition, the use of music technological innovations has led to the emergence of totally new ways of music making, including the practices of DJing and sampling (Goodwin 1990; Herman 2006; Killmeier 2001; Poschardt 1995: 40–96; Théberge 1999). Other musical authors who take part in the process of music making include music-video directors, engineers, record companies, distributors, managers and programme agencies, each of which has its own role in popular music culture, and hence, also in the designing, promoting and marketing of artists and their public images (Brackett 1999: 127; Shuker 1994: 99–100). Yet typically, there is only a select group of people whose authorial contribution is discussed and presented in public. Author images of popular music are often built around the *public artist*, whereas the input of producers, engineers and others is assumed (by representatives of the media and the music industry) to lie outside the area of public interest. By focusing attention on a single, originating individual, author images usually present artists as fascinating personas and mythical stars. As we will discover next, author images, because of their mediated nature, can be projected only in a certain light, while the meanings given to artists and their works are ultimately dependent on the individual subject position of each listener.

Specifying the image types – Presented, mediated, compiled

To elucidate the preceding discussion, I have specified three types of author image: the *presented*, the *mediated* and the *compiled*.[6] The purpose of the classification is to

6   The notion of author image is treated in parallel with the notions of public image, star image, star persona, public persona and artistic/authorial identity – depending on what kind of artists and their qualities is referred to. In contrast to the notions of presented, mediated and compiled author images, the terms listed in

help explain the mediation process and the various authorial roles and areas of responsibility of the agents involved (see *Table 1*). In addition, the three types make it easier for me to approach musical authorship from a variety of perspectives throughout the study. First, with the notion of (1) *presented author image*, I refer to the author image suggested by the text – for example, as suggested by a musical work or by the artist's commentary on it. The concept of presented author image, thus, stands for an image constructed by the artist and/or by the *marketing machinery*. This last term refers to agencies, publicists, managers and record companies who work within the music industry and whose job is to control and coordinate the so-called official information and images of popular music artists (see e.g. Turner 2004: 41–45).[7] This type of promotional material is intended to create or maintain a recognizable image with the help of which musical products can be marketed.[8] Second, the notion of (2) *mediated author image* refers to the image constructed by the media (the press, television, radio and the Internet). The media work, then, as promotional avenues through which record companies and other parties of the music industry seek to increase awareness of artists and their works in the hope of increasing sales. At the same time, the media work as the means by which popular music is consumed. (Turner 2004: 108.) The media should not, however, be seen as passive channels of transference, but as active, interpretative agents. Thus the author image constructed by the media is not identical with the presented one, since there is always an act of interpretation between them.[9] Third, members of the audience construct their own idea of the public artist, which is here referred to as a (3) *compiled author image*. In fact, by way of interaction with the presented and mediated images, and by co-compiling new author images, audiences themselves become another layer of mediation. In sum, these three types of image allow us to understand that author images in popular music are constructed in the relations between the public artist, the media, and the members of the audience.

(1) *Presented author image*	(image constructed by the artist and/or the marketing machinery)
(2) *Mediated author image*	(image constructed by the media)
(3) *Compiled author image*	(image constructed by the audience members

Table 1. The three types of author image.

---

the previous sentence are used to discuss the artist's image at a more general level, not to specify particular persons involved in producing the image.

7   The image presented by the marketing machinery may also be in conflict with the way the public artist would wish his/her image to be presented (see also Negus 1992: 64–65; Turner 2004: 41–45).

8   Also, the notion of *branding* is often used in this context (Marshall 1997: 245; Mäkelä 2002: 47).

9   The mediated construction of author images is discussed more in chapter 5.

The distinction between the presented, mediated and compiled author images is based on the idea that each type of author image is *produced by a different agent*, and therefore, through a different set of musical, literary, and visual media texts. Although I believe that the distinction is useful for explaining the construction of author images, it is essential to understand that because of their interrelatedness, the three types of image cannot be unambiguously separated from one another. The purpose of the notions is to call attention to the various agents who take part in the construction of author images in popular music, not to lay down strict or absolute distinctions. The aim, then, is not to promote some images as being more "right", "true" or "real" than others, since all three types share in the mediation process. It should be recalled here that this study deals with author *images*; hence no attempt is made to reach an author "behind" or "prior to" image construction. What we can reach, instead, are mediated constructions produced by various agents operating within popular music culture.

The distinction between the notions of *projected* and *reflected* cultural products, introduced by Marko Aho (2003), well clarifies the difference between the three types of image. According to Aho, the *projected* cultural products are produced by the artist, record company and the culture industry, while the *reflected* cultural products are produced by receivers of the projected images, that is, the media and the members of the audience. As Aho points out, the fundamental difference between these two productions is that in the former, the star and the backing team transmit a certain image of the artist, while in the latter, someone else reflects the projected image. The artist and the marketing machinery may, then, directly affect the former (in this case, the presented author image) and the other two (the mediated and compiled author images) only indirectly. (Aho 2003: 59–60.)

In *Table 2*, I have listed some of the main types of media texts in which the presented and the mediated author images consist, and also on which the audience constructs its compiled author image of the artist. The aim of the following classification is to give a picture of the analysed material and to explain the background for choosing the subject and methodology of the present study.[10]

---

10   The classification is indebted to the writings on (both film and pop) stardom by Richard Dyer and Janne Mäkelä (see e.g. Dyer 1986; Mäkelä 2002). Marko Aho's division, introduced above, between the two types of cultural products has also been useful in illustrating the way that the construction of author images is understood in the study at hand.

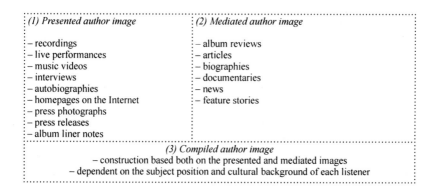

(1) Presented author image	(2) Mediated author image
– recordings – live performances – music videos – interviews – autobiographies – homepages on the Internet – press photographs – press releases – album liner notes	– album reviews – articles – biographies – documentaries – news – feature stories
(3) Compiled author image – construction based both on the presented and mediated images – dependent on the subject position and cultural background of each listener	

Table 2. The construction of author images.

The first type of author image, the presented one, consists of the actual works performed by the artist, including recordings and live performances. In addition to musical texts, the presented author image is made up of what the artist has said or written him/herself (or is presented as having said or written) by way of verbal commentary. These types of media texts include interviews, autobiographies, album liner notes and web blogs on the Internet. Finally, aside from the written or recorded material, the visual imagery, such as official press photographs and album covers, takes part in the construction of the artist's presented author image. It is, however, impossible to know what the power of decision of a single artist has been in the production of these texts, in proportion to how much publicists, managers and others within the music industry have been involved in the process. As noted earlier, what also complicates the tracking down of the authorial contribution of a single artist is the fact that the making of popular music is usually a collective process, in which the views of several music makers clash, mix, or blend with one another (Brackett 2000: 14–17; Gracyk 1996: 94–95; Shuker 1994: 99–111).

The second type of author image, the mediated one, refers to media texts that are produced variously through the press, radio, television and the Internet. The mediated author image, then, consists of a group of media texts – such as album reviews, articles, feature stories and unauthorized biographies – that are not produced by the artist and/or his/her marketing machinery; rather, it is the employees working in broadcasting and publication companies (journalists, critics, editors, publishers, directors, etc.) who construct the author image advanced by the media. It is often difficult to draw a strict line between the activities of the music industry and those of the media (see also Mäkelä 2002: 48; Turner 2004: 108).[11] Nevertheless, in the same way as we general-

---

11   It is, for example, possible for the companies (i.e. record companies and radio stations) of the music indus-

ized the three types of author image, we here shall classify their activities in terms of who is producing or said to produce (for example, an artist or a journalist) a particular media text, and also, an author image in question. For example, author images on artists' official Internet homepages are referred to as presented author images (despite their mediated nature), since it is the artist and/or the artist's marketing machinery which are controlling the accessible material.

Finally, the compiled author image, as it comes across to the members of the audience is based on both the presented and the mediated author images (cf. Goodwin 1992: 106; Grossberg et al. 1998: 151–153). Usually the compiled image is a mental structure rather than a material product – even though the constructed ideas are often embodied in people's behaviour and decision-making (see e.g. Straw 2001b). It is, for example, possible for audience members to publish their ideas (and to revise our understanding of musical authorship) through fan sites, discussion forums and self-written album reviews on the Internet, a medium that has greatly facilitated the distribution of audiences' opinions and views to other listeners of popular music. In addition to various written products, the audience members may express their musical preferences through certain modes of consumption: purchasing records, attending concerts, or consuming other products that have something to do with the music they like to listen to.[12] Thus, while seeing the compiled author image as a unique reading of each individual, and as being dependent on the subject position and cultural background of each audience member, it is many times also a question of an idea held in common by a certain (fan) community. The process of constructing author images does not stop when the compiled image is created. Rather, the designing and marketing of images is mutually affected by the audience's activities and choices; these last work as a useful feedback channel, with the help of which popular music culture is able to refine its own functioning and to plan its future.

Research material – Media texts and online sources

The research material of this study consists of a group of (written, visual and musical) media texts that fall into a number of categories presented in *Table 2*. The most essential set of texts are written media texts, including album reviews and artist interviews. Some of the texts have been published only in print, some only on the Internet, and some both in print and online. Even though most of the texts examined in this study

---

try and those of the media to work together in order to reach larger listenership, readership or sales (Turner 2004: 110).

12   For more about recent trends in studying the reception of popular music, see DeNora 2002; Mäkelä 2002: 49–50; Straw 2001b.

are written ones, it is clear that other media, such as television and radio, participate in the construction of images. Therefore, some music videos, artist websites and sound recordings are analysed so as to better explain the fragmented process by which author images are constructed. In addition, some online discussion forums, as well as album reviews written by fans, are examined in order to clarify the audience's point of view. Most of the research material in this study reflects the construction of author images from the artist's and/or the media's point of view, with less attention being paid to images compiled by audience members.

One of the most drastic changes affecting the mediated construction of artist images has been the emergence of the Internet. Hence a variety of online material – artist websites, interviews, album reviews and the like – plays an essential role in this study. Because of the centrality of the Internet in today's (popular) culture, the material that is published online both maintains and revises our thoughts concerning musical authorship, as do all other media texts. Ongoing, online discussions should thus be understood as different moments of narrating and signifying. Similarly to other texts, the meanings of online sources are formed during the process of interpretation, which leads to their independence from the moment of production. (Paasonen 2002: 8.) The texts published on the Internet do not, then, present a separate way of defining authorship, since they are intertwined with all the other material surrounding popular music. As pointed out by Sherry Turkle (1995: 10), when explaining the interaction between humans and machines, the boundaries between the real and the virtual are eroded in the formation of meanings in today's cultural context.

I have grouped the analysed online media texts into categories that are based on the types of context in which the texts have been published (see *Appendix*). The categories include music magazines, online magazines and dailies on popular music and culture, webportals on popular music and music technology, review and feature websites, other magazines and newspapers, miscellaneous websites, and finally, artist's Internet homepages. In the various contexts in which the texts have been published, the style of writing and the issues discussed therein have been chosen to fit the image and purpose of each specific publication. It is also possible that the style and the message of writings published in different contexts (and for different purposes) may be contradictory. Some websites and magazines are more popular and/or more accessible than others, thereby reaching a relatively wide audience; it is thus also likely that certain publications are more influential, in terms of affecting the ways in which people may wish to construct and revise their views and beliefs. It must be admitted, however, that no matter how large and varied the sample of media publications and sources one chooses to analyse, it is never possible to track down all the media texts that audience members use in constructing their author image of a particular popular music artist.

Some aspects of being online may decrease the reliability of certain materials as subjects of study. One such aspect is the uncertainty as to how long online material will remain available, as webpages are updated, servers fail, or other changes take place. From another point of view, the changeability of the material may be seen to reflect the fast pace at which trends come and go in popular music culture in general. Another challenged is posed by the fact that it is sometimes hard to find any information about the author(s) of certain texts or what their status as writers might be. While some of the texts are written by professional journalists, other pages may be maintained by music enthusiasts, who have founded their own website as a forum from which to issue their writings. Despite these reservations – whether the texts be written by artists, professional music writers, or regular listeners – all the media texts analysed in this study have one thing in common: they all participate in the ongoing discussion of popular music, its artists, and their public images.

Methodology – Social constructions and discursive readings

Media texts on popular music authorship are grouped around artists and their public personas. Altogether, these texts, including music videos, albums, artist interviews, usually make the artist appear as a coherent figure. It must be remembered, however, that no matter how unified an author image might appear, it is nonetheless made of texts and their relations to other, existing texts. In this respect, author images exist only intertextually, and involve only a certain set of meanings in constructing and maintaining that existence (cf. Fiske 1989: 124–125).[13] The intertextual nature of author images explains, among other things, why there can exist various, contradictory readings of a particular artist. The meanings given to each text are also dependent on the listener and on his/her knowledge of other existing texts and their intertextual relations (Fiske 1989: 124–125; see also Tiainen[14] 2005: 37). Author images are not produced randomly, but in contact and correlation with changing historical, political and social contexts (see e.g. Saukko 2003: 99). What also unites these textual constructions is that they are circumscribed by artists who impose limits on those texts – in the same way as Roland Barthes's (1990: 147) "author" is believed to "close" the writing.

13 Similarly, the brief "biographies" in the footnotes, used to introduce the case studies analysed here, present only one reading, though assumedly an established one, of the chosen star texts. Rather than critically discussing the artists' "histories" in these contexts, my purpose is to provide summary glimpses of the artists and their (mediated) images for those readers who are unfamiliar with the artists in question.

14 In Milla Tiainen's (2005) study, discourse analysis is applied in the context of contemporary Finnish artmusic culture.

If author images are made up of multiple and intertextual writings (Barthes 1990: 146, 148; 1979: 11), they nevertheless also repeat some of the established meanings of musical authorship (cf. Tiainen 2005: 18).

By now, we have learned that author images can be understood as intertextual constructions and culturally formed categories. This understanding brings us to the theory of *social constructionism*, which draws a line between the *material* world and the *symbolic* practices and processes through which representation, meaning and language operate (Hall 1997: 25).[15] To see author images as constructions of intertextual meanings is also related to the idea of language as a social construction of reality. The very notion of *discourse* emphasizes the link between social reality, language and subject (Tiainen 2005: 33–34; see also Burr 1995: 7; Lehtonen 1996: 29). According to Norman Fairclough (1997: 76; 1992: 64), each discourse builds subject positions, social identities, relations and constructions of knowledge and beliefs; every text moulds these social and cultural aspects. In addition to renewing and maintaining, discourses can also change some already established and shared conceptions (Fairclough 1997: 76; see also Jokinen et al. 1993: 18–24; Jokinen 1999: 39). Texts do not, then, only reflect social relations, but as Fairclough (1992: 3–4) puts it, "different discourses constitute key entities [...] in different ways, and position people in different ways as social subjects".

Also in this study, author images are treated as constructions that cannot be separated from their social and cultural contexts (cf. Thwaites et al. 1994: 112). As expressed by Bruce Horner (1999: 18), "the discourse used to describe popular music has material consequences for how that music is produced, the forms it takes, how it is experienced, and its meaning". From this perspective, my aim is to analyse the kinds of discourses on popular music authorship contained in the chosen media texts – produced by artists (and/or the marketing machinery), media and listeners – and also, how these discourses have affected the practices of music making and the way musical authorship is understood. When viewing author images as socially and historically constructed categories, the discourses on popular music authorship are also linked with the question of power. By examining author images we may, then, clarify, not only how musical authorship is defined, but what kind of authorship is valued and by which historically and socially justified criteria. The media texts analysed in this study also bring out the fact that the given meanings are not stable, but constantly changing. Through the examination of author images of various popular music artists, we may see that the notion of musical authorship is also in a state of constant redefinition.

---

15 The existence of the material world is not denied; it is just that the focus of social constructionist theories lies in the social agents that use linguistic and other representational systems to construct meaning (Hall 1997: 27).

As Alastair Williams (2001: 140) concludes toward the end of his book *Constructing Musicology*, by studying musical discourses and their functioning, it is possible to enhance the transparency of communication and to understand the construction of identity. Similarly, by analysing discourses on popular music authorship, this study aims at explaining the practices of making popular music and the way it is produced, distributed and consumed. The manner of understanding author images as discursive constructions links the frame of reference of the study also to postmodern and post-structuralist theories. Together these theories deny the existence of ultimate truths and fixed meanings (see e.g. Burr 1995: 13, 41), and highlight the possibility of contradictory readings that texts may carry (see e.g. Saukko 2003: 113–114). Also in this study, the examined author images are seen as sites of struggle through which meanings arise, power relations are contested, and subject positions constructed.

Context and focus – Defining the object of study

It needs to be specified that, in this study, the notion of "making popular music"[16] refers to the processes – i.e. writing, arranging and producing – through which music is transformed from an initial idea into a repeatable form. The actual process of music making is only one aspect of popular music authorship, and hence only one of the subjects to be discussed. The main focus of the study, however, goes to how the author images of a selected group of artists are constructed. By examining author images, it is also possible to explain what kind of assumptions and beliefs are linked with different forms of making popular music. It is equally essential to consider the ways in which economic circumstances, technological innovations and marketing strategies of popular music culture have affected the practices of music making (Goodwin 1990; Negus 1992; Schumacher 1995; Théberge 1997), and finally, to discuss their effects on the way we define concepts – such as musical creativity and originality – that are closely tied to the notion of authorship.

First of all, it should be noted that in this study I am using the term "popular music" in a sense that excludes the traditions of Western art music, jazz, and world music. Second, all the examined case studies may be categorized under the labels of con-

---

16 With the notion of *authoring* music, by contrast, I refer to the manner in which the artist represents the music (in the media) rather than simply speaking about making popular music, since not all public artists take part in actual music making.

temporary rock[17], pop[18] and electronic dance music[19]. The distinct styles, conventions and modes of production, which have variously been used in the labelling of genres, lead us to assume that the ways of constructing authorship might also vary according to the styles of music. The exclusion of genres like r 'n' b and rap does not mean that the question of authorship would be less relevant in these styles of music, but only that closer inspection of those and other genres lies outside the scope of the present study, and must await further research. By focusing on the three genres listed above, the case studies form a balanced and controllable whole, thus encouraging profound discussion of the various modes of author constructions and their underlying histories. Even if the genres under examination are, in a sense, treated as opposites of each other, the differences between the styles of music are not black and white; indeed, there are plenty of artists whose music making may be understood as a combination of several ways of constructing authorship. In this respect, the borderline cases and hybrid authorial constructions support the idea of musical authorship as a complex and fragmented category. We may also consider whether it is even possible to understand the question of musical authorship as a coherent entity, or whether we should discuss separately the authorship of each genre or artist in question.

Clearly and historically, technological innovations have profoundly affected music making practices (Buckley 2007; Frith 1996: 226–245; Goodwin 1998; Théberge 1997; Théberge 2004; Warner 2003). As a result, the notion of "author" is no longer automatically seen, if it ever was, as a fixed and coherent category. Technological

17 The term "rock music" is broadly used in reference to musical styles that are seen as having developed since the 1960s in North America and Britain, mostly among young white audiences and musicians. Seriousness and commitment are some of the characteristics that are typically linked with the ideology of rock and its performers. The strong beats and rhythmic patterns of rock music are often performed with amplified instruments. Punk rock, progressive rock and hard rock are some of the subgenres of rock music. (Middleton 2007a.) In this study, Bruce Springsteen and Coldplay are artists who are seen to represent this genre. Also Tori Amos, Björk and Jewel may be seen to represent the singer-songwriter tradition that is typically connected with rock music authorship – despite the fact that the musical influences of these artists vary between electronic dance music to dance pop and alternative rock, respectively.

18 Since the 1960s, pop music is usually defined in contrast to rock music. Generally, rock is thought to be harder, more aggressive and more improvisatory, while pop is seen as a softer and more arranged style of music. In addition to the stylistic differences, the genres are often seen to represent conflicting ideologies ("authentic art" vs. "commercial entertainment"). (Middleton 2007b.) In this study, Britney Spears and Kylie Minogue are artists who are treated as the representatives of the given genre.

19 By "electronic dance music", I refer to the genre of popular music that established itself at the end of the 1980s and into the early 1990s. In this type of music, the voice and the sounds of acoustic instruments are treated electronically (by means of synthesizers, drum machines, sequencers etc.; see Berk 2000: 190–192; Bogdanov et al. 2001: vi). Earlier, electronic dance music was often associated with the dance club scene, but along with less expensive music technology and the successful careers of Moby, Björk and others, the genre has become considered more mainstream. Trance, house, techno, disco and electro are some of the (sub)genres of electronic dance music, to name a few (Bogdanov et al. 2001: vii–xiv). There are also more experimental genres, such as IDM (intelligent dance music) and trip-hop, that are not primarily intended for dancing. That is also why the notions of electronic dance music and electronic music are used in parallel in this study, i.e. to put emphasis on whether the music is mainly intended to be played in dance clubs or is used, for example, in creating certain atmospheres – in both cases, the basic (electronic) means of music making remain the same. In this study, Daft Punk, Kraftwerk, Jori Hulkkonen and The Avalanches serve as case studies that are seen to represent the given genre.

changes, leading to more and more amateur musical performances, point up the activity of music making as a social and collaborative process during which authorial roles are shared among the members of a creative collective (Brackett 2000: 14–17; Gracyk 1996: 94–95; Shuker 1994: 99–111). Such ideas of social and collective authorship have also shaken the belief in a single originating author (see e.g. Toynbee 2000: 102–110). The boundaries between the various authorial roles and areas of responsibility may also overlap. Thanks especially to the Internet and the widespread use of computer technologies, practically anyone can make and distribute musical works, and thus, actually become an author (Connell et al. 2003: 267–269).[20] These kinds of thoughts may also be associated with the postmodernist notion of small-scale narratives replacing the "grand" or master-stories, as influentially argued by Jean-François Lyotard in his work *The Postmodern Condition* (1979). According to the postmodern mindset, everyone is authorized as a narrator (see e.g. Poster 1995: 38; Williams 2001: 119). When the same perspective is applied to the context of popular music authorship, even audience members can be seen as active agents, with intentions and meanings of their own.

Research questions, aims and execution – On the work at hand

This study consists of four main sections. In the first of these, titled "Starring the author – In the spotlight and underground", I deal with the construction of author images and the way they are used in creating artists' public personas. Here, the notion of author is understood as the point of origin around which the artist's authorial image is constructed. In the first chapter, I examine the idea of single originating authorship against the background of Björk's (an Icelandic singer-songwriter) author image as an individual and innovative artist. Functions of the celebrity-sign as well as theories of stardom are also discussed. Chapter two focuses on the artist's visual image and its role in the promotion of popular music artists and their works. The case study of this chapter deals with Daft Punk's (a French electronic dance music duo) disguised author image and the way it differs from star images based on the artist's celebrity value and personal appearance. Can we assume that Daft Punk's masked author image serves as another marketing tool and means of gaining attention?

In the second main section, "Authorship as a means of attributing value and fixing meaning", I analyse musical authorship as a category that is used in evaluating artists and their works. In this section, I first discuss the issues of *auteurism* and cover ver-

---

20   Pro Tools, Logic Pro, Cubase and Propellerhead Reason are some of the music software applications and digital audio workstations that allow their users to create music and work in their own virtual music studios. For more on the web communities of Propellerhead Reason users, see Sirppiniemi 2006.

sions as they apply to the authorship of Tori Amos (an American singer-songwriter). The underlying question here concerns Amos's status as an original and innovative artist. Based on the idea of auteurism, the following questions are asked: On the one hand, what does it take for an artist to fill the shared criteria of auteurism? And on the other, does auteur status give the artist license to experiment freely? Another typical notion that is used in evaluating popular music, is the artist's sense of *authenticity*, or the lack of it. In chapter four, the case of Jewel (an American singer-songwriter) and her stylistic and visual change is studied to explain some of the qualities that an artist is expected to have in order to be regarded as an authentic musical author. In relation to the question of authentic authorship, I deal with various themes, including the singer-songwriter tradition, the question of mediation, and the (so-called) "inauthenticity" that is often linked with the use of music technology.

In the third main section "Mediated author constructions", the construction of author images is treated as a mediated process through which artists' public images are produced, distributed and consumed. In chapter five, I analyse the images of three artists – Coldplay (a four-member British rock band), Britney Spears (an American pop singer) and Prince (an American singer-songwriter) – and the contradictory readings of their public personas. Also discussed here is the question of collective authorship as it relates to the artists' various authorial roles and areas of responsibility. In chapter six, I discuss the notion of *genre* and its relation to the construction of artist's images online. The chapter focuses on author images presented on the official homepages of Bruce Springsteen (an American singer-songwriter), Kylie Minogue (an Australian pop singer) and Kraftwerk (a German electronic dance music band). The online author image of each artist is analysed within the categories of music, biography and visual imagery.

In the last main section, "Rethinking musical creativity", my goal is to shed light on the ways in which making popular music has changed in step with the use of new music technology. The section considers what kind of effects the introduction of digital music technologies and new forms of authorship have had on the way the ideas of musical authorship and artistic creativity are understood. First, I discuss poststructuralist thought (mainly that of Roland Barthes and Michel Foucault) and its expanded notions of musical authorship. The ideas of *diffused authorship* and the active reception of musical works are discussed through the practice of DJing and the case of Jori Hulkkonen (a Finnish electronic music artist). The last chapter focuses on the practice of *sampling* and the changes it has brought to the field of musical authorship in terms of defining artistic creativity. These questions will be illustrated by the case of The Avalanches (an Australian electronic dance music collective) who use samples in their music making.

Overall, the author images examined in this study are connected with a number of themes, ranging from issues of auteurism and stardom to those of masked imagery and the blending of authorial voices. Author images of auteurs, stars, DJs and sampling artists are discussed alongside various topics, including collective authorship, evaluative hierarchies, visual promotion and generic conventions. Altogether, the examined case studies aim to clarify the functioning of popular music culture and the ways in which musical authorship is (re)defined.

I

STARRING THE AUTHOR – IN THE SPOTLIGHT AND UNDERGROUND

Because it is the storyteller, rather than the story itself,
that is the central fiction in popular music,
the construction of personality and identity
around pop musicians is fundamental to success.

Andrew Goodwin 1992

1. The author effect – Tracking down the source

The author as the point of origin

Musical works are commonly associated with the persons who perform them in public (Brackett 2000: 14–15; Toynbee 2000: 61). In a sense, then, artists' public images serve as recognizable trademarks that increase the attractiveness of those works and, by extension, the authors who created them. This author-based frame of reference is evident in the listener's tendency to perceive music through the mental "lens" of authorship (see e.g. Keightley 2001: 134; Straw 1999: 201). Upon hearing a piece of music for the first time, audiences tend to ponder a number of questions linked with the notion of authorship, such as: Who wrote the music to this song? Who wrote the lyrics? Did the performer(s) write this song, and what role does he or she play in the process of music making? Such questions call attention to the link between the author and his/her work as a central feature of popular music culture, which, in addition to enhancing the marketing of products, also influences the making and consuming of popular music (Wall 2003: 153).[21] For example, we have been so conditioned to the authorial frame of reference, that it requires a great stretch of the imagination to picture what album covers, TV commercials or music videos would look like without imagery based on the artist's public persona and visual appearance.

The artist's public persona also affects the listening experience, through which the audience is able to identify with the artist and/or with the music and lyrics of a song (Straw 1999: 202). Therefore, the meanings that the audience formulates during the process of interpretation are not only based on the music, but also on the public image of the artist who is regarded as the originating source of a given musical piece. The belief in a single, unitary author is also utilized in the marketing of artists and the musical products they represent (Frith 1983: 134–135; Wall 2003: 153). Musicologist Andrew Goodwin (1992: 103) recognizes two significant functions operating in the star persona. First, stars provide a *point of identification* for the listener-spectator. Second, the construction of stardom plays an essential role in the *economic functioning* of popular music culture. (Goodwin 1992: 103; see also Frith et al. 1987: 169.) The construction of a recognizable author image is also essential to any artist wishing to create a career of substantial longevity, which is a highly desirable goal, at least from

---

21   There is also music, e.g. certain danceable hit tunes, the marketing of which is rather (or besides) based on a specific impression that is built around a group of recognizable dance movements or a certain atmosphere. Such examples include so-called summer hits like "Macarena" by Los del Río or "Ketchup Song" performed by Las Ketchup, both songs having also introduced a certain dance style.

the viewpoint of popular music culture and its pursuit of commercial profit (Goodwin 1992: 103).

In the following section, I should like to clarify some ways in which the belief in single, originating authorship is used in the construction of author images in popular music. Whether one is speaking of stars, artists, auteurs, singers or performers, the rallying point here is that musical works are marketed in relation to the public image of the artist with which the music is associated. No matter what type of music the artist performs or whether the songs are self-written, the underlying strategy seems, in most cases, to be the same. Even though the collective music making of boy and girl bands usually differs a great deal from that of singer-songwriters, the ways the public images of these various artists are constructed do not appear to be all that different (cf. Wall 2003: 153–155). Their goal is the same: to create a recognizable author image through which musical products are introduced by the artist and the media to audience members that, it is assumed, conceive of the artist as an interpreter of "real life and true emotions".

Authoring identities and celebrity signs

In the history of cinema, star identities became more and more usable as commodities when it was realized that starring actors worked as more powerful sources of product differentiation than did the film studios themselves (Butler 1998: 345). The presence of the star anchors the fluidity and ambiguity of the film and music industries behind the making of movies (Croteau et al. 2003: 155). The star image has a similar effect in popular music: when the same song is performed by two different artists, the listener hears the song in two diverging ways. It is not, thus, only a question of listening to a piece of music, but listening to music *performed by a specific artist*. Therefore, the star images of Madonna or Robbie Williams, or any other artist, surround everything that is marketed and produced in their names. The artist's image is, thus, used as a classificatory item that unites a group of musical texts together and draws a line between other existing texts. This is what Nancy Spivey (1997: 212) refers to with the notion of *authoring identity*, that is, the identification of a person as the author of a particular work and the identification of works with a particular author. Moreover, the interpretation of musical texts is biased by the aura and the image of each artist in question.[22] As expressed by Rosemary J. Coombe (1994: 104), in analysing the value of celebrity image, "[t]he aura of the celebrity is a potent force in an era

22   Coombe refers to "aura" as Walter Benjamin (1992) used the term, in the sense of the unique, here-and-now character of the work of art and a precondition to the concept of originality. Benjamin (1992: 214–215), however, claims that the notion of aura has lost its meaning because of mechanical reproduction.

in which standardization, rationalization and the controlled programming of production characterize the creation and distribution of goods". Coombe (1994: 104) notes that the images and auras of popular music artists and other celebrities have become commodities, which are in turn used to sell products that would otherwise be indistinguishable. It is, then, the artist's public image that makes the musical product (at least appear) unique and original.

Media-culture theorist P. David Marshall (1997) clarifies the development through which popular music has become identified with its star performers. Firstly, Marshall links the trend with the *mass reproduction* of songs. In the nineteenth and early twentieth centuries, star-performers became tools for the publishing industry to expand their market. During that period of time, the function of the performer was to promote songs written by someone else. As a result, the performers became vital for the music publishing companies; while sheet music was a central commodity of popular music, the songs were associated either with their titles or by the names of their performers. The division of labour between stars and the (relatively anonymous) songwriters further elevated the performer's status. Another crucial development was the levelling out of regional differences, which led to the recording artist becoming the centre for production of similar songs. What also revolutionized the making of popular music were the technologies of reproduction. Thanks to recording technology, popular music was no longer dependent on the place of its performance; it was therefore possible to connect songs even more tightly with those who performed them. (Marshall 1997: 150–154, 156.) The technological innovations also made it possible to construct a more personal and individualized image around the artist's public persona.

Marshall refers to the celebrity as a sign or a text that *represents* something other than itself. Marshall (1997: 57) argues: "the celebrity is a way in which meaning can be housed and categorized into something that provides a source and origin for the meaning". Thus the image of each artist is an *intertextual sign* that is composed of texts presented in different media, such as newspapers, magazines and artist interviews. A specific image of each celebrity is constructed, based on media texts and the chains of signification they produce. Mediated texts also reveal the layers of connotative meanings that are embedded into each celebrity sign. As a result, the celebrity comes to be seen as a construct of highly mediated individuality. (Marshall 1997: 56–59.) In this manner, the public image of each artist works as a means of creating an image that appears fixed and permanent. In turn, the sense of permanency provides the artist with an aura that eventually makes him/her seem unique and exceptional. As Marshall (1997: 57) concludes, the celebrity sign is an important category because of "its power to organize the legitimate and illegitimate domains of the personal and individual within the social".[23] This statement also applies to popular music: when the public artist establishes a specific style or niche, the audience is able to construct a coherent image that influences the ways in which the works of a certain artist are, or are supposed to be, interpreted.

Tracing back the Romantic impact

The belief in a single originating artist is linked with the notion of the individual author, who is seen as the object of aesthetic attention and whose works are valued as the artist's true and honest expressions (Brackett 2000: 14–15; Keightley 2001: 134; Straw 1999: 201). As early as in the eighteenth and nineteenth centuries, the creating subject was placed at the centre in works of European Romantic poetry. At that time, the poet was seen as an original and originating genius whose work was believed to represent the author's thoughts and feelings. (Abrams 1953: 100–103; Bennett 2005: 55–71.) As literary theorist Andrew Bennett (2004: 65) summarizes, to read a text was to read its author. The idea of (literary) authorship also affected the ways in which poets, novelists and dramatists thought about themselves as writers, as well as the manners in which they wrote. One frequently mentioned poet in this regard is William Wordsworth (1770–1850), whose thoughts seem to well represent this type of notion of literary authorship; his views on the differences between poets and other men have been analysed thoroughly by M. H. Abrams (1953). In the Romantic idea of authorship, the poet is referred to as being "intensively sensible" and "susceptible to passion", and his/her poetic inspiration is considered effortless and involuntary (Abrams 1953: 189). According to Christine Battersby (1989: 13), Romanticism typically valued artists for their ability to express their personal feelings and imaginings in their work, turning authenticity and sincerity into the most important kinds of truth. Not only were the works themselves valued as expressing the artist's feelings and imaginings; the uniqueness and individuality of the artist's own character also became aesthetically significant (Battersby 1989: 13).

Jason Toynbee, among others, has criticized this Romantic ideal, instead preferring to understand musical authorship as a social phenomenon. According to Toynbee (2003: 102), cultural studies have paid too little attention to creativity; issues of authorship and creativity are still, quite commonly and exclusively, associated with high art. By contrast, Toynbee seeks to connect the question of creativity with all kinds of musics. He argues that creativity in music – whether classical, jazz or popular – needs

---

23   Thus, even when one conceives of stardom as a semiotic system of signs, it is necessary to pay attention to the ways in which signs and texts function as part of a wider social context (see also Gledhill 1991: xiv).

to be reconceived as a cultural and social process rather than as a heroic act. (Toynbee 2003: 102, 110.) Toynbee (2000: 61; see also 2006: 76) talks about the *expressionist mode* of performance by which he refers to the commonly held notion that the author uses music as a way of expressing his/her intentions. The expressionist mode is typically connected with singer-songwriters whose music is seen to be based on the author's autobiographical experiences. For instance, songs by the Canadian singer-songwriter Joni Mitchell are often taken as revelations of her personal life (Reynolds et al. 1995: 254–255). The following is an illustrative extract of a "confessional" reading of her work, from the liner notes of Mitchell's compilation album *Dreamland* (2004):

> Like her painting, like her songs, like her life. Joni Mitchell has never settled for the easy answers; it's the big questions that she's still exploring, like no one else, whether it's with a paintbrush, a guitar, a ukulele, or standing here, right now, in a room lined with fresh canvases. [...] Her songs belong so powerfully to those who hear them. How could you choose one and leave another behind? And then you realize, it's easy if you think about it. The masterpiece is Joni Mitchell. (Cameron Crowe 2004, liner notes of Joni Mitchell's *Dreamland*.)

As the citation illustrates, Mitchell's works are thought to express the author's life story. Toynbee (2000: 63) argues that such expressionist construals of performance obscure the fact that creativity consists in encounters between the artist and social contexts. Even if Joni Mitchell's songs are more likely based on the artist's intentions than are those songs written by a collective (and performed by a public artist who has not taken part in the creative process), the artist's image as an independent and omnipotent individual seems to come into conflict with the idea of the social nature of music making.

In Toynbee's (2003: 103) opinion, the main problem with Romantic thinking is that it sees music as coming from within, and being a direct product of, the creator's psyche. Toynbee lists three aspects that typify the Romantic idea of creativity.[24] First, the creative process is believed to take place within the creator's own psyche and to have no connection to other music making, past or present. Second, creation is seen as an involuntary action that is not subject to conscious control. Third, the creation of a musical work is supposed to proceed in stages, from a new idea to a definite form. Toynbee argues that there are problems with such ideas of creativity, which, according to the Romantic view, describe creation as a mystical process that is accessible only to a selected group of individual geniuses. Romantic thinking ignores the social nature of authorship, by recognizing the author as the only true source of meanings. (Toynbee 2003: 102–103.) The biggest problem with Romantic ideology, according

---

24 Toynbee bases his remarks on a comment by the Russian composer Pjotr Tchaikovsky.

to Toynbee, lies in the way it isolates the author from the outside world, thus ignoring the process of music making as dependent on the social and historical context in which it takes place.

Hans Lenneberg is another writer who takes a critical stance towards the idea of the artist as an originating genius. In his article, "The Myth of the Unappreciated (Musical) Genius", Lenneberg (1980: 221) observes that, in the Romantic tradition, great composers are usually seen as "not only destined to be gifted, but also innovative or radical and of extraordinary integrity". Composers are also depicted as moody and almost inevitably unappreciated or misunderstood. Like Toynbee, Lenneberg (1980: 221) believes that the image of the artist as an inevitably misunderstood genius is, in fact, a myth or at least an over-simplification. Although Lenneberg refers only to composers of classical music, such as Beethoven and Schubert, the idea of an artist who must suffer for his/her art has spread to all areas of music. Both Toynbee and Lenneberg view the Romantic idea of authorship as a myth that should be re-evaluated. Toynbee (2003: 111) explains the persistence of the traditional Romantic view mainly in political-economic terms; stardom brings a certain predictability to the marketplace, by which it is possible to reduce the uncertainties of supply and demand. Aside from economic factors, the cult of creativity encourages both music makers and audience members to believe in a single, originating authorship (Toynbee 2003: 111).[25]

Leading the way – The case of Björk

Here I present the case of Björk[26], to exemplify a popular-music artist whose author image seems to be based on the belief in the single originating author. Her public image is that of a mythical and autonomous character whose talent and uniqueness differentiates her from the average music maker. Besides enjoying a successful recording

---

25 Also, according to Nancy Spivey (1997: 215), autobiographical accounts of creative processes have, ever since the Romantic period, helped to increase and sustain the phenomenon of author-worship.

26 Björk Gudmunsdóttir was born in Reykjavik, Iceland on 21 November 1965. Björk started her musical career by studying classical piano when she was in elementary school, and at the age of eleven released her first album. Before her solo career, Björk was a singer in several punk-influenced bands. The first two of these, formed by Björk in 1979 and 1980, were called Exodus and Jam 80. In 1981, Björk joined with Exodus bassist Jakob Magnusson in assembling another group, called Tappi Tikarras, which two years later released a full-length album entitled *Miranda*. Björk was also the founder of the band KUKL, which in 1986 renamed themselves The Sugarcubes. With the success of their debut album, *Life's Too Good* (1988), The Sugarcubes became one of the few Icelandic bands to gain a following outside the boundaries of its homeland. After that band broke up, Björk moved to London, where she got interested in dance and club culture and started working on her solo album *Debut*. Released in 1993, the album yielded several hit singles, such as "Venus as a Boy" and "Big Time Sensuality". (Erlewine 2002a: 101.) Over the course of her career, Björk has made several full-length albums, including *Post* (1995), *Telegram* (1996), *Homogenic* (1997), *Selmasongs* (2000), *Vespertine* (2001), *Greatest Hits collection* (2002), *The Family Tree* (2002), *Medúlla* (2004) and *Drawing Restraint 9* (2005) and *Volta* (2007). (Erlewine 2002a: 101; Carew 2001; Collins 2004; Keefe 2007.)

career and international fame, Björk has gained acclaim as a solo artist and a vocalist who is known for her original and distinctive image. Media texts have referred to Björk as a "female sonic wizard", a "genius", and "a serious musician who creates her own distinct sound that continues to transform and mature" (Carew 2001; Widder 2001). She is also described as an artist who defies stereotypes and is in a league of her own (Greenwood 2001a; Widder 2001). Here is another typical characterisation of Björk, taken from an album review in *Ink Blot Magazine*:

> By now, we expect Björk to be different, to be slightly odd and evoke images of fairies hanging out with aliens. But somehow, with little tricks like recording music boxes and using her own vocals to create an enchanting call and response, she continues to rise above our earthly expectations. (Latimer 2001.)

Such descriptions accord well with the idea of the Romantic author as one who is "ahead of his [/her] time, avant-garde", and "somehow above or beyond the human" (Bennett 2005: 60). Nevertheless, some aspects of Björk's public image go against the traditional one of the artist as a self-sufficient genius. For example, her lavish use of music technology and the partly collaborative nature of music making are some of the features that might undermine the belief in single authorship. The present case study looks at ways in which Björk's author image is described in a group of media texts, and how those elements play into constructing her public persona. In addition to artist interviews and album reviews, the material analysed in this chapter includes six music videos that have also played a role in the construction of Björk's star persona.

It is difficult to give a succinct characterisation of Björk's music, since it joins together so many disparate elements. Critics, too, have had problems in deciding how to classify Björk's music (see also Tarvainen 2005: 88). While one writer calls her songs "electronic symphonies" (Latimer 2001), another wonders if Björk's creations might represent the start of a whole new genre of music (Lin 1997). The distinctive sound of Björk's music is often explained in terms of her production techniques, variously described as subtle, immaculate, pristine and grandiose (Appel 1995; Greenwood 2001a; Lin 2001). Such sophisticated production takes her music "to higher elevations" and "brings forth the creativity and originality" (Lin 2001). Amid the heavy use of music technology, Björk interposes musical elements that take "you back and forth between Gregorian chants and outer space" (Latimer 2001). It has been said that Björk's way of integrating choirs, harps and other performing forces from classical music makes "old fashioned strings, cutting-edge beats and radio-ready tunes" coexist within the same song (Dillard 2002). As the citations demonstrate, by combining a number of conflicting qualities into a coherent whole, Björk has gained the reputation of having created a distinct sound and image of her own, a "Björkian" reality.

Media texts and present-day myths

The public image of every artist consists of certain ideas and stories that are repeated in different media. Repetition of these narratives links one artist to other artists, to the media and to the public. In the same way, many special characteristics linked with Björk's music are explained through the artist's public persona, which musicologist Anne Tarvainen (2005: 88) describes as emotional and exaggerated, yet also contemplative and earthly. As noted earlier, the belief in an artist's uniqueness and individuality is what makes the branding of images possible. These commonly valued elements also dictate what kind of qualities the artist is expected and believed to have. As Marshall (1997: 57) argues with regard to film, the power of the image becomes activated only through cultural investment in the celebrity sign. Similarly, the construction of author images in popular music is dependent on a set of established beliefs, which we may also refer to as myths or stereotypes.

In his book *Mythologies* (1973), semiotician Roland Barthes argues that cultural myths are derived from the naturalization of signs. According to Barthes (1973: 109), a "myth cannot possibly be an object, a concept, or an idea; it is a mode of signification, a form". Barthes claims that a myth is a type of speech; it is a message that consists of material and/or other kinds of representation (Barthes 1973: 109–110).[27] Over time, certain dominant meanings crystallize as a hegemonic ideology that gains widespread acceptance among many groups and institutions (Thwaites et al. 1994: 157–158). Marshall (1997: 57) views this process as the generalization of connotative meanings, such that the members of society "no longer see the origins of the construction of representation and meaning and consider the given meanings as the real or natural meaning". The signification of the celebrity sign is under constant negotiation. Even if there was a governing consensus about what each artist represents, the positions and perspectives of the agents giving meanings to each text may vary a great deal. (Marshall 1997: 57–58.)

To all this should be added the media texts on popular music, which create and sustain certain conceptions of artists and their public images. In this regard, Björk is typically described as an extraordinarily talented person with a whimsical and eccentric character. A case in point is the following description of her second solo album *Post* (1995):

---

27 According to art theorist Vappu Lepistö (1991), a myth represents an area of cultural consciousness whose status and importance is of a fundamental nature for the community. In the context of art worlds, the notion of myth is used in referring to historically shaped, narrative beliefs and attitudes that repeat and produce the unique value of each artist. By contrast, the notion of stereotype is connected with the way people outside the art world understand artists and their works. Lepistö draws the conclusion that a myth represents cultural and literal ways of evaluating artists in a positive way, while a stereotype represents negative or questioning attitudes towards the artists. (Lepistö 1991: 42–43.)

Post breaks all the rules in the music industry and highlights humankind's most important and individualizing quality – the imagination. Bj[ö]rk's music, on all levels, is certainly one of a kind and *Post* allows the listener to partake in a collection of her creative, uncommonly insightful perceptions about reality, fantasy, the past and the future. (Jen Appel in *Nude as the News: Rock Writing for the Musically Obsessed*; Appel 1995.)

In the above citation, Björk is projected as one who makes albums according to her own wishes, not in order to sell records (Widder 2001). She is described as a groundbreaker, creating the future of music and a reality of her own, which she keeps renewing with every album she releases (Lin 1997). Björk is thus accounted as an artist that expresses her creativity through her songs and that reinvents herself with each new album (Appel 1995). Breaking new ground also seems to be Björk's own aim in making music. She says: "Not to be cruel, but I don't see the point in BritPop. I mean, it's kind of been done, you know? Either improve it or do something that hasn't been done before." (Björk in *westbrabant.net*; Björk 1997a.) Björk seems to think that artists should be able to discover new things and make music that people have not heard before. In addition to her music, such statements also strengthen Björk's image as an innovative artist.

Pieces of stardom

Pursuit of the intertextual construction of celebrity signs brings us to theories of stardom. In discussing film stardom, John Ellis (1982: 91) notes that it involves a "performer in a particular medium whose figure enters into subsidiary forms of circulation, and then feeds back into future performances". According to Ellis, the star image is not a set repertory of fixed meanings, but rather a composite of clues and representations that work constantly to make the image incoherent and incomplete. In his influential theory of film stardom, Richard Dyer (1986) analyses the star-text into four main categories. The first of these are promotional texts, which include press photos, advertisements, and the like. Second are those media texts under the control of studios, record companies and other gatekeepers. As a third category, Dyer mentions the films themselves as purveyors of the star-text. In the context of popular music, we may reckon films to be replaced by albums, live performances and other musical products (while acknowledging the fact that musical products operate in ways that not only differ from films, but even from each other). Finally, the fourth type of star texts consists of critiques and commentary, such as film or album reviews and artist biographies. (Dyer 1986: 68–72.)

The studies on stardom have mainly concentrated on film, with relatively little attention being paid to that phenomenon in popular music. Seeking to make Dyer's classification more applicable to theories on pop stardom, Janne Mäkelä (2002) has introduced the idea of a *starnet* that consists of four major components. First, there is the star him-/herself and his or her public activities; second, promotion strategies of the music industry; third, the media and their commentary on stars; and finally, the audience and its consumption of stars (Mäkelä 2002: 47–49). The artist's celebrity value and image surround the ways in which listeners interpret the songs that he or she might perform, and thus aid in the marketing of products, be they musical and otherwise (Frith 1983: 134–135; Wall 2003: 153).[28] Celebrity power explains why the artist commonly becomes the figurehead of a variety of by-products, such as TV commercials, movies, perfumes and fashion (Connell et al. 2003: 254–257; Marshall 2004: 9, 33–35). Like those, the public artist also becomes an object to be consumed.

In Ellis's writing on film stars, the film performance is described as a phenomenon wherein the star image is completed. Ellis also draws a parallel between the star system in film and in the rock music industry, where the function of film performance is replaced by that of live performance. (Ellis 1982: 92–93, 107.) Though Ellis's observation on the rock music industry is a valuable one, it should be noted that the construction of stardom varies a great deal according to the different genres of popular music. As suggested by Mäkelä (2002: 45–46), star images in music seem to be more complex than those of television and film, mainly because of issues relating to reception and public performance. There are also styles of music in which live performance is not automatically regarded as an indicator of the artist's creative capability (Mäkelä 2002: 46).

This is true in Björk's case, such that the live performance is not seen as the only way of affirming the artist's star potential; nor is it the only way of marketing the star persona to the public (Goodwin 1990: 269). Live performances of course aid in the construction of Björk's stardom; more important, however, is the fact that Björk's creations are regarded as "music for headphones" (Stefanos 1995), which alludes to a more intimate mode of musical listening. Also Björk's music videos may be seen as sort of culmination points through which she is able to put forward several essential elements of her public image, including music, visuality and public persona (O'Brien 1995: 201). As theories on stardom suggest, the construction of author images of popular music artists is a complex process that involves not only the people who take part in the actual process of music making, but the media and the audience as well

28 "Trademark value" is another term for the star's *cachet* through which different by-products are marketed (see e.g. Dickinson 2003: 84; Phillips 1999: 182).

(Coombe 1994: 105). It would, therefore, seem misleading to attribute the value of the star image entirely to the efforts of a single author.

Single authors with distinct features

Musicologist David Brackett (2000) explains the idea of single authorship in terms of the emotional charge of the music and the identification of the listener. Brackett argues that, although music is made collectively, it is common to hear the singer as the song's emotional source. This is because the listener associates the words and sounds with the most prominent voice in the recording. In this way, the audience usually perceives the singer as the song's emotional point of origin whether or not he or she is responsible for the other aspects of music making, such as songwriting, instrumental performance, arranging and engineering. As Brackett specifies, the song's emotional content is associated not only with the singer's voice but also with his/her body, public image and biographical details. (Brackett 2000: 2, 14.)

Brackett's views on the construction of musical authorship are reminiscent of Antoine Hennion's theory of the creation of artistic persona. As Hennion (1990: 188) points out, the image of a popular music artist is usually built so that the singer "must *be* the character who speaks in the first person in the song and not just *act* the part". The personage of the singer, then, becomes an image which the singer's own life history and the stories of which he/she sings are confused (Hennion 1990: 189). The artist is not believed to play a role, but to be one with the public image presented in the media. The sense of confessionalism also determines the way in which the artist's image is constructed by the media and, moreover, the way the listener interprets the music. Hennion explains the creation of the *artistic* persona by distinguishing three constituents of the *public* persona. First, there is the voice, by which Hennion does not only refer to the artist's vocal technique and capabilities; rather, it is that interesting and original sound that signals the artist's unique personality. The second element is the artist's visual image; the third, those biographical and historical elements that make the artist's voice and image appear meaningful. That history, Hennion (1990: 200) goes on to remark, may be "reconstructed according to the way it is projected visually, verbally, and musically" in the songs. As a result, the artist's personal (public) life and music become inseparable. What Hennion is saying here is that by making the song sound personal, the artist becomes more human and genuine in the eyes of the public. The "romanticized biography" not only enables the audience to identify with the artist, but it also works as the ground on which the construction of the artist's public image is based. (Hennion 1990: 199–202.)

42

In the case of Björk, her individual style includes several identifying markers. One of such features is Björk's voice, which plays a central role in her public persona. Much of Björk's special style is often explained in terms of her voice, which is "so distinct that its instantly recognisable tones stamp their character over all other sound" (Détourn 2001). Here is another typical comment in this regard, drawn from an album review of *Medúlla* (2004):

> Björk's voice is miked very closely, and with the dense layers of vocals surrounding her, it often sounds as if you're listening to the album from inside her larynx. Some of the heavy breathing, grunts, and ululating woven into the album come close to provoking physical reactions: the eerie sighs and throat singing on the feral "Ancestors" make the chest ache and suggest a particularly melodic pack of wolves. (Heather Phares in *All Music Guide*; Phares 2004.)

Because of the physicality of Björk's recorded voice, the singer becomes less distant to the listener, who may feel as if Björk is singing only for him/her. The voice may also be seen to bring Björk closer to the audience, leaving a personal imprint on the music. Some artists are often believed to have the ability to express their personalities through their distinctive and powerful voices (Cubitt 2000: 145–147; Negus 1992: 90). Anne Tarvainen (2005: 77) has observed that Björk's special use of voice is thought to reveal something intimate about the reality of the singing body.[29] In a sense, the voice is seen to work as a window through which the listener catches glimpses into the artist's more private side.

Simon Frith is another writer who stresses the centrality of the voice in the construction of the singer as a star. According to Frith (1996: 199), aside from all the packaging and publicity of the star, one's understanding of the artist persona is ultimately revealed by his/her voice. As Frith (1996: 199) puts it, "for the pop star the 'real me' is a promise that lies in the way we hear the voice".[30] Tarvainen (2005: 68) points out that the meanings given to a certain singing event are connected not only to the song's lyrics, melody and other musical elements, but also to the singer's physical movements and to the listening experience itself. Not least, both the singer's and the listener's cultural and individual backgrounds are involved in the process of listening (Tarvainen 2005: 68). Through these different functions, the singer's voice has a powerful impact on the construction of the star image – a fact that seems to hold true in the case of Björk.

Björk stands out also because of the exotic looks and idiosyncratic visual style, as imaged on her album covers, music videos and clothing. Another distinctive feature

---

29   Here Tarvainen (2005: 77) is referring to some of the rustling and creaking sounds of Björk's voice.
30   Frith (1996: 187) explains the personal expressiveness of singers by dividing the voice into four categories: voice as *a musical instrument*, as *a body*, as *a person* and as *a character*.

of Björk's public image is her geographical background[31], such that her music is often seen to reflect her life and experiences as an Icelander. According to media texts, Björk's geographical background extends into almost everything she does as an artist: "Björk is Icelandic through and through: an eccentric, unwavering individual who puts everything she has into every project" (Michael Heumann in *Stylus Magazine*; Heumann 2004). Nationality would probably not play such a central role if Björk had been born in some better-known country. In Björk's case, the Icelandic roots are a central element in the construction of her celebrity image and artistic persona, which are seen as unique, setting her apart from other artists (Appel 1995; Latimer 2001; Widder 2001). Björk's local identity is regarded as a characteristic that also strengthens the artist's image as a prodigy, who expresses her unique feelings and artistic visions by means of her music. Björk herself underlines the effect that her local identity has had on her music, as the following citation illustrates:

> In fact, I really don't think my music, or me, is especially Scandinavian, 'cause what is Scandinavian? I don't believe that there is a special Scandinavian style – or sound. [...] And yet I feel that my music is very Icelandic – exactly because I'm from Iceland. (Björk in *Agenda*; Ryming 1993.)

Björk, in the above quote, seems to be aware of the kind of eccentric image that people associate with the fact that she is from Iceland.[32] According to Björk, however, even Icelanders think her music is strange:

> In Iceland people think my music is weird. They say it sounds foreign to them. And here in England my friends say: 'Your music is strange. It must be because you're from Iceland'. (Björk in *Agenda*; Ryming 1993.)

In addition to her voice and visual image, Björk's local identity is, then, one of the elements that support the artist's star image as a peculiar figure.

Between nature and technology

Another characteristic linked with the belief in a single, originating authorship, and one of the central elements of Björk's public image, is the idea according to which the artist can express his/her feelings and thoughts only through creative activities (see

---

31 In fact, according to John Connell and Chris Gibson (2003: 91), a tendency to search for links between sites and sounds, and to locate the artist or the scene in physical space, is a common element of popular music literature. For more about Björk's geographical origins and the question of Icelandic sound, see Connell et al. 2003: 93–95.

32 The issue of locality is also brought out in Björk's video imagery, which will be discussed more later on.

e.g. Lepistö 1991: 48; Toynbee 2000: 102–103). Bennett (2005: 60) pays attention to this mysterious aspect of the originating author, who is seen "as a subject inspired by forces outside himself, forces that allow him to produce work originality and genius". The idea of an author's compulsive need to create seems to describe Björk's artistic persona and attitude towards the process of music making. For example, when asked how she spent her holidays, Björk replied that she would write tunes even in her spare time, because she loves doing what she does (Björk in *SpinOnline*; Björk 1997b). She also characterizes herself as "a freak who was born singing" (Björk in *Q*; Maconie 1995) – suggesting that her very nature compels her to sing and make music; it is the way she was born and she cannot imagine any other way of living. Björk's public image, thus, gives an impression that making music is not just a job or hobby for the artist, but a way of living instead. The presented image of Björk also recalls that notion which sees the artist's creative power as an innate ability.

On that view, creative talents are regarded as natural, inborn qualities that the artist either possesses or does not. Björk's image is further complicated by her lavish use of music technology. In the following extract, Björk explains how she perceives the relation between rural and urban, humans and machines, nature and technology:

> I think that in popular music today people are trying to come to terms with the fact that they are living with all of these machines, and trying to combine machines and humans and trying to marry them in a happy marriage: trying to be optimistic about it. I was brought up by a mother who believed fiercely in nature and wanted me just to be barefoot 24 hours and all of these things, so I was brought up with this big guilt complex of cars and skyscrapers, and I was taught to hate them, and then I think I'm, like, in the middle. I can see this generation who are ten years younger than me making music, trying to live with it. But everything is with those regular rhythms and learning to love them, but still be human, still be all gritty and organic. (Björk in *Dazed and Confused* 1996; Björk 1996.)

Along with her talk about machines and industrialization Björk uses concepts such as human and organic. With these terms Björk seems to stress the creative aspect of her music making.[33] On the other hand, the use of music technology seems to put her "in the middle", between nature and culture. Nevertheless, the idea of single authorship is still present with Björk: it is Björk who is presented as expressing her feelings and thoughts through the music, whereas music technology is used merely as a tool for carrying out the artist's visions. Björk seems to make little discrimination between making music with newer technology or with more traditional instruments:

---

33 Lepistö (1991) notes that another of the dichotomies linked with the Romantic myth is the juxtaposition of nature and culture. Because of that polarity, society and culture are seen to confine and suppress the artist's creative power (Lepistö 1991: 48).

I take technology personally. Machines are just tools, and in that way a synthesizer or a sequencer is no colder than a guitar or a flute. People tend to treat newly invented things as enemies, as a threat to their security. But it's a question of how you use them: A song will be warm if you put warmth in it. (Björk in *Wired*; Berry 1998.)

Björk feels that she – not technology – is in charge of things; she is the one making the decisions and the one presented as the songs' originator. She views music technology as a tool that enables the artist to be more independent and free from intermediaries. As the following comment makes clear, for Björk, the development of music technology is not an obstacle, but a possibility:

Orchestras used to need 50 people in order to fill a whole room with sound. Then the rock band could do it. Now you just need one person. It's cheaper. It's easier. You've got more control. (Björk in *Wired*; Berry 1998.)

In a sense, technology enables artists to take even more control of their music making (see also Christophe Den Tandt 2004: 150; Rojola 2004: 64–65; Théberge 2004: 143). This is how Björk describes her feeling of power over a number of different stages and authorial roles during the creative process:

Technology used to complicate things, and now it's simplifying. I've gone up, like, nine points in being a business woman because I've got a little organizer, and I can, write songs and arrange things. You just need a machine, and you can put out records. So companies, you won't need them, and you won't need media because of Internet. (Björk in *Rolling Stone*; Udovitch 1994.)

Technological innovations have also affected the development of the star system. In explaining the relation between technology and stardom, David Buxton (1990) argues that the nuances of "personality" in each singer were heightened by the invention and further developments of the microphones used in recording. The development of radio technology, too, made it possible to distribute recordings, and thus, to market musical stardom on a mass scale (Buxton 1990: 429–430). As Buxton concludes, it was no longer a question of what artists *did*, but what they were *like*:

Rock stars, as agents of consumer discipline, help to define the norms and limits of the existing sociohistorical consumer, and thus individual possibilities. They anchor a chaotic aesthetico-ideological discourse and represent it in a "humanized" form by investing the human body itself. (Buxton 1990: 434.)

According to Björk's public persona, recording technology is one of the main reasons her music sounds as it does. Nonetheless, the image of the self-expressing artist and her celebrity power seem to exceed the sense of impersonality that is often related to the use of music technology (Frith 1986: 265; Schumacher 1995: 264; Warner 2003: 103). As Björk herself hints above, the artist is still presented as imposing her personal imprint on the music, since it is the author, and not the technological equipment, that is believed to be in charge.

The taskmaster and her crew

From the beginning of her solo career, Björk has collaborated with many celebrated artists within the field of electronic dance music. Björk produced her first two solo albums *Debut* (1993) and *Post* (1995) with Nellee Hooper, and later worked with artists such as Underworld, Tricky, Graham Massey, Howie B. (on *Post*), as well as Matmos and harpist Zeena Parkins on *Vespertine* (2001). The most significant impact of those contributors lies in the areas of production and arranging. Björk comments on the writing as distinct from the arranging of her music:

> Most of my songs I write on my own, and it's like a diary thing, like a relationship I have with myself. When it comes to arranging them, I almost like need a midwife to sort of get it out of my system. (Björk in an interview by Dustin Rabin; Rabin 2005.)

Although it seems to be important for Björk to maintain her own individuality and authorial power, she is willing to acknowledge the contributions of artists with whom she collaborates. She states: "But I always collaborate and it always says in big letters on the record that these are Nellee Hooper's beats, or this is a song written and produced by Björk and Tricky" (Björk in *Q*; Elliot 1997). Björk's desire to be in charge of her own music making also comes through in the following remarks, about why she wanted to pursue a solo career after first being a member of The Sugarcubes:

> When I worked with The Sugarcubes, it was never my music – my ideas. It was a conglomeration of a whole bunch of people's ideas, the people who were The Sugarcubes. When I decided to make *Debut*, I told myself: "Ok. I've tried to satisfy all of these people and it has been tremendous fun". But it was always other people's dreams we made alive, now, I want to realise my own little vision. (Björk in *Agenda*; Ryming 1993.)

Björk relates elsewhere that, after letting go of the idea that making a solo album would be a selfish act, she finally decided that she had to make a recording with her own face on the front and containing only original songs (Aston 1996: 184–185).

The above citations indicate that artistic self-sufficiency and collective collaboration are central elements of Björk's authorship. Collaboration is emphasized on her album *Medúlla*, which features the input of miscellaneous beatboxers, vocalists, songwriters, choirs and programmers. That album also works as an indication of what can be done with the help of digital music technologies and sound manipulation, since all the sounds on it were created by using the human voice as a source of both sampled electronic and acoustic effects (Collins 2004). The album may thus be seen to represent Björk as an experimentalist who is unrivalled in both creative power and in adapting and combining disparate musical elements and traditions. Confirming this view is the following extract from an album review:

> On the surface, *Medúlla* swoops and hums like a typical Björk album, showcasing her spastic and solemn sides in dramatic songs that suck up all the air around them. The denser track feature swaths of voices in unorthodox settings – odd choral chants, human-beatbox drum lines, nasal noise riffs – but they basically mimic the avant-pop backings that first made Björk a futuristic throwback to crooner-era swing, Bollywood soundtracks, hyperactive jungle, and fidgety glitch electronica. (Andy Battaglia in *Audio Video Revolution*; Battaglia 2004.)

Even though the co-artists' input is often mentioned in album reviews, there seems to be no question of who is regarded as the main and controlling force behind the songs (Battaglia 2004; Beaumont 2004). In fact, despite the great number of contributors involved in the music making, Björk's way of collaborating with various artists is often seen as another implication of her strength, as demonstrated by her careful choice and usage of collaborators (Battaglia 2004; Détourn 2001). Even when the input of a guest vocalist may dominate a song, and even if Björk is said to cross "the fine line of collaboration and guesting on her own album" (Beaumont 2004), the resulting album is still seen as another creation by Björk, the artist.

What explains the way of emphasizing Björk's autonomy and individuality in her author image? Again, it is the functioning of the celebrity sign. The latter is also underlined when an artist's public image is imported into a context other than the one in which it was first introduced. This is what happened when Björk played the leading role in the film *Dancer in the Dark* (2000), directed by Lars von Trier. In the film, Björk plays a Czech immigrant Selma who, with the help of imaginative musical scenes, escapes the misery of daily life. The separation of Björk's star image from that of her screen character, Selma, was made even more difficult by the fact that Björk composed the music for the resulting soundtrack album, *Selmasongs* (2000). Many reviewers regarded the album not only as a soundtrack but also as another album by Björk the artist (Phares 2002; Widder 2000). For example, the striking vocals and shuffling, industrial beats on the album have been seen to "reflect Selma's life in the factory as well as Björk's distinctive style" (Phares 2002: 101–102). In this case, Björk's character Selma is regarded as the authorial source of the songs, while the album's sound is connected with Björk's earlier output and her public persona. In the end, the album is seen as another indication of Björk's artistic vision, although the songs on it were originally written for the film and even though the boundaries between the personalities of "Selma the character" and "Björk the artist" are blurred every now and then. Björk produced the album together with the American arranger-conductor Vincent Mendoza, and she co-wrote the lyrics with the film's director (von Trier) and the Icelandic poet Sjón Sigurdsson; still, critics regarded the album as an outcome of Björk's unique vision (Phares 2002; Widder 2000). Despite the collaborative authorship of the project, Björk is viewed as making all the decisions and credited with the dominant creative input of the final product. As the reactions of the critics prove, the impact of the celebrity sign is so powerful as to make receivers of the work see the artist's creative signature in everything that the celebrity chooses to do.

Visual reflections of Björk

In connection with the construction of the artist's public image and his/her celebrity status, *music videos* function to present the artist's persona in detail.[34] By analysing music videos, it is also possible to gain a better understanding of the elements that make up the artist's public image.[35] In Björk's authorship, visuality has always played an important part, which makes it interesting to examine the ways in which her music videos support the artist's image as both innovative and originary (see also Nielsen 2006: 168–169). The music videos do not, however, represent Björk's artistic vision as such, since it is the director who is responsible for the final outcome. Rather, the videos reflect the director's perspective on the artist, as represented through the chosen themes and imagery. Hence the videos serve to reaffirm the visual imagery that is already linked with each artist. Through such imagery, it is also possible to expand and revise an artist's established image by introducing styles and looks that differ from the more familiar ones. The clips may provide the audience with material that forces them to amend their views on the artist. A more or less renewed visual appearance is usually introduced in connection with the release of each new album. The renovated looks also support the sense that "progress" is taking place in the artist's career. Overall, the visual imagery provided by music videos – together with album covers, photographs and other visual material – builds up an artistic identity that is easy to recognize.

---

34 Antti Alanen (1992: 127) notes that, since the 1970s, music videos have worked as an important tool for introducing new artists, as well as for presenting new images by already known artists.
35 Antti-Ville Kärjä (2005: 62) suggests there are at least four analytical strategies for analysing music videos; namely, in terms of: structural elements, relations between image and sound (synaesthetic aspects), intertextual connections (between other works, artists or styles), and genre, this last making it easier to examine the musical and visual elements as part of a larger socio-cultural context.

In the following, I analyse six of Björk's music videos directed by the French director Michel Gondry. The songs of the videos are from three different Björk albums: "Human Behaviour" is from *Debut* (1993); three songs – "Army Of Me", "Isobel", and "Hyperballad" – from *Post* (1995); "Jóga" and "Bachelorette" from Björk's third solo album, *Homogenic* (1997). In addition to Björk's videos, Gondry has worked with artists like The Rolling Stones, Sheryl Crow, Radiohead and The White Stripes.[36] It was, however, the videos he made for Björk that helped Gondry to establish his value as a director, prompting many other artists to seek collaboration with him (Beauvallet 1999). Gondry, who directed Björk's first solo video, *Human Behaviour*, has become particularly instrumental to Björk's career. The visual world that Gondry introduced in that video became not only the starting point for Björk's future videos, but it also defined the singer's visual image and conveyed it to audiences.

Gondry's unique style of working suggests that he tries to include something of his private artistic vision in the videos he directs. In the end, Gondry is responsible for the video's overall imagery, though Björk and the director are said to consult with each other at length during the filming process (Beauvallet 1999). In fact, Gondry and Björk are told to have rather dissimilar points of departure for planning videos. While many of Gondry's ideas are said to originate in his dreams, Björk's views are held to be more biographical in nature, departing from the writing process and history of her songs. We may say, then, that even though the videos present the director's overall vision, the artist's star persona makes its own imprint on each video. In fact, it is often suggested in media texts Björk chose Gondry as her collaborator because she finds his style of directing suitable to her ways of making (and representing) music. (Beauvallet 1999.) Nevertheless, Björk's videos do in fact constitute *fusions* of both her and Gondry's artistic visions.

All the videos directed by Gondry are built around Björk's character. Each video includes close-ups of the artist's face, thus emphasising whose video the viewer is watching. There is no doubt as to who is playing the leading role – it is Björk who forms the centre of attention, even though four of the videos (*Human Behaviour, Army of Me, Isobel* and *Bachelorette*) also involve a number of minor characters. In the two other videos (*Hyperballad* and *Jóga*) Björk is the only figure shown. The emphasis on Björk's character may be seen to reflect her image as an independent artist who is a "lonely traveller" in the field of popular music. Björk is therefore presented as an eccentric persona, who disregards the opinions of others, and makes music as she would have it. Even in videos such as *Army of Me* and *Bachelorette*, which have a more or less distinct plot, all events revolve around Björk's character. In these videos, Björk is pictured as an active agent that is undertaking some kind of a mission. For example,

36   See www.michelgondry.com, as accessed 8 November 2006.

at the beginning of *Army of Me*, there is a scene in which Björk sits in the cab of an impressive truck (see *Picture 1*). Although Björk looks tiny when steering the enormous vehicle, it is she alone who is presented as being in charge. Gondry's way of portraying the artist as an active agent may also be connected with Björk's desire to exert full control over her career and music making. As a result, Björk is depicted as a self-sufficient artist, who needs no helpers, but does everything herself – whether it is a question of writing songs, driving a huge truck, fighting against a powerful gorilla, or saving the one she loves by blowing up a museum – just to list some of the events in *Army of Me*.

Picture 1. Björk, in video Army of Me: Truck-driving character assertive of industry and self-sufficiency.

Gondry's videos typically feature close-up shots of Björk, which naturally put emphasis on her facial features and expressions. By showing the artist's face in close-up, Gondry focuses the viewer's attention on Björk's singing. The close-ups of Björk's mouth further stress the uniqueness of her voice. Also, Björk's intense facial expressions strengthen the impression of the artist's vocal expression as a particularly pow

Picture 2. Björk, in video Jóga: Icelandic landscapes, emphasizing the artist's native country.

erful one. Shots showing the inside of Björk's mouth make it clear to viewers that she is the authorial and emotional source of the songs. *Jóga* is the only video by Gondry in which Björk is not shown singing. Even though the imagery of *Jóga* consists of pictures of landscapes, the video contains features that ally it with Björk and her usual public image. The most obvious connection between the digitally postproduced video imagery and Björk's background is the fact that *Jóga* was shot in Iceland (see *Picture 2*). The beginning and ending sequences of the video present Björk in a white shape, first lying on the ground and then standing on a mountain top. Although Björk's character is mostly absent from view, the video is coordinated with elements of the song. First, the shooting is synchronized with the song's rhythm throughout the video. Second, the visual material supports the song's lyrics. Björk sings: "You don't have to speak / I feel / emotional landscapes / they puzzle me". Also in the opening and closing scenes, Björk's character has her mouth shut and eyes closed, or she is not looking at the camera, as if to underline the artist's strong relation with the surrounding landscapes.

Björk is also placed in the heart of nature in other of Gondry's videos. *Human Behaviour*, *Isobel* and *Bachelorette* are partly shot in a forest setting. The three videos form a trilogy about a girl who lives in the woods, visits the big city and eventually re-

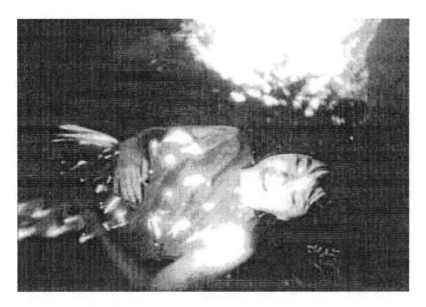

Picture 3. Björk, in scene from Isobel, her figure shown merging with water.

turns to the forest. In *Human Behaviour*, Björk lives in a cottage, until she gets chased and eaten by a bear. Björk's relation to nature is even more emphasized in *Isobel*, as Björk's figure is overlapped with pictures of woods and water (see *Picture 3*). In the middle sequence, skyscrapers rise from the ground when Björk is visiting the city, but she returns to the forest at the end of the video. The beginning of *Bachelorette* carries on the black-and-white theme of *Isobel*, but in contrast to *Isobel*, it becomes colourised as the video progresses. Early in *Bachelorette*, Björk leaves for the city, bound for a publisher to whom she is delivering a book that tells her life story. Björk's character looks perplexed throughout the sequence shot in the urban surroundings. By contrast, in the closing scene, which takes place in the forest, she appears more confident in the bright lighting, as the beats (i.e. noises of the city) fade away, replaced by a lone accordion that accompanies Björk's singing.

Given its central position in Björk's videos, nature may be seen as an important source of inspiration for her music making. Shots of the city and the flashing lights, on the other hand, feature the use of music technology and industrial beats. Such scenes, then, bring us back to the dichotomy between nature and culture, or rural and urban, respectively. By showing Björk in a prone position, as if merged into the landscapes of mountain and water – a scene that is repeated in *Human Behaviour*, *Isobel*, *Hy-*

perballad and *Jóga* – the videos give the impression that she is "at one with nature", whereas the urban surroundings are something that she wishes to get away from. The natural environment may also be seen to describe the artist's overall public image: raw and whimsical, wearing only a touch of make-up, as if stressing the sense of honesty and truthfulness that is linked with Björk's music and star persona. The unusual imagery, camera angles, lighting and other effects in Gondry's videos make them into something like absurd fairy tales, which tend to leave the viewer confused about how to interpret them. In *Isobel* and *Hyperballad*, for example, the sense of ambiguity is heightened as pictures of Björk's face are set one atop the other, or when Björk's character is morphed into an animated figure. Gondry's play with images and surreal characters may also be seen as correlates to the mixture of different musical styles and elements typical of Björk's music. Despite the ambiguity of Gondry's video imagery, one message is fairly clear: the videos are just as peculiar as Björk's music and public persona are typically thought to be.

Conclusion

Author images serve as a means of uniting and classifying everything an artist does into a coherent body of works. A recognizable style and public image link the music to its authorial source, drawing a line between other artists with their own distinct styles and images. Because of the established connection between the music and its author, the process of music making is often seen as a form of the artist's self-expression. This way of thinking is not confined just to the listening audience; the media also use the belief in an originating artist in the aid of marketing and promoting various artist-related products. In this manner, the music becomes identified with the public artist, whose star image and celebrity power make the products appear unique and original and, thus, desirable.

Author images can be seen as intertextual signs that consist of specific types of narratives, such that a specified image is connected with each artist. In the case of Björk, her public image is constructed around such elements as her Icelandic roots, distinctive voice and personal visual style. Also coming together in Björk's star image are many features associated with ideas of artistic peculiarity, self-sufficiency, and the artist's pursuit of control. Björk's star persona is further established through the unique imagery of her music videos. The emphasis on Björk's local identity and other distinctive features enable the artist to stand out in today's global world of popular music.

According to her authorial image, Björk appears either as a type of prodigy for whom the music works as a way of expressing her feelings and artistic visions, or as an exceptionally creative individual whose creations represent the future of music. The belief in a single, originating authorship remains firmly fixed in Björk's public image, despite her use of music technology and collaborations with various artists. Björk's mysterious authorial image seems to occupy a unique position in the general field of popular music. Still, she is clearly not the only popular music artist to be presented as a single, originating author. The persistence of the belief in single authorship reveals audiences' penchant for considering popular music artists as exceptional, different or special as compared to "ordinary" people.

2. Stardom in disguise

Author image as a marketing asset

The authorial input of popular music artists is not limited to making and performing music. The artist also represents the music through his/her personal appearance, as shown in photographs, music videos, TV commercials, live performances, album covers and homepages on the Internet (cf. Ahonen 2006a; Goodwin 1992: 51; Negus 1992: 67). The visual image also helps audience members to recognize the artist. Sometimes listeners may become familiar with an artist's looks even before hearing his or her music. It is quite possible for the audience to identify artists based on celebrity criteria alone, without being able to name any of their songs. The use of visual imagery also intensifies the impression that the artist is sharing something personal through the music.

Despite the centrality of visual marketing in the construction of star careers, some popular music artists have author images that are not defined by personal appearance (see e.g. Den Tandt 2004; Herman 2006; McLeod 2003: 352). David Buxton (1990: 437) links the sense of anonymity in star images with the decline of the star system and with the emergence of computer technology in music. Faceless imagery is often connected with certain musical styles, most notably electronic dance music, in which music technology commonly plays a large part in the music making. As an example, Buxton (1990: 437) mentions the German group Kraftwerk[37], whose pioneering electronic music may be described as robotic, as was their visual imagery. Other groundbreaking bands also became known for having author images based on the artist's nonimagery; these include art-rock bands of the 1970s and 1980s, such as New Order and Pink Floyd, who favoured faceless designs for their album covers (Den Tandt 2004: 145; Goodwin 1992: 113).[38] The minimal visual presence of band members does not, however, mean that such artists have no public image. Quite the contrary: by questioning the familiar imagery of popular music, it is possible to create alternative ways of promoting artists and their works.

---

37 The author image of Kraftwerk and its relation to the genre of electronic music is discussed in chapter 6.
38 It should be noted that the idea of the artist's facelessness does not apply only to electronic dance music or to the mentioned art-rock bands; artists with masked identities can be found in other genres as well. The American glam rock band KISS and the Finnish hard rock band Lordi (winner of the 2006 Eurovision Song Contest) are some examples of groups whose members only perform in certain outfits. In contrast to Daft Punk, all the members of KISS and Lordi have stage names and wear recognizable and unchanging outfits. An earlier band that became known for its secrecy was The Residents, which was formed as early as 1966 (Ankeny 2006).

In this chapter, I deal with the question of the *visual author image* – or rather, its rejection – and the role of visuality in the marketing of popular music. The focus of the examination is on the visual promotion of popular music, even though it is clear that visual imagery is only one of the elements – together with the musical works, album reviews, interviews, etc. – that make up the artist's author image. In addition to artists whose author images are based on the idea of single originating authorship and whose music is marketed with the help of their recognizable star personas, there are some artists whose public images are presented only in disguise. In such preservations of anonymity, the visual imagery that is normally built around the artist's personal appearance must be replaced by another set of images. Star identities and author images are also used as a means of predicting the public's taste. In such cases, the author serves as means of regulating aspects of popular music culture. As Andrew Goodwin (1992: 105) points out, "[s]tardom and persona are the mechanisms through which record companies seek out career longevity for their investments". Goodwin (1992: 110–111) distinguishes two opposing ways of bringing the artist and his/her star image together. On the one hand, there are artists who take on a star persona to the extent of "becoming" that character (e.g. Bruce Springsteen); on the other hand, some artists are continually adopting new personas (e.g. David Bowie). Despite their apparent differences, all star images are built around some concept of authorship. As Goodwin (1992: 110) remarks, the narratives used to construct that authorship do not inhere in any given musical product, but rather in popular music culture in general. Needless to say, the driving purpose of such narratives is to promote public awareness of the artists and their music.

(Non)visual promotion

According to Tim Wall (2003: 111), the music industry and record companies see other media as promotional avenues for the music they produce and represent. The media by which the music of each artist is promoted are not chosen randomly, but picked according to market segmentation. That is to say, audiences are divided into groups that are believed to be potential buyers of specific styles of music. For example, dance music is mostly promoted directly through club DJs, whereas the promotion of a mainstream rock band is more likely focused on reviews and interviews published in certain music magazines. (Wall 2003: 111.) Keith Negus (1992: 42) argues that the marketing of music is also based on the relationship between the artist's (constructed) identity and the lived experience of consumers. Negus views the artist's visual image as a product manufactured by record companies, rather than as an inseparable part of his/her personality. On this basis, record companies may be accused of treating performers like puppets, by exerting control over the artist's appearance, statements and behaviour.[39] However, visual marketers do not consider themselves manipulators or propagandists, but rather as persons whose job it is to bring out and cultivate an artist's inherent personality and innate style. In short, marketing personnel would claim that they enhance the artist's image rather than impose it. The degree of enhancement, as Negus makes clear, depends largely upon the artist involved – some artists have a strong idea of their own image, while others consider visual imagery relatively unimportant. (Negus 1992: 64–65.) All the same, the artist's visual image, regardless of what it is like, must be established no later than, and preferably before, that moment when the artist's persona is first introduced to the public.

According to Negus, much promotional imagery is based on the imitation of pre-existing, genre-specific styles. To a great extent, then, the artist's author image consists of a set of codes and connotations that reinforce the artist's musical identity. (Negus 1992: 65, 67.) The visual imagery connected to the artist's public figure does not just give evidence of physical appearance. Rather, as Cynthia Fuchs (1999: 18) points out, images also embody social, commercial and political representations through which artists express their values and beliefs. When conjoined with the meanings to be linked with each artist, the image conveys something more than just a visual surface. The imagery linked with the public persona should also accord with whatever musical style the artist represents. Negus (1992: 70) also stresses the artist's ability to carry his/her image convincingly in a range of settings. As Negus (1992: 72) concludes, the visual marketing of an artist usually involves an attempt to articulate a specific image which operates as a ground for the artist's entire musical identity.

The foregoing observations on visual marketing and promotional material demonstrate the fact that the activities of popular music culture rest heavily on artists and their star images. The notion of author in popular music does not, then, necessarily refer to the source of meaning of a musical work. As media culture theorist John Hartley (2002: 15) puts it, "authorship is more a way of organising marketing strategies and conferring value on intellectual property than a way of accounting for meaning". Hence the artist's effort to be as self-sufficient as possible is valued for a number of reasons. The artist's sense of independence may also work as a way of acquiring a lot of credit – both in terms of financial gain and artistic respect among peer musicians,

---

39   Graeme Turner (2004: 41) makes a similar point about the agents, managers and publicists of the celebrity industry. According to Turner, these so-called third parties try to mask and naturalize their professional practices. The job of the agents, managers and publicists is, for example, to find work and to arrange publicity for their clients, to write press releases and to negotiate with magazine editors and other media representatives about how their client will be represented in photographs, articles and other media. At the same time, Turner remarks that "what these industries do is not easy to distinguish and therefore their importance is not easy to assess". (Turner 2004: 42–45.)

the media and the members of the audience (Shuker 1994: 111–114; see also Frith 1986: 134–135). As an example, Fuchs (1999: 181) mentions Madonna and Prince as stars who have managed to take charge of their own public images. Madonna, especially, is known for her use of music videos as a means of playing with various personalities (Fuchs 1999: 181; see also McClary 1991: 150).[40]

Another act that controls its public image is the French duo, Daft Punk. The duo's faceless image seems to question marketing strategies that are based on the artist's personal appearance and star value. The purpose of the following examination is to clarify the ways in which the band's masked identity differs from author images that are based on an artist's visual star persona. Artists with faceless images commonly understand the artist's image as a fragmented category. (The relation between disguised images and incoherent identities will be discussed more closely later, in an analysis of the imagery of Daft Punk's music videos.) In addition to music videos, the material analysed in this chapter consists of written media texts, including artist interviews and album reviews. Also addressed are the following questions: Is it possible to use a faceless author image as a protest against the conventional star system and visual marketing? Or is the use of mysterious imagery merely another way of gaining recognition?

The masked anonymity of Daft Punk

Daft Punk is a French electronic dance-music duo that was formed by Thomas Bangalter and Guy-Manuel de Homem-Christo in Paris in 1992. Before Daft Punk's international breakthrough, the two men were members of an indie band called Darlin.[41] Bangalter and Homem-Christo played bass and guitar in their first line-up; after Darlin's break-up, they switched to synthesizers and samplers, and started making house and techno-based electronic dance music.[42] Though Daft Punk relies heavily on new music technology, a number of earlier musical influences on the band members, including the genres of pop, indie rock and hip-hop, receive frequent mention in descriptions of the band's music. (Cooper 2002: 278; see also Poschardt 1995: 428.)

---

40 It is worth noting that the slipping in and out of various subject positions, typical of Madonna and other similar artists, does not lessen the artist's control over his/her own image and artistic identity (Williams 2001: 93).

41 The name Daft Punk was inspired by a review written on Darlin's release that was published in *Melody Maker*. In the review, the writer described Darlin's sound as "daft punk" (Collin 1997).

42 In 1996, Daft Punk released its debut album *Homework*. Soon after its release, *Homework* became one of the albums of electronic dance music that brought the genre to mainstream audiences. Since then the group has released two more albums: *Discovery* (2001) and *Human After All* (2005). In 2006 the band also published a compilation album, *Musique Vol. 1 1993-2005*. Daft Punk's songs, such as "Around The World" and "One More Time", have become well known, especially by dance-club audiences. (Cooper 2002: 278; Woholeski 2001.)

Picture 4. Daft Punk, dressed in trademark futuristic outfits. (Photo by: Kai Jünemann.)

In 1994 the duo made a decision to remove themselves from the public eye, after a photo-shoot heralding the release of their first single. Ever since that shooting, the men have appeared only in disguise, wearing robot helmets for example, or having their faces distorted digitally.[43] (Osborne 2001.) Since the release of the band's second album *Discovery* in 2001, the futuristic robot outfits have become Daft Punk's main visual trademark (see *Picture 4*). The duo has created a somewhat fabulous tale that explains their disguised image. This is how Bangalter tells their story[44] in an interview:

> We did not decide to become robots. There was an accident in our studio. We were working on our sampler, and at exactly 9:09 a.m. on September 9, 1999, it exploded. When we regained consciousness, we discovered that we had become robots. (Thomas Bangalter in *Remix*; Gill 2001.)

---

43 Daft Punk is not the only group to use faceless imagery. For example, distorted facial pictures of the British electronic-based dance pop duo, Pet Shop Boys, appear on the cover of the band's *Nightlife* album from 1999. One of the band members, Chris Lowe, commonly wears sunglasses in publicity shots and on album covers, whereas the other member, Neil Tenant, is less hesitant about revealing his "true" visual identity.
44 It seems that Bangalter usually acts as the band's spokesman.

Despite the fact that the story is obviously fictitious, it nevertheless has become a part of Daft Punk's public image and artist biography. Though they are opposed to the star system of popular music, Daft Punk needs to have some kind of a history and visual image, even if these elements are hidden behind masks and fiction. To operate within popular music culture, each artist needs to have an image – whether it is based on the idea of the artist's facelessness or on star appeal. In the case of Daft Punk, the band's disguised author image has become its trademark: the robot masks represent the men's faces, while the fictional tale works as the band's biography.

Though viewing Daft Punk's masked imagery as just another way of constructing stardom, we may still ask if there are any underlying differences between the images that are built around the artist's star value and those based on the use of faceless imagery. According to Bangalter, the difference between the conventional star system and Daft Punk's public image lies in the band's way of emphasizing the creative use of promotional material. In the following quote, Bangalter describes the duo's aim to exploit the marketing in a creative fashion:

> To present our faces would just be information data and we like to work with artistic data. This way we can transform any promotional activity into creative activity. (Thomas Bangalter in *Guardian Unlimited*; Osborne 2001.)

Here Bangalter is claiming that the artist's publicity should not be an end in itself; rather, the main focus should be on the music, not the artist's public persona. Through its faceless author image, Daft Punk wishes to lay greatest emphasis on the music and how it is used, with less attention going to the persons who create and perform it. However, the faceless image does not mean that visuality plays no role in Daft Punk's authorship. Instead, in Daft Punk's case, its image seems to work as a comprehensive entity that includes the imagery presented on album covers and music videos. One detail that indicates the band's interest in the visual is the fact that their *Discovery* album also serves as the soundtrack of a Japanese-style, animated musical entitled *Interstella 5555: The 5tory of the 5ecret 5tar 5ystem* (2003).[45] Though Daft Punk does not wish to focus attention on the band members' personal appearance, they clearly evidence a concern for the band's overall visual image.[46] Here is Bangalter's comment on the matter:

---

45 Daft Punk co-produced the film with the Japanese director Leiji Matsumoto. The film tells a story of five extraterrestrial musicians who are kidnapped and taken to Earth. (Www.leijiverse.com, as accessed 8 November 2006.)

46 There are also artists whose music is categorized as electronic music, but whose faces are not necessarily replaced by logos and labels. Moby, The Chemical Brothers, and Fatboy Slim are some of such artists who have adopted more conventional ways of constructing stardom, which rely on the artist's star persona (see e.g. McLeod 2003: 350).

> We are completely interested in the visual concept on the whole – album covers, videos. How we look is irrelevant. It has always been irrelevant in house or techno music. (Thomas Bangalter in *Montreal Mirror*; Silcott 1997.)

Bangalter (Silcott 1997) prefers to see the band's logo as the star; the artists' personal visual appearance should not be the focus of media attention.

Home-made musicianship

In media texts, Daft Punk's music is generally referred to as a combination of several musical styles, ranging from house, rock and funk to baroque-style electronica (Richert 2001). Techniques of collage and pastiche, inevitably linked with the mixing of styles[47], complicate the band's status as the only authorial source of their music. Instead of emphasizing the author's status as a creator, the sense of multiplicity brings out the social and intertextual nature of music making (cf. Novitz 2001: 163). Yet despite the various stylistic influences, the duo still wishes to be in charge of its music making. Bangalter seems to especially appreciate the opportunity to work in his own studio as long as needed, while otherwise, "you have to go to a studio and you never get the time or result you want" (Thomas Bangalter in *Guardian Unlimited*; Osborne 2001). The role of studio technology is implicit in Bangalter's way of describing the band members' artistic identities:

> We consider ourselves musicians at some point because we write songs and play some instruments, but I guess we prefer to consider ourselves producers. A producer is not about just the music, but instead making something happen, having an idea and making it real. (Thomas Bangalter in *DJ Times Magazine*; Woholeski 2001.)

Bangalter's comment suggests that the studio is no longer used merely as a means of documenting a performance (see also Negus 1992: 88; Poschardt 1995: 278–279), but it works as a tool used by producers and artists to prove their artistic skills and creative capabilities. The studio is regarded as an instrument as such – one that plays a central role in the process of music making (Des Pres et al. 2000: 138; Théberge 2004: 143).

Working in their home studios enhances the duo's ability to be in charge of their music. According to culture and music theorist Christophe Den Tandt (2004: 150), the home studio is a domesticated space in which musicians may seek, at their own pace, to master various production skills (see also Rojola 2004: 64–65).[48] Ulf Poschardt

---

47 See e.g. Hartley 2002: 22–23; Strinati 1995: 232–233.
48 Dent Tandt (2004: 150) links this type of studio wizardry to solitary musicians and producers like Brian Wilson.

(1995: 429) points out the rather obvious association of the title of the band's *Home-work* (1996) album with something that is done in the home.[49] Though Daft Punk's author image and music are combinations of various eclectic elements, it is important for the band to be in charge of its public image and music making. In addition to its faceless image, Daft Punk's control over their own music making helps to isolate the band from the familiar star system and create a unique image of its own.

Rejecting regulations

Daft Punk has remained in charge of its author image by retaining control over all its affairs. As Bangalter notes: "We write everything, we do all the creating, we say exactly how it's going to be recorded. There is no compromise." (Thomas Bangalter in *Yahoo! Music*; Adcock 1997.) In order to rebel against the regulations of popular music culture, the band produces and manages everything it does. First, the duo has its own production company, Daft Life, through which they can license their tracks to the record company, Virgin, while remaining in control of their musical output. Then there is the management company, Daft Trax, and Daft Music, which oversees publishing of the band's music in France. Finally, there are Daft Arts and Daft Life, which are responsible for Daft Punk's photography, logo copyright and multimedia material. (Osborne 2001.) Both men also have their own record labels, named Roulé (that of Bangalter) and Crydamoure (that of Homem-Christo), which makes it possible for them to release solo works or material that they make in collaboration with other artists (Osborne 2001).[50]

With the help of its various self-owned enterprises, Daft Punk remains in charge of its musical activities. Bangalter describes the band's authority over its music making in comparison with the control exerted by some less independent artists:

> Controlling what we do is being free. People should stop thinking that an artist that controls what he does is a bad thing. A lot of artists today are just victims, not having control, and they're not free. (Thomas Bangalter in *Yahoo! Music*; Moayeri 2001.)

Bangalter (Woholeski 2001) also suggests that some artists who sign regular deals with record companies do not even try to strive for control, but rather for fame. The band's pursuit of control can also be linked with the Do It Yourself (DIY) ideology of punk (and to the self-ruling author of rock in general), which, in Deena Weinstein's

---

49 Seeing the album as a representation of the do-it-yourself type of authorship, Poschardt (1995: 429) describes the album's sound and snapshots on the cover as incomplete and sketchy.
50 In 1998, Thomas Bangalter released, with *Stardust* (Bangalter, Benjamin Diamond and Alan Braxe), a well-known single, "Music Sounds Better with You" (Cooper 2002).

(1999: 60) words, substituted the artist's authenticity for autonomous amateurs. However, as Weinstein (1999: 60) sees it, it is not the style of music as such that makes punk
musicians appear more independent, but the amount of freedom that record labels and
other mediators are willing to give to the artist.[51] Ken McLeod (2003: 346) has linked
the artists' desire for control to (progressive) rock bands such as Pink Floyd, King
Crimson and Yes. Another factor that seems to unite the image of artists such as Pink
Floyd with those of, say, David Bowie in his Ziggy Stardust period, is the usage of alien and space themes (McLeod 2003: 340–341).[52] This futuristic theme is also evident
in the public image of Daft Punk, with its use of robot outfits and fictitious biographies. Perhaps the history of Daft Punk's faceless, self-sufficient and futuristic image
may be best connected to such artists and musical traditions as described above.

The most striking difference between Daft Punk and other artists seeking artistic
control (e.g. independent singer-songwriters) seems to be that the members of the
French duo prefer to keep their private lives undercover. Instead of appearing in the
media spotlight or regarding music making as a form of confessional storytelling, the
duo wishes to be presented as a pair of artist-engineers, in contrast to actual celebrities (Collin 1997). By drawing a line between the private and the public, Daft Punk
makes a distinction between its way of making music and the one built around the idea
of single, originating authorship. Whether or not the artist actually tells about his/her
own personal experiences in the songs and interviews, the audience and the media are
provided the necessary material in order to assume as much. In the case of Daft Punk,
the fictitious story about the band's origin seems to work as another element that
presents the band's author image not as confessional, but imaginary.

According to Daft Punk, the disguised image does not automatically mean that the
band's music is impersonal in nature. Quite the opposite: the duo claims that the making of personal music does not require the artist to show his/her face in public. This is
how Bangalter views the matter:

> I think that giving people our music to listen to is the most personal thing we can give be-
> cause it is really us. And showing that is much more of a commitment to our audience than
> showing ourselves physically. We show instead our taste. (Thomas Bangalter in *Montreal
> Mirror*; Silcott 1997.)

In order to emphasize their status as independent artists, the members of Daft Punk
have also given up remixing[53] and DJing (Gill 2001), since they rather wish to concen-

---

51 For the DIY ideology of punk, see also Sabin 1999: 3–4.
52 Interestingly, another musicologist Kenneth Gloag (2001: 401) refers to this increased sense of distance,
    as one finds with such artists as Pink Floyd, Roxy Music and David Bowie, as a break with the optimism
    of the 1960s (see also Poschardt 1995: 428). Gloag (2001: 401) associates the image of these artists also to
    the historical moment of postmodernism in relation to the stylistic identities of modernism.
53 The history of remixing goes back to the 1970s and the introduction of multitrack recording technology

trate on recording original tracks. Also, the men claim (Collin 1997) that they do not need to show their faces on magazine covers in order to make good music; rather, the music can speak for itself. In connection to Daft Punk's low public profile and masked imagery, Homem-Christo tells about the duo's wishes of not becoming famous and not being recognized on the streets:

> In France, you speak of Daft Punk and I'm sure millions of people have heard it, but less than a few thousand people know our face – which is the thing we're into. We control it, but it's not us physically, our persons. We don't want to run into people who are the same age as us, shaking our hand and saying, "Can I have your autograph?" because we think we're exactly like them. Even girls, they can fall in love with your music, but not with you. You don't always have to compromise yourself to be successful. (Guy Manuel de Homem-Christo in *Mixmag*; Collin 1997.)

To some, however, the band's masked author image does not appear as a form of rebellion against the music industry. Bangalter responds to accusations relating to the duo's crafty use of their disguised image:

> People amaze me. We fought tooth and nail to bring out *One More Time* without any kind of advertising or music video and then people turn round and say "They've got such a cunning marketing strategy!" [...] I mean, if trying to be innovative and make changes in the record industry is considered "marketing", then OK let's just say Daft Punk's *all about "marketing"*! (Thomas Bangalter in *RFI Musique*; Richert 2001.)

According to Bangalter, some people see Daft Punk's faceless image as merely another means of attracting attention.[54] Whatever the intention behind its disguised identity, Daft Punk relies on its visual image as a means of marketing its music. The group has a recognizable imagery, with its logos and masks, even though its author image is not built around the band members' identities and physical appearance. Though the duo wishes to stay invisible, it can still express its ideas through public commentaries and masked imagery.[55] Daft Punk may wish to channel public opinion in a certain

---

(Diakopoulos 2005: 1; Manovitch 2005). According to Will Fulford-Jones (2007a), a remix version is a recording that is produced by combining sections of existing tracks in new patterns and with new material. With the help of innovative remixing, the DJ may be accorded the status of a recording artist, while when making records for other artists, the DJ is typically seen as a producer (Fulford-Jones 2007a; Souvignier 2003: 155; see also Ahonen 2005: 43–45; Diakopoulos 2005: 6; Grimshaw 1998). The producer-DJ can establish an author image with a distinctive personality, by turning creative remixing into a means of expressing his/her own artistic visions. Another practice close to remixing is the making of so-called *mashups*, which are made entirely of parts of other songs (McLeod 2005: 82–87; O'Brien et al. 2006: 1–3).

54 It is also possible that the band's hiding behind obscure names serves as another ploy to prevent the music from becoming labelled as mainstream (Taylor 2001: 140; see also Negus 1992: 16–17); by being categorized as "underground", the artist is able to maintain his/her low profile and strengthen their separation from the star system. Ulf Poschardt (1995: 434) describes a tension between the ideas of mainstream and underground in the case of Daft Punk, noting that the band's image is skillfully disguised as mainstream, but constantly referring beyond it. The notion of underground and its relation to dance club culture is discussed more thoroughly by Sarah Thornton (1995: 116–122).

55 Interestingly, with the release of their latest album *Human After All* (2005), the band's public comments

direction. In the end, however, the audience decides whether they see the artist's author image as a means of making a statement against the music industry or merely as another form of public promotion.[56]

Fragmenting the subject

As noted above, the images that Daft Punk has come to represent are not those of the band members' natural looks, but images of contrivance and disguise (Gill 2001). Also, Daft Punk's public image is marked by constant transition, the duo having appeared in various masks and outfits during its career. Dominic Strinati (1995: 238) explains the sense of *diffused identity* through the gradual disappearance of those traditional frames of reference that used to help people define themselves and their place in society. Along with the diffusion of collective identities, the sense of personal identity has also become more fragmented. The traditional sources of identity – such as social class, family and local communities – have declined, and no new institutions or beliefs have arisen that would help people to form coherent identities to take the place of the previous ones. (Strinati 1995: 238–239.) In contrast with the modernist conception, identity is no longer understood as a fixed, solid and stable category, but as a myth or an illusion. The subject is often regarded as a fragmented and disconnected agent who does not possess the depth and coherency typical of the modern subject. (Kellner 1995: 233.)[57]

McLeod (2003: 351–352) connects the use of alien imagery to the temporary transcendence of time, space and place. Even though McLeod does not mention Daft Punk, it is clear that the band's futuristic imagery transcends the personal histories of the band members.[58] Also, the notion of diffused (postmodern) identity (see e.g. Björnberg 2000: 348; Strinati 1995: 238) seems applicable to Daft Punk, whose fictitious characters lead a separate existence that bears no relation to the private lives of

about their work have decreased substantially. Even on their official homepage (www.daftpunk.com; as accessed in 5 July 2006), users may only view the band's latest video, without being given any background information about the duo or its earlier career.

56 When discussing the authorship of the virtual band Gorillaz, John Richardson (2005) draws a similar conclusion: despite the band's critique of the traditional construction of star images, it seems that the artist must still remain engaged with the music industry. Though the band's music is performed by animated characters, the real members of Gorillaz are still willing (or forced) to give interviews – which may be regarded as another means of stating their anticelebrity agenda, but which also brings the real band members into the spotlight. (Richardson 2005: 3, 7.)

57 However, as Douglas Kellner (1995: 259) suggests, the subject's complete dissolution in contemporary culture seems exaggerated, since media culture still provides images, narratives and spectacles that produce pleasures, identities and subject positions that people embrace. Rather than thinking the subject has vanished completely, it might be better to understand new modes of identity as alternatives to the old ones.

58 This is not to say that the band's image is independent of any historical background, since it retains, for example, traces of the Romantic notion of authorship and the DIY-ideology typical of punk music. These traces still exist even though the band's image is seen to go against certain values, such as the artist's public visibility.

the band members.[59] On the other hand, the line between the masked imagery and the band members' private personas becomes partly blurred in some of the information presented in the media. For example, from interviews the band has given, it is easy to discern that two Frenchmen are wearing the masks, despite the fact that people are not familiar with the duo's personal looks. Yet by hiding their faces, the duo undermines traditional modes of stardom and author presentation, since it is impossible to know if it is always the same men who are wearing the masks.

If the use of disguised imagery is read as a counteraction against the traditional star system, then Daft Punk's masked author image might also be understood as a rejection of previous ways of constructing stardom. In order to go against more traditional values, Daft Punk must have chosen other ways of presenting its image. When the duo hides their faces, they seem to stress the gap between the star system of popular culture and Daft Punk's own designs regarding visual (non)imagery. It may, however, be asked whether the notion of authorship is, contrary to designs or intention, underlined all the more when the band seeks to establish itself outside that traditional discourse of stardom which is based on the artist's public visibility. Is the differing (or *différance*, to use Jacques Derrida's term) just an illusion that only adds to the power of the absent star discourse? The answer would seem to be affirmative, if we accept Derrida's thesis that "the sign represents the present in its absence". (Derrida 1991: 61; see also Burke 1998: 119.) Might one suppose that, by not showing their faces in public, Daft Punk makes the audience all the more eager to find out who the author is behind the band's disguised imagery? Although Daft Punk's author image is based on the idea of hiding from (visible) stardom, it is nevertheless possible to speak of the band's distinct identity – no matter how blurred it may be. Daft Punk's image seems to be a combination of elements that are believed to be both fact and fiction, personal and fabricated, innate and constructed.

Futuristic imagery and faceless travellers

Because it is important for an artist to have a recognizable public image in order to sell records, the promotion of "faceless" artists might seem a daunting task. Daft Punk has solved the problem by wearing masks or by showing their faces digitally distorted in photographs. The band's music videos, as well, line up with the idea of facelessness. In them, the band members are usually not shown; but when they do appear, they are always wearing masks. The concept of artistic invisibility seems to problematise the

---

59   If the lines between the artist's private and public lives seem unconnected, it is certain that the star system and the media take part in this blurring of boundaries. Thus, the disconnect between the public and private realms of the artist may be seen as another theme that is central to image construction.

idea of the artist as the song's originator, by not exposing the artist's face, body and movements (Cubitt 1991: 57). In the following, I look more closely at six Daft Punk videos. Five of them – *Da Funk, Around the World, Burnin', Revolution 909* and *Fresh* – are singles from the album *Homework* (1996); the remaining video, *Robot Rock*, was released on Daft Punk's third full-length album, *Human After All* (2006). Two of the videos (*Fresh* and *Robot Rock*) were directed by the members of Daft Punk; each of the other videos has a different director: *Da Funk* was directed by Spike Jonze, *Around the World* by Michel Gondry[60], *Burnin'* by Seb Janiak and *Revolution 909* by Roman Coppola.[61] The purpose of the analysis is to examine what *is* shown in Daft Punk's videos, when no band members are visible. Are there any similarities between the videos? What kind of plots do the videos include? And how is the artist's masked identity brought out in the clips?

In Daft Punk's videos it is often difficult to find points of contact between the chosen themes and the band's public image. If viewers have not heard the song before or if they do not recognize Daft Punk's trademark sound (the vocoder vocals), they may have a hard time telling whose video they are watching. In the Daft Punk videos under examination, there are some tell-tale markers as to the artist's identity. First, in the video made for the song *Robot Rock*, the two men are presented performing on stage.[62] One is playing the guitar and the other the drums. The video seems to imitate the live show of a rock band, as the men move in time with the music and seem to "pour out their souls" while playing. What distinguishes the figures from ordinary rockers is that they are wearing robot costumes, replete with helmets. The metallic surface of the outfits reflects lights of different shades, in a manner that is reminiscent of "disco balls" and of dance culture in general. The robot costumes resemble the ones worn by the band in promotional photos (e.g. presented on the inner sleeves of album covers and in magazines). The costumes alone may cue viewers to the fact that the artist is Daft Punk – though the men's faces are revealed nowhere in the video. *Robot Rock* may also be seen as a parody of rock culture and the rock-related star system, since the performers in the video imitate poses and gestures typical of rock music performances.[63]

---

60   Both Jonze and Gondry have worked also with Björk.

61   One wonders if this duo, which seeks control over all aspects of its work, would have rejected any suggestions by video directors that did not accord with the band's overall author image.

62   The video is accessible on the band's homepage: www.daftpunk.com (as accessed 27 July 2006).

63   This video also poses a contrast to the stereotypical image of the performing electronic-dance musician, who stands motionless behind a computer (see also Ahonen 2004: 17). Though combining features from rock and dance cultures, the video does not seem to aim at fusing the genres together, but rather at mixing the typical characteristics of both traditions into a new aesthetical form. As remarked by E. Ann Kaplan (1987: 145), it is common for postmodern video to incorporate rather than to quote texts, and to blur even more the preexisting boundaries between different traditions.

Picture 5. Cover shot of DVD collection, D.A.F.T. A Story about Dogs, Androids, Firemen and Tomatoes (1999), showing Charles the Dog-Boy and other characters in Daft Punk videos.

Another video, *Da Funk*, tells the story of a dog-boy named Charles and his one night in a big city. Charles has a man's body, but the head and paws of a dog (see *Picture 5*). The dog-boy wanders the streets of Manhattan in casual clothes, with a plaster cast on his right foot, while all the other characters of the video look like ordinary people, with no masks over their faces. Charles behaves like a human being: he gets teased by two teenage boys, buys a book from a street vendor, and later meets a girl name Beatrice, who used to live next door to him. Since the plot of *Da Funk* centres around Charles's character, there are not many allusions to the song heard in the background. In fact, the only musical reference in the clip is a radio that Charles carries with him throughout the video. The video's soundtrack reflects the sounds that Charles hears. The video begins with traffic noise and the sound of a drawing pen, used by a man who is writing a good-luck wish on Charles's cast. Other ambient noises on the video include the open-and-close sound of a cooler door and the jingling of Christmas decorations that Charles spots in a display window. The volume of the radio is lowered in scenes where Charles is talking with another person or when he is shot through a shop window. By contrast, the song plays louder in scenes where

Charles's attention is focused on the radio. As Charles starts his walk at the beginning of the video, he strolls in time with the song's rhythm. The radio also causes Charles to miss the bus that Beatrice gets on, when he sees a sign that forbids passengers to bring a radio inside the vehicle. Here and throughout the clip, Daft Punk's music is highlighted, even though the main focus is on Charles and his lonesome walk in the night.

The song is placed in the background also in the clip for *Fresh*, another video about Charles the dog-boy. The video opens with a shot of Charles, apparently in low spirits, standing on the seashore. After he has a talk with himself and then meets a little girl with a sea shell in her hand, a film crew is revealed. No music is heard in the beginning and end sequences of the clip. Instead, the video starts and ends with the rushing sound of the sea shown on screen. Next come the sounds of a dialogue between Charles and the little girl. That scene is followed by another chat, this time with a man who is directing a film in which Charles plays the leading role. The song is heard most clearly only in the middle sequence of the video, when Charles is walking through the film set as the crew is packing up their equipment. The song fades out as Charles steps into Beatrice's car. Finally, the couple rides into the sunset while having a discussion about dinner, as the sea sounds continue to rush in the background. Like *Da Funk*, the video for *Fresh* is, above all, a story of Charles. The dialogue between the characters mostly draws the viewer's attention to the plot instead of the music. This emphasis on storyline diverts attention from the artist, to what is happening in the video – not to the way in which the video fits together with the music. Both *Da Funk* and *Fresh* build up a story of their own without having a clear connection with Daft Punk the artist. The videos are not, then, made to support the artist's star persona as such; rather, the clips seem to echo the image of Daft Punk as a band that aims to reject the artist's visibility and star value not only in its musical product, but also in terms of its video imagery.

Unifying the videos of *Robot Rock*, *Da Funk* and *Fresh* are the combinations of human/Other: human and robot, or human and dog. The robots of *Robot Rock* do not move mechanically or forcedly, as robots are thought to move. Instead, their movements are elastic and natural, more like those of human bodies than those of machines, even though their facial expressions are hidden behind the helmets. Also, the character of Charles the dog-boy raises several questions: Why is Charles the only one with a dog head? Where does he come from? Where is he going? Poschardt (1995), when discussing the video of *Da Funk*, notes that, except for the character of the dog-boy, there is nothing to suggest that the story is fictitious. It is, thus, the dissonance between Charles's appearance and his surroundings that makes the video seem absurd. (Poschardt 1995: 433.) The characters in the videos seem to live in a timeless moment and to make their decisions quite randomly. Pertinent here is McLeod's description

(2003: 351) of the subject used in the imagery of electronic dance music, as a faceless traveller "from another world who transcends the socio-cultural baggage of Earth". A similar aura of disconnectedness, together with themes relating to human/Other identity, seem to unite all the characters – both the performing robots and Charles the dog-boy – presented in Daft Punk's videos.

Confused timelines and circular subjects

Except for the use of the robot helmets and the dog head, few visual elements link the described videos to Daft Punk and its music. (One might, of course, expect as much, since the band members wish to stay invisible and the songs are mostly, or completely, instrumental.) To make definite identification of the artist, then, the viewer of the clips would need to be familiar with Daft Punk's sound and style of music making. The two other videos to be discussed – *Burnin'* and *Revolution 909* – also feature stories with a distinct plot; in them, too, the band members are nowhere in sight. *Burnin'* tells the story of a boy's fantasy of becoming a fireman; *Revolution 909* follows the life of a tomato, from a seed to a stain on a policeman's white shirt. Although it may at first appear that the two videos have nothing in common, they are in fact connected, visually, by scenes showing a dance or a rave party.

These scenes play an important part also because they link the videos to dance culture. By moving in time with the music, the dancing people also call the viewer's attention to the music, which moves into the foreground of the video soundtrack.[64] In the middle sequence of *Burnin'*, the dance scene takes place in a skyscraper, when firemen arrive to extinguish the flames of a fire that has broken out (see *Picture 6*). At the beginning of *Burnin'*, a family is shown grilling steaks in the yard, while a little boy is playing with a toy fire truck and daydreaming of being a fireman. As the boy is lying on the grass, a parallel scene takes place in an actual fire station, where firemen are boarding a real fire truck. Throughout the video, the pictures of the boy and the heroic fireman are shown by turns. At the end, the fireman is shown putting out the flames in the skyscraper, as the boy throws a bucket of water on the smoking barbecue. As occurs in many music videos, the transitions between different chains of events may seem to break up linear narrativity, causal logic, and temporal and spatial coherence.[65] Instead of providing narrative closure, the transitions of *Burnin'* open up

---

64   In the dance scene of *Burnin'*, there is also a concrete reference to the music: a girl on the dance floor is wearing a shirt with the song's title, "Burnin'", printed on it.
65   These are also characteristics that Alf Björnberg (2000: 348) lists when analyzing the relation between the expression typical of music videos and the theoretical viewpoints of postmodernism. The link between certain postmodernist aesthetics and the fragmented aspects of music videos have also been discussed by

Picture 6. Daft Punk, Burnin' video: Fireman shown in dancing scene on skyscraper.

new possibilities, making the viewer wonder whether the scenes taking place in the skyscraper are real, whether the boy is merely having a daydream, or whether he is able to see into his future.

In the second video, *Revolution 909*, the dance segment takes place in the opening and ending scenes. The beginning of the clip occurs at an illegal rave party where a large group of youngsters have gathered together. Only the young people's dialogue is heard, until interrupted by the howling siren of a police car. The music starts playing when a police officer talks with a girl who is on drugs. The girl's attention is focused on a red stain on the policeman's white shirt, after which the next scene shows a tomato's life from a seed to being sold in a grocery store. The tomato is bought by an elderly lady who cooks lunch for her son, that is, the police officer introduced in the beginning. Throughout the cooking scene, subtitles show a recipe for the pasta that the lady is preparing. As the song's beat is altered, the next scene pictures the officer having his lunch in a police car. While he is eating, a spot of pasta sauce falls on the officer's white shirt. The video ends with the same scene with which it began: two policemen come to disperse the crowd at the rave party, and the girl notices the stain on the policeman's shirt – only this time the stain also catches the officer's attention, at which point the girl manages to escape unnoticed.

Dominic Strinati (1995: 227), E. Ann Kaplan (1987: 55) Andrew Goodwin (1992: 16) and Christophe Den Tandt (2004: 140–146).

Picture 7. Daft Punk, Around the World video: Dancers shown encircling a podium.

Will Straw (1999: 205; see also 2001a: 158–159), whose writings focus on dance culture, finds the rejection of the traditional idea of authorship to be reflected in the unbroken sequence of music tracks played in performances of electronic dance music. The authorship that is usually invested in the public artist is broken down as the songs' individuality disappears into the mix (Herman 2006: 24). Ideas relating to the loss of subjectivity extend beyond the making of electronic dance music, finding their counterparts in rave culture and its participants, who lose themselves to the beat (McLeod 2003: 352; see also Reynolds 1998: xv–xvi; Thornton 1995: 111). In the same manner, the dancing people in Daft Punk's videos are presented as a communal whole rather than separate individuals. In addition to the similar dance scenes, both *Burnin'* and *Revolution 909* include the narrative device of two separate timelines. In *Burnin'*, pictures of the dreaming boy and the rescue operation alternate with each other; in *Revolution 909*, the middle sequence of the video portrays the girl's hallucination, triggered by her seeing the stain of pasta sauce. In both videos, the sense of unified linearity is replaced by the alteration of two parallel timelines. The plots also share a similar cyclical structure, such that the beginning scenes are repeated in the endings. In both videos, notions of time and space become blurred and incoherent, without definitive articulation of closure.

The idea of circularity is also present in the video for *Around the World*. First of all, the stage setting of the clip is in circular shape, around which the characters move in time with the music. The backdrop, echoing the circularity motif, consists of round, glimmering disco lights. In the video, there are five groups, each of which includes four dancers. Each group represents a different instrument that has been used in the making of the song: the athletes stand for the bass sound, the mummies for the rhythm boxes, the skeletons for the guitars, the robots for the vocoders, and finally, the disco girls for the synthesizers. The mummies are placed on a round podium in the middle of the stage, which is surrounded by a staircase. The athletes and disco girls go up and down the stairs, and the skeletons stand in the foreground, while the robots move in the outermost circle of the stage (see *Picture 7*). The staircase, too, is based on the music: it has the same number of steps as the ascending and descending notes of the song's bass line. The change of camera angles and intensity of lighting serve to fix the audience's attention on the dancer associated with a particular instrument, as fore-grounded on the audio track. For instance, when the guitar is silent, the skeletons sit motionless on the ground, with no light directed on them.

Though the focus occasionally shifts to each group of dancers individually, the choreography of all five groups fits together seamlessly throughout the video. The movements of all dancers are quite mechanical, though only four of them are dressed as robots. Besides the robots, two other groups, the mummies and skeletons, are non-living creatures. Whereas the living figures of disco girls and athletes looking like hip-hop dancers are connected with dance culture, the three other groups of instru-ments – rhythm-boxes, guitars and vocoders – are represented by lifeless characters. When the mummies, skeletons and robots move, a human element seems to enter into the characters' bodies. The result is a creation of hybrids: living/dead or machine/hu-man. All the characters move in time with the music, even though it is not clear to the viewer how they originally came together or why they are dancing. Are the dancing figures destined to circle around endlessly, representing the undying nature of mum-mies, skeletons and robots? Or is this motley assortment of dancers something that reflects Daft Punk's public image in general – drifters running in a circle, wearing various costumes that separate their carriers' identities from one another?

Conclusion

Visual imagery is one component of the artist's author image. The use of distinctive imagery helps to convey the artist's public persona as an individual and original figure. The artist's visuality also works as a means of promoting artists and their works. In addition to artists whose author images are constructed around their personal appearance and star persona, there are those artists whose imagery is covered with masks and fiction. In this chapter, I have examined the French duo Daft Punk and its disguised public identity. Even though the duo wishes to hide from the public eye, it nevertheless projects a recognizable author image through which its music is marketed.

What is typical of Daft Punk's authorship is the band's desire to have full control over its music making, visual promotion and marketing. By wearing masks that are often connected with futuristic themes, the band members are able to keep their personal lives and identities undercover. Fictitious characters and histories also "fill in" for the band's real visual appearance. In Daft Punk's authorship, it would seem to be more a question of creating a disguised author image than having no image at all. In addition to photographs, music videos and other visual imagery, the band can express its thoughts (and revise its image) through commentaries published in the media. If the members of Daft Punk insist on keeping the reins of authorship in their own hands, the band's visual imagery almost seems to lead a metamorphic life of its own. Through the play of assorted visual representations, Daft Punk's author image may also be seen as connected with the idea of fragmented identity. The characters presented in the music videos are responsible for marketing and representing the band's music – a task that is usually taken on by the public artist. In Daft Punk's case, the actual music makers prefer to remain in the background, behind the music, the masks and the ambiguous video imagery.

II

AUTHORSHIP AS A MEANS OF ATTRIBUTING VALUE AND FIXING MEANING

Star images, then, continue to point backwards
in the individual performances and are part of the template
we use to make them meaningful, but they also point forwards
to general representations of cultural ideas that are part of the way
in which the music takes its place in a popular music culture.

Tim Wall 2003

3. Auteurism and the issue of cover versions

Auteur theory – From screen to music scene

A number of evaluative criteria, such as originality, autonomy and authenticity, have proved essential to the construction of authorial hierarchy among popular music artists (see also Frith 1986: 134–135; Keightley 2001: 134; Mäkelä 2002: 155). These criteria are not applied to musical works alone, but also to artists, who are evaluated in terms of their authorial responsibility and artistic creativity. Members of the creative collective – including writers, musicians, singers, producers, engineers and arrangers – are always changing; thus so does their relative artistic significance (Brackett 1999: 127; Frith 1986: 267–268). Also, in general discourse about musical texts, the created products are often personified through identification with those who have, or at least are believed to have, produced them.[66] As art philosopher Paul Thom (1993: 23) concludes, "Works of art are actually valued not solely for their intrinsic properties but also for the fact that they are authored".[67]

While some artists collaborate with a number of songwriters, musicians and producers, others seek full control over their music making, image and whole musical career (cf. Fuchs 1999: 181). Regardless of the degree of personal autonomy, the authorship of each artist is connected to the dynamic interrelationships of the production context, which includes musical works and their creators, and not least, the audience (Shuker 1994: 99). Thus, in order to understand the artist's authorial responsibility in music making, we must take account of the whole production context – that is, the available technology and expertise, economic factors, and audience expectations. Roy Shuker (1994: 100) defines the making of popular music as "a distinct form of labour process, with identifiable characteristics and various specialist roles within it". Stars, artists, auteurs, session musicians and cover bands are some of the categories into which those who make and perform music are classified. Though all the participants in music making work within essentially the same production context and commercial medium, some artists appear to utilize the same medium as a means of expressing their own unique visions, instead of simply carrying out their duties. (Shuker 1994: 99–100, 110.) (The idea of the artist's exceptional creative power has already been

---

66 This is also the case with background music (*Muzak*), which consists mostly in recordings by the original artists. Even nondiegetic film music (i.e. coming from outside the space of the narrative) may not be regarded as anonymous, since a number of film composers have an authorial presence. For more about the use of diegetic and nondiegetic music in film, see Kassabian 2001: 42–49; Kärjä 2005: 138–148.
67 Cf. Foucault 1979: 147; discussed more in chapter 7.

seen in the case of Björk, the focus of chapter one.) Not all areas of authorial responsibility in the process of music making are valued equally; there exists an evaluative hierarchy both between and within various categories (see also Brackett 1999: 127; Frith 1983: 52–55; Keightley 2001: 134; Wall 2003: 153–155). Here the notion of *auteur* comes into play, pointing up an artist's (supposed) special quality, which is believed to supersede the mode of commercialism.

Auteur theory was originally developed by a group of French film critics and directors in the 1950s. Auteurism was first formulated in the French movie journal *Cahiers du Cinéma*, when François Truffaut introduced the so-called "*politique des auteurs*" in his essay *Une certaine tendence du cinéma français* in 1954 (Hietala 1992: 12; Lapsley et al. 1988: 106; Stam 2000: 83–84). The main purpose of the theory was to identify those artists in Hollywood cinema that had transcended the limitations of the studio system, and to exhort respect for the Hollywood cinema as a significant art form. The notion of "auteur" was introduced to describe those directors whose creative style displayed individualism, in contrast to the unremarkable methods of so-called *metteurs-en-scène*, whose works were regarded as less unique and less exceptional. (Bennett 2005: 104; Bordwell 1996: 4; Buscombe 1981: 23; Crofts 1998: 311; Phillips 1999: 195; Shuker 1994: 113.) The cinematic auteur was believed to bring signs of his/her personal style to a film; for example, in the way the narrative is constructed, the way certain themes are explored, or in the visual techniques (Phillips 1999: 195). As another film theorist, Edward Buscombe (1981: 23), describes the author's special abilities, "Instead of merely transferring someone else's work faithfully and self-effacingly, the *auteur* transforms the material into an expression of his own personality".

Auteur theory is based on the assumption that the works of some film directors consist of a set of identifiable thematic and stylistic characteristics that rise above the common patterns of more formulaic filmmaking. Instead of focusing on the industrial and collective aspects of filmmaking, auteurism centers on the director's individual creativity and control. The auteur is also regarded as the main creative force, who is able to impose his/her unique authorial mark onto the text. By contrast, the metteurs-en-scène are those directors who have no distinctive style and who apply their competence to working on films to which they bring no overall artistic vision. As we may notice, auteurism is ultimately a construct of criticism that is used as a tool for evaluating films. Often the auteur's name in itself offers insurance value to the film industry and trademark value to the audience. (Phillips 1999: 195–196; see also Lapsley et al. 1988: 106; Stam 2000: 83–84.) The promotion of films on the basis of the director's name resembles the way in which music is marketed through public artists and their celebrity value. The evaluation and promotion of both films and music rely on granting certain artists a special status, which is used as a means of sorting musical authors and their creations into a hierarchy, ranging from best to worst.

By stressing what is perceived as the director's individual creativity and control, auteur theory echoes the image of the artist as an individual creator. Auteurism also refuses to acknowledge the collective and social nature of creativity, which is typical of both films and popular music (Gracyk 1996: 95; Livingston 1997: 132). By suggesting that cinema works as a means of the director's self-expression, auteurism individualizes what is in fact a collaborative process. Auteur theory also promotes evaluative hierarchies within popular music, along with the belief in the individual author, one ramification of which is the notion of creative "genius". In discussing the history of this notion, Hanna Järvinen (2003: 13) remarks that discussions of genius always include "talk about artistic hierarchies, about the experts who wield the magic wand that makes something art, placing an art work within a context of previous and subsequent events". Similarly, in the context of popular music authorship, auteurism is used as a means of celebrating those authors who are regarded as the most artistic and innovative. Auteur status is therefore seen to correlate with the artistic quality of the works the author has created. A blind allegiance to auteurism can even lead to the idea that it does not matter what kind of work a certain auteur may create, since all his/ her works will be seen automatically as artistically valuable, or at least more so than the output of non-auteurs.

In search of musical auteurs

Dave Laing (1990), in his study of Buddy Holly's career, discusses musical authorship in relation to the film-director concepts of auteur and metteur-en-scène. According to Laing, the auteur – in this case, a vocalist – can articulate a text in ways that may change certain meanings that it initially had. The metteur-en-scène does nothing more than faithfully transfer a text to the screen. In Laing's view, a musical equivalent to the latter kind of author is the performer whose aim is to render the lyrics faithfully. By contrast, an auteur's performing style instead is not determined by the song's features, but by his/her personality and total ensemble of characteristic vocal effects. (Laing 1990: 327.) The musical auteur, like that in film theory, is regarded as an individual artist whose name and personality function as a sign(ature) referring to a specific and recognizable set of stylistic and thematic features (Phillips 1999: 196). The auteur, in film and in music is believed to have special inner qualities and artistic visions that he/ she is able to express in and through his/her works.

In popular music, auteur status requires that fellow artists, the media and audience members regard the would-be auteur's visions as unique and original. As Roy Shuker (1994: 111) notes, artists with auteur status are ranked as topping the hierarchy of performers. The notion of auteur can, then, be understood as an evaluative criterion, the use of which indicates that the music community has acknowledged the artist's skills and artistic competence. The less an artist meets established criteria, the less he/she is valued in the hierarchy. Shuker summarizes the criteria that both media and audiences use in determining musical auteurs and in according chosen artists an iconic and mythical status:

> [T]he ability of the auteur to break new ground, innovating, crossing or blurring genre boundaries; the ability to perform their own "original" material, especially by writing their own songs; the exercising of a fair measure of control over various facets of the production process; and some sense of personal overarching vision of the music and its relation to the canon. Furthermore, auteurs are usually considered to maintain their high profile over a period of time. (Shuker 1994: 114.)

As we may see based on Shuker's definition, many of the criteria that a musical auteur is supposed to have support the idea of single (Romantic) authorship. An auteur is, then, expected to have unique, creative visions that he/she is able to express in an innovative manner. The auteur is also supposed to play a significant role in the process of music making, since it is the auteur's creativity that is expected to be evidenced in the outcome. As a result, it is often believed that the artist's personality is somehow present in the music he/she performs (Straw 1999: 202; see also Williams 2001: 97). Because of a belief in the artist's confessionalism, auteurs are typically judged in terms of the honesty and sincerity which they are perceived to project. Music made by auteurs is thus expected to consist of something more than the mere technical competence or straightforward renderings of song lyrics. (Straw 1999: 201–202.)

In writings about popular music, one finds the auteur concept permeating biographies of critically acclaimed artists who are believed to express their personal thoughts and emotions through the music (see also Brackett 1999: 127; Mäkelä 2002: 39). To take just one example, the following quote hails Stevie Wonder as an exceptionally gifted musician who has the ability to pass on his *joi de vivre* to the audience:

> Stevie Wonder is a much-beloved American icon and an indisputable genius not only of R&B but popular music in general. [...] Nearly everything he recorded bore the stamp of his sunny, joyous positivity; even when he addressed serious racial, social, and spiritual issues (which he did quite often in his prime), or sang about heartbreak and romantic uncertainty, an underlying sense of optimism and hope always seemed to emerge. (Steve Huey in *All Music Guide*; Huey 2004.)

It is not only media representatives and audience members who elevate some artists to the status of auteurs. The artists themselves engage in honouring and admiring one another. For example, the official homepage of Brian Wilson (www.brianwilson. com[68]) cites such famous artists as Paul McCartney, Neil Young and Bob Dylan, who tell about their personal relationships with Wilson and heap praises on his music. Billy Corgan, the singer and songwriter for The Smashing Pumpkins, says the following about Wilson and his long-awaited album, *SMiLE* (2004):

> Brian Wilson the astronaut, peering down from the Heavens, cooly dreaming of California girls. An idealized pop utopia that widens the senses and soothes the ears. Lands the spaceship, finds nothing but disco and platform shoes and decided to take another trip around the moon for good measure and to search for the elusive lonely harmony. Landing back down for the millennium, our astronaut decided it's time. Time to stop and hear what he's brought back. (Billy Corgan on Brian Wilson's homepage; Corgan 2005.)

In Corgan's quote, Wilson is depicted as a supernaturally talented individual who has managed to create his own way of making music. According to Corgan, Wilson's songs form a reality of their own, which only their creator has access to. Wilson is, thus, presented as a mediator whose works are believed to originate from divine inspiration.

Although auteurism plays a central role in the evaluation of popular music artists, its theoretical premises have been called into question (Crofts 1998: 322; Livingston 1997: 132; Toynbee 2000: xiii). Most often the critique is directed against the concept of a single, controlling author, which diverts attention from the collaborative and social processes of making popular music (cf. Gracyk 1996: 95). Critics of auteur theory argue that musical authorship should not be considered solely the action of a single individual, but understood as a combination of various responsibilities and special skills, such as composing pieces, their assorted vocal and instrumental performances, the arrangements of works, as well as the engineering of recordings (Straw 1999: 199). In film theory, too, authorship is often understood nowadays as part of a larger social process, system or structure – rather than the work of an individual filmmaker (Livingston 1997: 132). Despite such criticism, however, the belief in a single, originating authorship continues to hang on. It is interesting, then, to analyse the reasons for the persistence of auteurism – both in film and music. Film theorist Stephan Crofts (1998: 322) remarks that auteur theory is no longer central to discussions of the legal and contractual bases of production and distribution, yet it still has an enormous influence within cultural discourse. The idea of auteurism is also used to emphasize the independence of artistic products from social determination, which necessarily bids up the cultural status of the art form in question (Crofts 1998: 322).

68   As accessed 8 November 2006.

Auteurism in rock

Because of belief in an originating author, auteur status is typically connected with those singer-songwriters who perform their own songs (Keightley 2001: 134). In some cases, other authors involved in music making – such as songwriters, sound engineers, producers and session musicians – are acknowledged to provide the most dominant input (Shuker 1994: 115).[69] Yet it is the public artist with a self-sufficient and creative star persona who is most likely to be referred to as an auteur, and elevated to the top of the hierarchy of musical authors. In regards to particular musical styles, auteurism is usually associated with the genre of rock and especially its singer-songwriter mode (Keightley 2001: 134; Shuker 1994: 110–111). Historically, what explains the connection between auteurism and rock is the latter's status as art. That status dates back to the late 1960s, when rock music was increasingly linked to the idea of the artist's individual sensibility, which was seen as an opposition to the facelessness of mass culture (Frith 1983: 53; Middleton 2001: 215; Wicke 1990: 91, 112).[70] At that time, as Frith (1983: 53) notes, critics and competent audience members took on the task of revealing the auteur, who was seen to stand against the machine of commercialism. Using such criteria as self-awareness, frankness, musical wit, the use of irony and paradox, critics labelled some artists as auteurs in contrast to "less artistic" musicians (Frith 1983: 53). David Hesmondhalgh (1996) argues that the evaluation of certain musical styles, in addition to performers, is based on a set of conventions and a system of values that critics and writers have institutionalised and circulated. Once a certain set of conventions is established, it is used as a means of drawing lines between styles and genres of music. Through various mediated material, the established assumptions are passed on to readers, who supposedly absorb the same set of meanings. As a result, the ideology of rock was institutionalised as the fans became both writers and critics who circulated a particular set of assumptions and value judgements. (Hesmondhalgh 1996: 195.)[71]

Jason Toynbee presents a different perspective on the historical legitimation of authorship within rock culture. As Toynbee (2000: 30) sees it, celebration of the artist's autonomy was linked to the *rock album*. When the album came to be viewed as a sub-

---

69 In discussions of filmmaking, too, the studio, star and spectator are sometimes referred to as auteurs (Phillips 1999: 199–200).
70 Another element said to typify rock music is its celebration of masculinity (see e.g. Walser 1993: 108–138).
71 Stuart Hall (1996) has described the process by which a particular set of values, including those relating to musical authorship, becomes the predominant one. According to Hall, the semantic field within which any particular chain signifies, "leaves the traces of their connections, long after the social relations to which they referred have disappeared". Hall refers to the possibility of entering the field of such ideological struggles, and to transform its meaning by changing or rearticulating the warring ideologies. Such interventions thus attempt to win a new set of meanings for a preexisting term or category. (Hall 1996: 31.)

stantial work of art, rock artists began to build long-term careers around periodic album releases and synchronized tours in the 1960s (see also Théberge 2004: 143–144; Thornton 1995: 26–32).[72] The belief in a single autonomous author was inscribed in the LP-text and its accompanying material, such as liner notes and album credits. A new kind of journalism, which highlighted and helped create star personas, served to fuel more middle-class consumption of popular music. In the 1970s, the established idea of rock auteurism also increased the artist's musical control over the means of production. In big studio productions, some artists were able to share creative control with record producers. Thus, in addition to financial compensation, those artists got the opportunity to leave their authorial mark on aspects of sound engineering and production. (Toynbee 2000: 30.) With the artist's expanded areas of creativity, the notion of auteurism was further confirmed.

The commonly-held notion of artistic autonomy becomes apparent also when one compares auteurism to stardom. When explaining the difference between these two types of authorship, Shuker (1994) calls attention to the fact that, unlike auteurism, stardom is not so clearly based on the music which the artist performs. Thus, in comparison with auteurs, film stars are more likely to arouse wider interest and fascination through their public personas. According to Shuker, some popular-music artists embody characteristics of both auteurs and stars. As examples of such artists, Shuker names Prince, Bruce Springsteen and The Beatles. Not only are such artists commonly seen as creative and innovative, their musical works have also gained high public visibility. Therefore, while stardom is usually seen to require commercial success, auteurs are not necessarily evaluated in terms of record sales. (Shuker 1994: 110–111.) As we have discovered, auteurism is often used as a means of elevating certain styles of music (mostly notably, rock genres), regardless of their economic value. On the other hand, the auteur concept holds sway even in genres that are adjudged inferior to rock, such judgments obviously holding to a different set of evaluative criteria.

The link between auteur theory and rock music is somewhat ambiguous. According to Frith (1983), there are at least two problems in referring to rock as art in comparison to other musical genres. First, just as all other popular music styles, rock music is dependent on a complex structure of people and machines. Rock music is not, then, more self-governing or free of mediation than are other ways of music making. Still, representatives of the media and members of the audience continue to celebrate the notion of single authorship, by viewing everyone else involved in the music making, except the rock auteur, simply as part of the means of communication. Second,

---

72 Will Straw (1999) notes that the evaluation of musical recordings or concerts is not generally based on ideas of multiple authorship. Instead, music is usually perceived as the product of a single individual or an integrated group. (Straw 1999: 199–200; see also Brackett 1999: 127; Gracyk 1996: 94.)

rock – like any other creative action – is expected to require interpretation and active reception from the audience, whereas "mere entertainment" can only be enjoyed.[73] As Frith points out, the problem with the latter assumption is that it denies the fact that all musical texts, including rock music, are social products rather than artifacts made by isolated creators. Rock musicians, too, must rely on the marketing and the commercial success of their music. As Frith concludes, the real question here is not the presumed distinction between commercial and non-commercial music. Rather, the ideology of rock is meant to establish and underscore the criteria by which various kinds of rock music can be evaluated as either good or bad. (Frith 1983: 52–55.) Regardless of the fact that all popular genres are dependent on production machinery, the ideology of rock and its established criteria set expectations as to what a musical auteur should be like (see e.g. Keightley 2001; Shuker 1994: 110–111). The shared notion of auteur does not, however, guarantee the continued expression of auteurism, even within the genre of rock music (Mäkelä 2002: 156).[74] As with other evaluative terms, it is a question of interpretation. The constructed interpretations are also dependent on the subjective position of each member of the audience as well as on the expectations that the media and peer musicians share within different musical traditions.

As a case study, I shall examine the author image of the solo artist, Tori Amos[75]. The purpose of the examination is to clarify some of criteria by which certain artists are valued more highly than others and, moreover, to elucidate the historical background of current ways of evaluating musical authorship. I approach the question of evaluation in terms of two themes: first, through auteur theory as it is used to esteem some artists above the others, and second, through issues concerning cover versions. Common to both of these themes is the idea of a pre-existing set of criteria according to which an artist's skills and artistic competence are estimated. The purpose of the

---

73 Many rock fans see other kinds of popular music as superficial, artificial and corrupted, whereas rock is connected to ideas of the artist's self-expression and creativity (Butler 2003: 14–15; Fornäs 1995: 99, 102–103; Williams 2001: 85).

74 The varieties of auteurism within different rock (sub-)genres is linked with the varying and competing definitions of authenticities (Mäkelä 2002: 157).

75 Tori Amos (birth name, Myra Ellen Amos) was born on August 22, 1963 in North Carolina, and raised in Maryland. Amos sang in a church choir, and by the age of five had won a scholarship and was invited to study piano at the Peabody Institute in Baltimore. Amos was supposed to be trained as a classical concert pianist, but she was expelled from the school at the age of eleven, after having problems in adapting to the conservative surroundings. She took private piano lessons and performed in local clubs throughout her high school years, then moved to Los Angeles after graduating. In time, she became the lead singer of a hard-rock band, Y Kant Tori Read, which secured a contract with Atlantic Records in 1987. After the band's debut album failed both commercially and critically, Amos began writing her piano-based songs. In 1991, Amos moved to London where she focused on her solo career. Later that same year, the EP *Me And A Gun* was released. Amos's first critically acclaimed solo album, *Little Earthquakes*, came out in 1992, and later, an EP called *Crucify* was released. (Rogers 2004: 10–39; Erlewine 2005.) Since her debut release, Amos has made seven full-length albums: *Under The Pink* (1994), *Boys For Pele* (1996), *From the Choirgirl Hotel* (1998), *To Venus and Back* (1999), *Strange Little Girls* (2001), *Scarlet's Walk* (2002), *Tales of A Librarian* (2003; a compilation album with four new songs), *The Beekeeper* (2005) and *American Doll Posse* (2007). (Erlewine 2005; Mazur 2007.)

case study is to discuss Amos's image as an artist whose authorship is based on the idea of auteurism, with its belief in a single originator. In linking auteur theory with the question of cover versions, my aim is to examine how essential auteur status is to the evaluation of popular music.

I shall first look at those qualities on the basis of which auteur status is granted. The notion of auteur is connected with certain assumptions that determine what kind of an image the popular music auteur is supposed to have in terms of music making, creativity, style and visual image. For instance, the auteur of popular music, as previously noted, is typically expected to be innovative and to write his/her own material (Shuker 1994: 114). In the case of Amos, I will concentrate on presumptions linked to auteurism by considering what a musical auteur is expected or allowed to do. The analysed material consists of artist interviews, album reviews and a specific album by Amos. I also discuss closely one of the cover songs from the album, by contrasting Amos's reinterpretation with the song's original version. That discussion focuses on her album *Strange Little Girls* (2001), which consists of cover versions of other artists' songs, and more specifically, on how that album may have affected her status and image as a unique and original author.[76] Was Amos's auteurism significantly damaged by that album? Or was her auteur status strong enough to support the temporary dropping of one of the main conditions of musical auteur-ship – that is, the songwriting? Through this case study, I also consider the extent to which the value of popular music is, in fact, rooted in the auteur. By combining the issue of cover versions with the question of auteurism, I hope to shed some light on some of the ways in which different hierarchies within popular music are constructed.

Tale of an auteur – Tori Amos

The music of Tori Amos is often compared to that of Kate Bush, Laura Nyro and Joni Mitchell (Erlewine 2005). What is common for the public images of such artists is the biographical reading of their works by the media and the audience.[77] In the case of Amos, her songs are often interpreted against her personal history (Reynolds et al. 1995: 267–269). In their writings about autobiographical music, Simon Reynolds and Joy Press (1995) refer to the work of artists such as Courtney Love, Joni Mitchell, Kat Bjelland and Sinead O'Connor. Amos's songs, too, are typically described as purely

---

76   Before the *Strange Little Girls* album, Amos had recorded other cover versions; for example, of Led Zeppelin's "Thank You", Nirvana's "Smells Like Teen Spirit" and the Rolling Stones' "Angie" (Brown 2001).
77   The history of autobiographical readings of texts goes back to the belief in an author who controls the meanings given to each text. The idea of confessionalism is also seen as guaranteeing the truth of a text. (Anderson 2001: 2.)

autobiographical, records of the tensions between her religious background and sexually rebellious spirit. (Reynolds et al. 1995: 249–275.) For example, many of her songs include references to Christianity, through which Amos is seen to criticize the patriarchal repression of women (Koivisto 1997: 23).[78] Another example of Amos's image as a self-expressing artist is the song "Me And A Gun", in which she tells of her own experience of being raped.[79] Another biographical vignette appears on the album *From the Choirgirl Hotel* (1998), in which artist discusses, or so it is told, the miscarriage which she had prior to starting work on the album. (Carmon 2001; Erlewine 2005; Rauch 2003.) The songs based on Amos's personal tragedies are, then, often seen as sounding forth the artist's inner, painful experience (Carson et al. 2004: 47).

Other authors oppose these kinds of exclusively personalized, autobiographical readings of Amos's work (Lafrance 2002). Such critique has mainly been directed against the idea that the categories typical of confessional music – such as guilt, apology and sin – seem to be reserved mostly for female artists (Lafrance 2002: 63–65). Despite such critiques, most readings of Amos's work are still characterized mainly by a search for similarities between the author's personal experiences and her lyrics. In the following album review of *Little Earthquakes*, the confessional reading of Amos's music becomes evident:

> In my mind, there's no one else out there whose work is so intensely personal and emotional. I've always thought of *Little Earthquakes* as the closest thing you can get to pure emotion distilled onto a CD. Tori's debut album [...] shows her at her most intimate – indeed, many have likened *LE* to "Tori's diary", and while the album sometimes teeters on the edge of sounding too confessional, there is ample room for the listener to inject her or his emotions and experience. (Stephen Rauch in *PopMatters Music Review*; Rauch 2003.)

In addition to the artist's official homepage[80], several other websites[81], maintained by fans, have been dedicated to Amos and her star persona. There are also various online discussion forums and message boards[82] where Amos's fans can exchange opinions and trivia about their idol, regardless of the geographical distance that may separate them (cf. Sibilla 2006: 153). According to Katja Laitinen (2003: 41), who has studied the artist's fans online, Amos's fan base consists of an especially heterogene-

---

78 The critique Amos presents in her songs is often connected also with her being raised in a religiously charged environment (her father was a Methodist preacher). Amos's upbringing was, however, a mixture of several traditions; in addition to the religion espoused by her father, Amos was exposed to her Cherokee grandparents' teachings about nature and American Indian mythology. (Laitinen 2003: 39.)

79 The song was originally released on the EP *Me And A Gun* (1991), but the reduced version, an *a cappella* tune, aroused wider public attention, as issued on Amos's debut album *Little Earthquakes* (1992) (Erlewine 2005).

80 www.toriamos.com; as accessed 8 November 2006.

81 Such as www.toriamosonline.com, www.thedent.com, and www.toriamos.org; as accessed 8 November 2006.

82 See www.atforumz.com, http://toriforum.proboards13.com; as accessed 8 November 2006.

ous group of people of different ages, backgrounds and nationalities. Typically, many of the fans consider themselves to have something in common with Amos, in terms of personal experiences and beliefs. Some of them are former victims of sexual assault; others have had a religious upbringing, some still religious, others having abandoned their faith. Despite their various backgrounds, most of the fans seem to share the idea of Amos as some kind of mythical creature, a saviour, or even an omnipotent goddess. (Koivisto 1997: 25–26; Laitinen 2003: 39–51.)

Cover versions – Reconstructing the past

Amos's author image, thus, seems to include many of the elements that a musical auteur is expected to have, such as performing self-written songs and embodying the figure of an original and creative individual. Another indication of Amos's artistic control is the fact that she has either produced or co-produced all her albums. Also the autobiographical reading of Amos's works seems to support her public image as an exceptional and self-sufficient artist who deserves a special place in the authorial hierarchy of popular music. Because of the pervasive image of Amos as an innovative and independent persona, it may thus be assumed that the audience, peer musicians and media representatives generally consider her to have earned her status as an auteur. What distinguishes *Strange Little Girls* (2001) from other albums by Amos, is that it consists exclusively of *cover versions*, i.e. new renditions of previously recorded songs (see e.g. Weinstein 1998: 138). By covering songs instead of performing self-written material, Amos poses a challenge to her acclaimed status as an auteur.

Looking back in history, one finds that artists' motives for doing cover versions have changed greatly throughout different eras of popular music. In the 1950s, most rock 'n' roll covers were made to serve commercial purposes, namely, in order to reach a wider audience. As Deena Weinstein (1998) points out, Elvis Presley built his early career on performing cover versions, many of which were originally performed by black r 'n' b artists. At that time, most of the original songs were relatively unknown by the intended audience. Also, many of the original versions were released only a few months prior to covers, and therefore had no well-established history. In contrast, the 1960s saw British bands doing cover versions in order to validate their own authenticity as musicians. For example, the early Beatles covered songs that had previously been successful in the United States, including Chuck Berry's "Roll Over Beethoven" and Little Richard's "Long Tall Sally". The original sources of rock 'n' roll thus came to be seen as a new source of authenticity. With the emergence of Bob Dylan and the singer-songwriter style, it became increasingly essential for an artist to write his/her own songs in the late 1960s. As a result, the value of cover versions decreased. In the 1970s, heavy metal and punk musicians found new reasons for doing cover versions. If heavy metal used covers of classical music to flaunt the performers' virtuosity, punk bands parodied familiar songs to engage audiences in their raw, back-to-basics style. During the 1980s and 1990s, the reasons for covering songs became even more varied. Also, audiences have become more knowledgeable about the history of popular music, and thus may be expected to be familiar with the original version of a covered song. (Weinstein 1998: 137–146.)

Doing cover versions of songs by others is usually thought to be more acceptable if the artist has already proved his/her skills as a songwriter and a competent musician (Gracyk 2001: 209–210; Weinstein 1998). Otherwise, audiences may take cover songs as a sign that the artist is incapable of creating anything of his/her own, or is trying to take advantage of the familiarity of the original song. Weinstein (1998) lists a number of possible reasons why artists may do cover versions:

> [T]he commercial advantage of familiarity, homage, introducing obscure artists to a wider audience, gaining credibility, criticizing the past, appropriating a song from one genre into another, demonstrating one's roots, finding the original song to express the cover artists' views or feelings as well as if not better than anything they could write, and lack of creativity (Weinstein 1998: 146).

In the case of Amos and her cover album, it seems that the artist is not trying to gain artistic credibility or to take commercial advantage of familiarity, given that her previous albums have proved she is capable of writing songs of her own.[83] Rather, it is thought to be a question of criticizing the past by re-interpreting songs from a female perspective (Brown 2001; Carmon 2001; Coan 2001).

Another author, another set of meanings?

Amos describes the making of the *Strange Little Girls* album in several interviews and press releases. After having her first child, Amos began to consider the similarities between being a "song mother" and a human mother, and then, got the idea of making a cover album (Nelson 2001). Eventually, she decided on the content of the album by asking some of her male friends and acquaintances to tell her about songs that had

---

83   In her autobiographical book, *Piece by Piece*, published in 2005, Amos claims that, in making a cover album, she actually was attempting to end her recording contract with Atlantic without providing the company any new self-written songs (Amos et al. 2005: 322–326). Such claims were not voiced, however, when the album was released in 2001. Such comments evidence the power that an artist's comments can exert over the listeners' attitude towards his/her work, even when applied anachronistically. In this study, reception of the album is examined based on knowledge that was available at the time it was released.

Picture 8. Tori Amos, Strange Little Girls (2001): Visual represen- tations of song narrators. (Pic- tures by: Thomas Schenk.)

strongly affected them (Brown 2001; Carmon 2001). With the help of this "laboratory of men" (Amos's term; see Brown 2001), Amos conceived the following track listing: "New Age", performed by The Velvet Underground (from the album *Loaded*, 1970); "'97 Bonnie & Clyde", performed by Eminem (from the album *The Slim Shady LP*, 1999); "Strange Little Girl", performed by The Stranglers (a single, 1982); "Enjoy the Silence", performed by Depeche Mode (from the album *Violator*, 1990); "Rattle- snakes", performed by Lloyd Cole & The Commotions (from the album *Rattlesnakes*, 1984); "I'm Not in Love", performed by 10cc (from the album *The Original Sound- track*, 1975); "Time", performed by Tom Waits (from the album *Rain Dogs*, 1985); "Heart of Gold", performed by Neil Young (from the album *Harvest*, 1972); "I Don't Like Mondays", performed by The Boomtown Rats (from the album *The Fine Art of Surfacing*, 1979); The Beatles' "Happiness Is a Warm Gun" (from their *White Album* 1968); "Raining Blood", performed by Slayer (from the album *Reign In Blood*, 1986); and finally, "Real Men", performed by Joe Jackson (from the album *Night And Day*, 1982).

On the album cover, there are pictures of each of the female figures who are repre- sented as the songs' narrators (see *Picture 8*). All these narrators come with their own stories, voices and looks.[84] None of the female narrators' pictures resemble Amos's physical appearance (red curly hair) or public persona. Hence none of them illustrate the artist's usual author image. Rather, the images are meant to represent the songs' female narrators, as if the woman's voice in each song was a distinct character (Coan 2001; Nelson 2001). By representing her appearance in the form of the female characters on the album cover, Amos stresses the difference between the cover album and those containing material she has written herself. In contrast to Amos's albums where she is the primary author of each song, in *Strange Little Girls* there is no one-to-one relationship between the performer (i.e. Amos) and the recorded songs. By contrast, Amos is the only person presented on the jackets of her other albums; such presentation may be seen to strengthen the belief in a single, originating authorship, as well as enhance her image as a soloist (Rauch 2003).

Amos is not the only female artist to cover songs written by men (see e.g. Middleton 2006: 154–155). In a discussion of the destabilization of gender, Theodore Gracyk (2001) lists some famous cases of women performing songs that were originally popularised by and strongly identified with male performers. The list includes songs like Marvin Gaye's "What's Going On", performed by Cindy Lauper, and John Lennon's "Working Class Hero", covered by Marianne Faithful. As Gracyk points out, the issue of gender emerges whenever a song that is associated with a masculine identity is delivered by a woman's voice. (Gracyk 2001: 209–210.) In this same regard, Alastair Williams (2001: 59) argues that women who engage in musical activities will inevitably bring feminine qualities to music.[85] Frith (1988: 120–121) emphasizes that it is not just what the artist sings, but the *way* of singing that determines how the audience is situated in relationship to the singer(s). Frith's argument also seems to be applicable to the case of cover versions, differences between the original version and the reinterpretation usually result from the artists' various singing styles, while the lyrics of the original version remain mostly untouched (Gracyk 2001: 63–66).

For Amos, cover versions also seem to work as an effective means of calling attention to parts of the song's original version that would otherwise be ignored. She describes the process of expanding and changing the meanings of the songs:

---

84   There are actually twelve songs, but thirteen characters, since one of the personas is a set of twins (Coan 2001; Nelson 2001).

85   As also discussed by Roland Barthes in his essay "The Grain of Voice" (1990: 182, 188–189), the author should be understood as a body within the music instead of the source of unified intention or the guarantor of meaning (see also Williams 2001: 60). Questions linked with the issue of embodied music, as well as the distinction between pheno-song and geno-song and their relation to feminine writing (*écriture feminine*), have also been discussed by writers such as Julia Kristeva, Kaja Silverman, Hélène Cixous etc. See also Aho 2004: 23–38; Middleton 2001: 219–221; Negus 1992: 89–90; Välimäki 2005: 148–156.

You take a man's word; you take his seed. So I'm going to take his seed and plant it in a woman's voice. And using their words was the best way to do it. [It] wouldn't have meant the same if I had just written a response. (Tori Amos in *Denver Post*; Brown 2001.)

For Amos, then, the artist can use covering as a tool for contrasting the revised version with the original one. In revealing her aim to give voices to the silenced women of the songs, Amos also issues guidelines as to how audiences should hear the songs. The artist's aim is to make the listener hear familiar songs in new ways, by offering an alternative reading of the original text. As the following comment shows, Amos intends to reinterpret the songs from a female perspective: "Each woman [of the songs] approached me and said, 'I have a point of view on this song, that you may want to know, that may change how you hear this meaning'" (Tori Amos in *Georgetown Voice*; Coan 2001).

Auteur status as a licence to experiment

As an established songwriter, Amos is sensitive to the differences between doing cover versions and writing her own material. This is how the artist describes her authorial role as a songwriter:

When it's your own work and you're the mother of it, the DNA adds up and there's a certain genetic bond you have with your own song children. These [songs on *Strange Little Girls*] are the children of the men, and I went in with that respect. (Tori Amos on *MTV. com*; Nelson 2001.)

Amos acknowledges her discovery that, when doing a cover version, the artist must first reinterpret the song:

What I didn't really count on was discovering that if you build a bridge to travel into a sonic structure and you crawl inside, the fair exchange is that it can crawl back inside of you (Tori Amos on *MTV.com*; Nelson 2001).

Amos's remark seems to suggest that, by first reinterpreting the song, it is possible to make a cover version sound as if it were one's own, even though the song was originally written by someone else.

Many reviewers have referred to the *Strange Little Girls* album as an innovative and creative work, even though it consists exclusively of covered material (Brown 2001; Oliver 2001). The main reason for such a positive response seems to be the artist's long career and earlier merits as a respected singer-songwriter. Amos's creative approach to making the album, especially in terms of the female perspective imposed on the songs, seems to play a central role in the positive critical reception of the work (Brown 2001). (One wonders if the media's response would have been just as positive, had the album been recorded by a lesser known artist.) Whereas reception of *Strange Little Girls* was generally positive, some reviewers questioned the artist's motives for making cover songs. For example:

> If you are going to make a career of covering songs you have to show ingenuity, you have to make it different from how the original composer had created the songs. Otherwise you are just a poser wishing you were someone you're not. (Dan Cooper in *Stylus Magazine*; Cooper 2003.)

> The concept: an album of cover songs written by males sung from a female's perspective. The guilty party executing said concept: Tori Amos. Thrill to hardcore fans alternately scratching their heads over this one, trying to decide if Tori created yet another "great" album, misfired completely, or just handed in a contract-fulfilling product. (Jason Thompson in *PopMatters Music Review*; Thompson 2001.)

In view of her previous output, critics seem to regard this album as a passing experiment rather than a permanent change of Amos's style (Carmon 2001; Thompson 2001). In this respect, the auteur concept may also be seen to aid in building a coherent image of the artist. As Will Straw (1999: 202) remarks, the sense of a unified artistic career allows the coexistence of heterogeneous compositions by the same performer. An established public image makes it possible for an artist to explore different musical styles, and thus, to do cover versions of songs by others (Straw 1999: 202). In most cases, a recognizable author image also gives an artist more creative freedom, since the audience is likely to find his/her experimentations meaningful. It seems, then, that the mostly positive attitude of the media towards the experimenting artist depends greatly on earlier stages of his/her career. In the case of Amos, her decision to make a cover album is not generally seen to nullify the artist's talent as a skilful songwriter (Carmon 2001; Oliver 2001).

According to album reviews, Amos has managed to combine inventiveness and imaginative experimentation in such a way that the album *Strange Little Girls* gets credit as a justified and meaningful career move (Brown 2001; Carmon 2001; Oliver 2001). Here is a typical extract from an album review in which the writer pays homage to Amos's creativity: "Each track is a classic in its own right but Amos shows such creativity and love that she is able to claim [each one] as her own" (Lisa Oliver on *Yahoo! Music*; Oliver 2001). Amos herself alludes to the creative contribution that a covering artist may bring to music making: "I think because I'm not the songwriter here, as a composer, the writing will probably show itself somewhere" (Tori Amos in *Rolling Stone*; Falik 2001). With this comment, Amos seems to refer to the musical arrangements and vocal interpretations by which she modified the originals to suit her own authorial vision in the covers. Though in this case the public artist is not the writer of the original songs, it is nevertheless assumed that Amos's creative input is present in the covers, causing them to be heard in new and unique ways (Nelson 2001).

The interplay of authors

The notion of intertextuality was introduced in the 1960s by Julia Kristeva, who used the term to describe the fact that every new text is a transformation of other texts (see e.g. Gracyk 2001: 56; Modinos 1994: 32–33). According to Kristeva (1986: 37), "Any text is constructed as a mosaic of quotations; any text is the absorption and transformation of another. The notion of *intertextuality* replaces that of intersubjectivity, and poetic language is read as at least *double*". Or as expressed by Roland Barthes (1979: 77), "Every text, being itself the intertext of another text, belongs to the intertextual". On this view, each text can communicate its individual meaning only when situated in dialogue with other texts (Gracyk 2001: 56). In this respect, all of culture might be regarded as an instance of intertextuality (Jensen 2002: 186). To quote Barthes again (1990: 146): "The text is a tissue of quotations drawn from the innumerable centers of culture".

The phenomenon of intertextuality is also at play in the case of cover versions, which act as commentaries on other musical styles and works (Butler 2003: 1).[86] Gracyk (2001: 59, 63) refers to cover versions as "[t]he most obvious example of *specific intertextuality*" – a notion applied to texts whose recognition demands that audiences be familiar with a specific earlier text.[87] By analysing the way one text uses other texts to make its own points – or the way one artist uses a song by another artist – it is possible to understand how texts adapt their meanings and implications to new contexts (Thwaites et al. 1994: 109). As literary theorists such as Tony Thwaites et al. (1994: 108) suggest, intertextual links are one of the most significant means by which texts enable the exchange of values and beliefs. This also explains why a covering artist may inject new meanings that usurp those of the song's original version.[88] According to Gracyk (2001: 64), a remake is more often a substitute for, rather than

---

86   The notion of intertextuality is generally applied to all musics in which one is able to find signs of allusions, borrowing etc. Intertextuality also obtains in other areas of music making (including remixing and sampling) in which the authorial voices of more than one artist are interconnected (e.g. Gracyk 2001: 63).

87   In contrast to specific intertextuality, Gracyk (2003: 51–58) speaks of *general intertextuality*, which is "supposed to account for complex significance even when the audience knows nothing of that history".

88   Allan F. Moore (2001) points out that intertextuality may be seen as an opposition to the concept of authenticity. Whereas the notion of authenticity is usually linked with such positive values as integrity, sincerity and honesty, intertextuality may be joined with such attributes as borrowing, fakery and simulation (Moore 2001: 198–199).

a distinctive interpretation of, familiar music. Straw (1999: 202) argues that covering and borrowing have, in the course of time, become personalized. If performing the songs or adopting styles of others used to be seen as a part of working within a shared cultural system or as a way of establishing professional relationships, covering and borrowing are nowadays often regarded as gestures of affinity and allegiance. In this way, the ability to choose and cover the kinds of songs that gel with the artist's earlier career may, in fact, shed light on the performer's own creative sensibility, cleverness and historical connoisseurship. (Straw 1999: 202–203.) The skill an artist displays in selecting the songs he/she decides to cover can thus act as yet one more means of supporting that artist's image as an innovative author.

Gracyk (2001: 64) describes various ways in which an original version may be altered. The covering artist is typically seen as a "new 'speaker' who usurps the place of the historical author generally by changing the emphasis of elements *within* the song". Gracyk notes further that the most significant alterations are usually musical and emotive instead of verbal. The artist may also *change* the music or lyrics of the original version. It is, thus, possible for the covering artist to supplement and revise the intentions of the song's historical writer.[89] In addition to any musical alterations made by the covering artist, the latter's public image affects the way the revised version is interpreted by the audience.[90] (Gracyk 2001: 63–66.)

In the case of *Strange Little Girls*, the outcome that listeners hear (in addition to the musical and emotive alterations) derives both from the songs' original versions and performers, which interact with Amos's own authorial image as a strong, outspoken female artist. This type of intertextual reading of Amos's cover versions is evidenced in album reviews that discuss the covered tracks in relation to the original versions (Carmon 2001; Oliver 2001; Thompson 2001). Amos herself remarks on the tight connection between the original songwriter and his/her self-written material:

> We as writers cannot separate ourselves from what we create. All of these songs [on *Strange Little Girls*] were created by powerful wordsmiths, whether you agree with them or not. (Tori Amos in *Georgetown Voice*; Coan 2001.)

The effectiveness of Amos's revised versions derives not only from their original identification with male performers, but also from her musical alterations and her status as a musical author. When Amos reinterprets the songs by going beyond the original artist's consciousness – perhaps by finding something in the original record-

---

89 This is not to say that artists themselves are, or even can be, fully aware of the various influences to which they are subjected.
90 As literary theorists Michael Worton and Judith Still (1991: 2) point out, we should pay attention not only to the texts that arise via authors, but also those which come about via readers. When discussing the twofold nature of intertextuality, Still and Worton (1991: 1) stress the fact that, firstly, the writer is a reader of texts, and secondly, texts are available only through a process of reading (see also Moore 2001: 24).

ing that the original artist did not choose to bring out or did not realize he had put in – she presents her own reading of the original text. Nevertheless, Amos's interpretations cannot be fully separated from their authorial sources, which in this case include both her and the writers of the original versions. The public images of both the original and the covering artists also affect the way in which the audience interprets the song – that is, if the listener is familiar with the original version and its performer. The artist's public persona, then, acts as a textual foundation upon which the reading of each text produced by a certain artist is constructed.

Recasting the speaker of " '97 Bonnie & Clyde"

The cover version that has received the most attention from reviewers of Amos's *Strange Little Girls* is a song originally performed by Eminem.[91] This song, titled " '97 Bonnie & Clyde", tells the story of a man who kills his wife, then takes the couple's daughter with him on a ride to dump the wife's body in a lake. The original version describes the events from the murderer's viewpoint; by contrast, in her remake Amos adopts the persona of the woman in the song, i.e. the victim of domestic violence. Amos tells about the first time she heard Eminem's version: "When I first heard the song the scariest thing to me was the realization that people are getting into the music and grooving along to a song about a man who is butchering his wife" (Coan 2001). In the following comment, Amos discusses her relation to the representation of characters in the original version:

> Eminem wrote a powerful work[92]. [But] I did not align with the character that he represents. There was one person who definitely wasn't dancing to this thing and that's the woman in the trunk. (Tori Amos on *MTV.com*; Nelson 2001.)

The first-person narrative of a man soothing his baby daughter as he murders her is, in Amos's remake, changed into that of a woman soothing her daughter before her own body is thrown into the water. Amos explains her choice of giving voice to the formerly silent and faceless character: "[A] hand reached out of that trunk and pulled at me and said, 'You need to see how I heard it'" (Tori Amos in *Village Voice*; Carmon 2001).

---

91   Eminem is an American rapper who was born in 1972 in St. Joseph, Missouri. He released his first album *Infinite* in 1996, followed by *The Slim Shady LP* (1999), *The Marshall Mathers LP* (2000), and *The Eminem Show* (2002). In addition to his eventful private life, much attention has been paid to Eminem's controversial lyrics. (Ankeny et al. 2006.) For more about Eminem's public image and the construction of authenticity, see Armstrong 2004.
92   Eminem wrote the original version in collaboration with Marky and Jeff Bass.

The atmosphere of Amos's version differs greatly from that of Eminem's original. Whereas his version is a danceable and accessible rap song, Amos's interpretation – a softly spoken, chilling lullaby – invokes the atmosphere of a horror movie.[93] By emphasizing the song's sinister story, Amos brings out the cruelty of the plot (Oliver 2001). In her version, the rhythmic, danceable beats and sound effects are replaced by a spectral piano and string arrangement. Because of these changes, the mood of Amos's interpretation is hushed and tranquil, the lyrics whispered gently against a plain musical background. The song is thus transformed into a dramatic and disquieting argument; it is no longer an accessible, pop-influenced rap song. The original version closes by slowly fading out, but Amos's version ends abruptly, further highlighting its dramatic impact.

Although Amos took on the wife's role rather than the husband's, she made few changes in the song's lyrics. In both versions, the verses are nearly identical. Amos has slightly revised the choruses of the original version by reducing or excluding some of the phrases (see *Example 1*). The new, critical and subversive meanings of Amos's version do not result from the minor changes to the lyrics, but rather from the musical alterations. Still, the feminine perspective of Amos's version is not established solely through the musical amendments; rather, it also derives from her authorial image as a powerful female artist. Amos's authorial voice and public image add to the impact made by the change of narrating perspective in the cover version. In addition, Amos's and Eminem's rather polarized author images help to widen the gap between the two versions: Amos's self-written lyrics usually are sympathetic to women's experiences, whereas Eminem is well known for his misogynist comments (Ankeny et al. 2006). In the following, I compare the lyrics of both versions to illustrate in which ways Amos's version differs from the original one:

Just the two of us[94] (x8)

Baby your da-da loves you (*hey*)
And I'm always **gonna** be here for you (*hey*) no matter what happens (*iih*)
You're all I got in this world (*iih*)
I would never give (*iih*) you up for nothing
Nobody in this world is ever gonna keep you from me
I love you

C'mon Hai-Hai, we going to the beach (*ii-iih*)
Grab a couple of toys and let da-da strap you in the car seat

---

93   In order to simulate the song's settings and the dead woman's location in the car's trunk, Amos recorded the vocals inside a small box (Nelson 2001).
94   It may noted that the phrase "Just the two of us" links back (parodically) to Will Smith's single by that name (from the album *Big Willie Time*, 1997). In turn, Smith's single was inspired by Bill Withers' song of the same title. Together these songs may be seen to add at least two more sets of authorial voices to Eminem's and Amos's versions.

Oh where's mama? She's taking a little nap in the trunk
Oh that smell (*whew!*) da-da musta runned over a skunk
Now I know what you're thinking: it's kind of late to go swimming
But you know your mama, she's one of those type of women
that do crazy things, and if she don't get her way, she'll throw a fit
Don't play with da-da's toy knife, honey, let go of it (*no!*)
And don't look so upset, why you acting bashful?
Don't you wanna help da-da build a sand castle? (*yeah!*)
And mama said she wants to show you how far she can float
And don't worry about that little boo-boo on her throat
It's just a little scratch - it don't hurt, her was eating
dinner while you were sweeping and spilled ketchup on her shirt
Mama's messy isn't she? (*ii-ii-ih*) We'll let her wash off in the water
and me and you can pway by ourselves, can't we?

** [chorus] **

Just the two of us *(x2)*
And when we ride!
Just the two of us *(x2)*
Just you and I!
Just the two of us *(x2)*
And when we ride!
Just the two of us (x2)
Just you and I!

**

See honey, there's a place called heaven and a place called hell
There's a place called prison and a place called jail
And da-da's probably on his way to all of em except one
Cause mama's got a new husband and a stepson
And you don't want a brother do ya? (*nah*)
Maybe when you're old enough to understand a little better
I'll explain it to ya
But for now we'll just say mama was real real bad
She was being mean to dad and made him real real mad
But I still feel sad that I put her on time-out
Sit back in your chair honey, quit trying to climb out (*wahh!*)
I told you it's okay HaiHai, wanna ba-ba? (*a-ha*)
Take a night-night? Nan-a-boo, goo-goo ga-ga?
Her make goo-goo ca-ca? Da-da change your dia-dee
Clean the baby up so her can take a nighty-nighty
Your dad'll wake her up as soon as we get to the water
Ninety-seven Bonnie and Clyde
Me and my daughter **(x3)**

** [chorus as above] **

Wake up sweepy head we're here, before we pway
we're gonna take mommy for a wittle walk along the pier
Baby, don't cry honey, don't get the wrong idea
Mama's too sweepy to hear you screaming in her ear (*ma-maa!*)
That's why you can't get her to wake, but don't worry
Da-da made a nice bed for mommy at the bottom of the lake
Here, you wanna help da-da tie a rope around this rock? (*yeah!*)

We'll tie it to her footsie then we'll roll her off the dock
Ready now, here we go, on the count of free
One, two, free, whee! (*whoosh*)
There goes mama, swashing in the water
No more fighting wit dad, no more restraining order
No more step-da-da, no more *new* brother
Blow her kisses bye-bye, tell mama you love her (*mommy!*)
Now we'll go play in the sand, build a castle and junk
But first, just help dad with two more things out the trunk

** [chorus as above] **

Just the two of us (x4)

Just me and you baby
is all we need in this world
Just me and you
Your da-da will always be there for you
Your da-da's always gonna love you
Remember that
If you ever need me I will always be here for you
If you ever need anything, just ask
Da-da will be right there
Your da-da loves you
I love you baby

Example 1. The lyrics of *'97 Bonnie & Clyde*. The lyrics are identical in both Amos's and Eminem's versions, except for words and phrases marked in bold (parts found only in Amos's version) and italics (parts found only in Eminem's version). Additionally, Eminem's version features baby screams and sound effects (indicated in parentheses) that reinforce meanings of the lyrics.[95]

Amos's revised version of "'97 Bonnie & Clyde" may be understood as an intertextual construction that combines the views and intentions of two divergent artists, neither of which exerts full control over the reading of his/her work. When recording the original version, Eminem probably did not expect that someone would make a contrasting reinterpretation of his song. Equally, Amos could at the most suggest, not dictate, how the audience should interpret her remake of Eminem's song. Because of its (specific) intertextual nature as a cover version, Amos's version involves a more complex interpretation than does a reading of Eminem's original. A thorough interpretation of Amos's remake calls for attention to the blending of Eminem's and Amos's authorial voices, and also to the kinds of meanings that arise in various receptions of her cover version.

---

95   The baby sounds on the recording are those of Eminem's daughter. In using those sounds, Eminem makes the baby of the song an accomplice to her mother's murder (i.e. Bonnie to Clyde). Eminem's version also includes sounds of the wife's body being dragged and put it into the car trunk.

Conclusion

The idea of auteurism works as a hierarchical construction that is used in the evaluation of artists' musical skills and artistic capabilities. Auteurism also represents a notion of musical authorship in which the artist achieves his/her artistic vision despite the constraints of popular-music commercialism. Auteur status is typically accorded to artists who are seen to meet certain criteria, such as being innovative, independent, and the writer of one's own material. The authorial role and practices of music making also determine the artist's place in the hierarchy of popular music and its performers.

In this chapter, I have examined the artist's auteur status in relation to the making of cover versions. Cover versions by unknown artists are often seen as ploys for gaining popularity and credibility. By contrast, covers done by established auteurs (like Tori Amos) can be viewed as yet another indication of the artist's creative sensibility – an episode of experimentation, after which the artist returns to his/her musical and authorial origins. Recognized auteurs may use covering as a tool for underlining differences between the remake and the song's original version, as we saw in the case of Tori Amos's cover of Eminem's "'97 Bonnie & Clyde". Because of their author images as innovative and original artists, auteurs can take advantage of the familiarity of cover versions, without losing their credibility and fame as skilled musicians.

As Amos's case demonstrates, those popular music artists considered to be auteurs may use covers as a powerful means of reconstructing the past, as seen from a critically charged perspective. Covering artists may also use their creative abilities in such a way as to make the remake an inseparable part of their own musical careers. The remake also prompts audiences to reinterpret a song's original performance. When that happens, the cover and its revised meanings can sometimes supersede the song's original version. After hearing the cover version – which is a reconstruction of the past – one can no longer hear the original in the same way as one first heard it.

4. Authentic authorship vs. inauthentic calculation

Demystifying authenticity

By "authenticity" in music, what is usually referred to is a performance that is faithful to the sounds of past performances (see e.g. Young 2001: 385). The notion of authenticity is traditionally applied to performances that purport to be "'historically informed' or 'historically aware', or employing 'period' or 'original' instruments and techniques" (Butt 2007; see also Middleton 2006: 200). In the context of popular music, the notion of authenticity does not simply refer to specific historical performance practices. Even though it is common also in popular music to regard earlier artists, techniques and instruments as more authentic in comparison with more recent ones, the idea of authenticity in popular music seems to be primarily connected with the public artist and his/her star persona (Dyer 1991: 133; Marshall 1997: 150). This notion of authenticity and its functioning is reminiscent of auteurism.[96] In both of these evaluative systems (of discourse), it is a question of bringing the public artist to the centre of attention, as well as differentiating among musical genres, styles and practices (Frith 1983: 52–57; Keightley 2001: 125–131).

In this chapter, I explore ways in which authenticity is understood and used in evaluating authorship in popular music. I take the position that there exists no firm and unchangeable notion of authenticity that is applicable to all styles and genres of music. Instead, I adopt the critical perspective of cultural studies and poststructuralism, which understands authenticity as a socially and historically formed construction that is constantly being reshaped within different musical practices (Moore 2002: 210; Mäkelä 2002: 157; Scott 1998). As Derek Scott (1998: 142–143) remarks, authenticity may be seen as a constructed style, the values of which are established by such elements as the artist's dress-code, style of singing, or the instrument he/she is playing. By unravelling some of the meanings embodied in the notion of authenticity, we may come to know the history behind various uses of the term. More importantly, those meanings shed light on the different values and qualities by which musical authorship is evaluated, and on which artists' public images are constructed.

---

96   To attain auteur status, an artist must be viewed as "authentic," since authenticity is generally seen to implicate the artist's resistance to the commercial logic of the music industry (Frith 1987: 136). Nevertheless, as Frith (1987: 136–137) points out, both auteurism and authenticity are also vital ingredients in the marketing of popular music. The celebration of auteurism thus works as another means of legitimating the generally shared assumptions as to what kinds of music should be valued more highly than others.

The making of popular music has undergone radical changes during the past few decades. Yet, amidst all those changes, the concept of authenticity seems to have maintained its central position in the thinking of artists, the media and audience members (Butt 2007; Fornäs 1995; Frith 1987: 136–137; Keightley 2001: 131–139; Moore 2002: 210). The idea of authenticity is generally used as an evaluative concept by which to distinguish the "true" from the "false", the "original" from the "copy". In the context of popular music, authenticity is typically regarded as an attribute of respected artists or performances. (Butt 2007; Middleton 2006: 200.) Hence, authenticity can be used as a powerful tool for framing and evaluating music (Mäkelä 2002: 155). The definition of authenticity varies according to different styles and eras of music. In the course of time, new kinds of desirable features emerge that people start to regard as authentic, after first getting used to them (Frith 1986: 263–265). New hierarchies have been constructed by which to evaluate even the most current ways of music making (Goodwin 1988; Porcello 1991; Sanjek 1994; Thornton 1995: 29). Still, the hierarchy of musical authors continues to be headed only by those artists that musicians, critics and audiences consider to be the most authentic, original and creative.

Musicologist Allan F. Moore (2002: 210), in questioning where and how authenticity manifests itself, claims that it is a construction based on the act of listening. In Moore's opinion, authenticity is not an inherent characteristic of specific combinations of sound. Instead, it is a question of interpretation, since each member of the audience interprets music from his/her own cultural and historical position. Thus, views on authenticity will vary according to the background of individual listeners, different social contexts, and the times in which the interpretation takes place. (Moore 2002: 210; see also Scott 1998: 142.) Janne Mäkelä (2002: 157) defines authenticity as "a cultural construction which is deployed with considerable symbolic force and is constantly used as an argument to justify and legitimate certain forms of music". In fact, it is up to each audience member to decide whether a certain kind of music is or is not authentic. Yet authenticity and other evaluative terms may be used in attempts to supersede the power of individual interpretation and to fix particular interpretative practices (Williams 2001: 37). Authenticity can thus be understood as yet another means of elevating certain public artists, by emphasizing the "special" qualities that they and their musical works are held to possess.

As a case in point, I take the Alaskan singer-songwriter Jewel. I concentrate on the stylistic and musical changes that have taken place in her career, as well as the media's and the audience's reaction to those changes. Through an analysis of media texts (including artist interviews, album reviews and comments by audience members) and Jewel's recordings, the case study aims to explain some ways in which the idea of authenticity is understood, not only in terms of Jewel's author image, but within popular music in general. The purpose of the chapter, then, is to explore what kind of shared notions exist, on the basis of which some artists and types of music are believed and presented to be more authentic than others. I also inquire about the specific ways in which "authentic musical works" are supposedly made. The themes discussed in this chapter include the question of mediation, the use of music technology, and the supposed gap between fabricated commercialism and true, authentic forms of music making (Frith 1986: 263–265; Keightley 2001: 133–134; Thornton 1995: 29). I begin with a look at some biographical details and an examination of the artist's author image, against which the notion of authenticity is more thoroughly examined.

From folk-rocker to pop singer – The case of Jewel

At the beginning of her career, people got to know Jewel[97] as a singer-songwriter who played the guitar and performed self-written songs. Media texts often present Jewel's life as a rags-to-riches story: she used to live on the edge of poverty, in a van in Alaska, before succeeding in the music business. (Dickison 2001; Dimartino 2003.) A crystalline, yet strong and versatile voice, along with sensitive lyrics, became Jewel's trademarks (Ankeny 2002b: 590). Jewel's first two albums were thought to be quite similar musically, each one featuring "pretty melodies, gentle folk-rock, and sweetly naïve lyrics" (Erlewine 2002c: 590). If her music remained fairly consistent through the first two albums, her next major release, *Spirit* (1998), abandoned the ragged and rough arrangements of her debut album, in favor of more refined and polished production techniques (see also Erlewine 2002c: 590). After a third seasonal Christmas collection, she recorded an album entitled *This Way* (2001). Some country and folk influences could still be heard on this album, but overall, the earlier, down-to-earth sound was replaced by lighter, more energetic pop tunes (Crossing 2002; Paoletta 2001). As a result of the stylistic change, both the media and the audience did not know quite how to respond to Jewel's new album. Some writers claimed that "the recording [was] buffed and polished to within an inch of its life" (Crossing 2002), while others described *This Way* as Jewel's "most ambitious effort" so far, or as the record

---

97   Jewel Kilcher was born in Utah on May 23, 1974, but spent her childhood in Alaska. Starting at the age of six, she performed music at local hotels with her parents who both were singer-songwriters. Later, after attending Michigan's Interlochen Fine Arts Academy at the age of seventeen, she began playing the guitar and writing her own songs. Jewel performed in several coffeehouses until signing a record deal with Atlantic in 1995. Since then Jewel has released several full-length albums, including *Pieces of You* (1995), *Spirit* (1998), *Joy: A Holiday Collection* (1999), *This Way* (2001), *0304* (2003) and *Goodbye Alice in Wonderland* (2006). In 1997, Jewel won the American Music Award for "Best New Artist" and the MTV Video Music Award for "Best Female Video". In the same year, she won two prizes at the Grammy Awards. Jewel has also published two books of poetry, *A Night Without Armor: Poems by Jewel* (1999) and *Chasing Down the Dawn: Stories from the Road* (2001). (Ankeny 2002b: 590.)

on which she "finally comes into her own" (Dickison 2001; Paoletta 2001). The fourth album can also be seen as a bridge to the artist's following release, titled *0304* (2003), which had an even more controversial reception.

In contrast with Jewel's previous folk-rock[98] records, *0304* is clearly a dance-pop album, featuring a mixture of dance-oriented electronic beats and up-tempo melodies (Diamond 2003; Foley 2003). Jewel describes the mixture of styles as follows:

> I loved hip-hop and rap when I was first exposed to it in the '80s. [...] I also like the hyp-
> notic nature of dance music; there is something very primordial about it. And, of course,
> I love folk music – love storytelling and socially driven music. The tone of some of the
> new songs also leans towards jazz. So you are going to hear my love of all these types of
> music on the new album, and I tried to combine them in a way that makes sense. You have
> folk melodies against hip-hop beats against a French accordion against hand-clapping and
> whistling solos but it still really sounds like me. (Jewel in a press release by *Warner Music
> Australasia*; Warner Music 2004.)

A comparison of *0304* to Jewel's debut album reveals a striking change, both in the artist's musical direction and in her public image. On the album liner notes, Jewel comments on this transition: "This album may seem different to you. To me, it's closer to what has been in my head for years". The artist also addresses her stylistic change in an interview: "I wanted to make a record that was a lot more layered, as well as being a lot of fun. I haven't really changed musical direction, but broadened my influences".[99] (Jewel in *iVillage*; Dutta 2003.) Despite Jewel's explanatory comments, the album met with divided opinions, in both the media and the audience, when it was issued in June 2003. It would seem that the music of *0304* is not in itself a sufficient reason for the contradictory reception of the album, since scores of dance-pop records are issued every week. Rather, the main issue here seems to be the change in the artist's musical and visual style, which one critic refers to as "the most dramatic image overhaul you're ever likely to see" (Alex Petridis in *Guardian Unlimited*; Petridis 2003).

This polarization of opinions is evident in a number of album reviews. Whether the writers see the *0304* album and Jewel's transformation in a negative or positive light, they usually understand the record in relation to their earlier knowledge of the artist,

---

98   Folk-rock refers to a broad range of popular music in which contemporary amplified instruments are used in reinterpreting traditional music or in accompanying contemporary songs in a folk idiom (Laing 2007; see also Connell et al. 2003: 29–43). The tendency to see Jewel's former musical style as a more authentic one may well be connected to the fact that the music she wrote at that time was categorized as folk-rock. This is because one aspect of authenticity that works as a basis of rock musicianship and rock stardom is seen to derive from the American folk-music movement and its ideology (Laing 2007; see also Frith 1983: 48–52, 159–162).

99   Jewel (Warner Music 2004) also says that one of her reasons for making a "fun" record was that, when recording it, she knew that the U.S. was heading for war, and she hoped that the album would provide a place where listeners could escape the real world and forget about reality (see also Petridis 2003).

her public image and the music she used to perform (Diamond 2003; Erlewine 2003; Smith 2003). Jewel (Rutkoski 2004) herself stresses the importance of the past when speaking about her change of style and image. According to Jewel, her earlier output is what enabled her to play with her image later on. The artist seems to suggest that the moment her fans got to know who she was and what she stood for would be an opportune time for her to start expanding both her visual and musical styles. (Rutkoski 2004.) Some, but not all, reviewers welcomed Jewel's new style, which was seen as too radical a break from her previous output:

> For a singer who has been making low-key singer/songwriter albums so unassuming that her two debut singles had to be re-recorded for mass consumption it is a big shock to put on *0304* and hear that she has abandoned folkiness and adult pop to make her dance-pop album. (Stephen Thomas Erlewine in *All Music Guide*; Erlewine 2003.)

> *0304* isn't going to make anyone forget *Pieces of You*, but it's not a bad job at all of keeping with the times. Give Jewel the benefit of the doubt and listen to the album with fresh ears, instead of comparing it to her past, and you'll most likely enjoy it. (Alex Diamond in *Pop Entertainment*; Diamond 2003.)

> We liked Jewel because she seemed honest, unsure of herself, wrote and performed songs that were raw and emotional. [...] *0304*, her latest, is a 180 degree turn from any of her previous works. It is slick pop, produced in such a way as to pander to the pop radio audience. (Brian A. Smith in *Tollbooth*; Smith 2003.)

While some reviewers would have preferred that Jewel remain the way they first got to know her, others were more willing to give the artist a chance to change her style and to reinvent herself. Those that oppose Jewel's stylistic makeover seem to conceive of her author image and musical style as wilfully planned constructions (Smith 2003). The assumptions about her image being a calculated career move also prevent critics from seeing Jewel's music making as a way of expressing the artist's personal feelings and creative visions (Erlewine 2003; Smith 2003). On her official website (www.jeweljk.com[100]), Jewel expresses her own idea of authenticity as being the foundation of everything she does: "To me, relevance means staying honest about where you are. The most important thing to me is maintaining my authenticity". Here Jewel seems to identify "authenticity" with truthfulness and allegiance to one's roots. Ironically, negative reviews of the album would suggest that, due to the musical and stylistic change, Jewel has lost something precious, something she once had, that is, her authenticity – "the most important thing" she wished to preserve.

---

100   As accessed 10 April 2006.

Twisting the image

The largely scathing criticism of Jewel's *0304* album seems to derive mainly from the artist's original author image as a traditional singer-songwriter. Jewel's earlier public image presented the artist as a humble girl-next-door, whose lyrics and poetry were often considered biographical (Dickison 2001).[101] Jewel's original artist-image gave one the impression that her music was a form of autobiographical storytelling, through which the artist learned to know and accept herself and her own deficiencies (see e.g. Swiss 2002: 176). Because of the artist's surprising stylistic change, media representatives and the general public saw Jewel's new image to be in opposition to the original one. Whereas "the first and the authentic Jewel" was regarded as a more truthful and honest one, "the new dance-pop Jewel" was seen as fake and inauthentic (Erlewine 2003; Petridis 2003; Smith 2003).

One website, www.metacritic.com[102], has posted audience reviews of the *0304* album. Here are two examples, one positive, the other negative:

> OK, so Jewel has completely changed her image and turned in her folk guitar for modern-day pop mechanics on *0304*, but that is not the point. The album is a sheer, unadulterated pleasure to listen to, and how many of her previous albums can that be said about? With only few small missteps, *0304* is one of the most fresh and exciting albums of 2003. (Username Matt M. on *Metacritic*.)[103]

> Jewel has given into the devil on her shoulder and become what sells. [...] This type of garbage can be produced by anyone with a microphone, an ibook, and a copy of garage band. You can make any voice sound "great" with effects. But very few can actually sing from the heart and without effects like Jewel does. She didn't need a pop album! She was fine the way she was. (Username David W. on *Metacritic*.)[104]

The former writer seems to prefer Jewel's new album over her previous records; the latter writer is claiming that he used to like Jewel's music, but is annoyed by the artist's new album and use of music technology. While the former writer seems to have reshaped his image of Jewel and her music, the latter, Jewel's ex-fan, insists on preserving his previously established ideas of the artist's "genuine and authentic style". These opposing comments demonstrate the fact that, even though the author images constructed by listeners may not be identical, each audience member draws upon those images in producing his/her own reading of the artist.

---

101 Some of Jewel's poems are printed on the cover sleeves of her debut album, which bring out the artist's status as a poet.
102 As accessed: 8 November 2006.
103 Username Matt M., http://www.metacritic.com/music/usercomments.jsp?id_string=838:O$ZNpjAuUcLJ RpllrFkgew** (accessed 8 November 2006).
104 Username David W., http://www.metacritic.com/music/usercomments.jsp?id_string=838:O$ZNpjAuUcL JRpllrFkgew** (accessed 8 November 2006).

It has been shown that the notion of authenticity plays an essential role in evaluations of an artist's capacity for self-expression and of his/her "true" personality (Dyer 1991: 133). P. David Marshall (1997) characterizes the relationship between authenticity and the performer as follows:

> [H]ow he or she expresses the emotionality of the music and his or her own inner emotions, feelings, and personality and how faithful the performer is to the intentions of the musical score are all part of how the individual performer is determined to be authentic (Marshall 1997: 150).

The artist's authenticity is also believed to refer in some way to his/her existence in the real world (Dyer 1991: 135). As Richard Dyer (1991: 133, 135) remarks, through the sense of immediacy, spontaneity, sincerity and other elements connected with the idea of authenticity, the artist proves his/her image to be something real and genuine, not a manufactured construction.

An aura of authenticity adds to the artist's star power, which in turn is used in the marketing of musical products. The artist's celebrity value and confirmed artistic identity help popular music culture to push toward the future (see also Goodwin 1992: 103). As Will Straw (1999: 203) puts it, through the idea of continuity, the musical past becomes "a complex map of unfolding careers and lines of biographical development". The pursuit of fixed identities also explains why artists usually do not seek to change their public personas and star images (cf. Rojola 2004: 56). If predictability serves as a dependable marketing tool, an unpredictable change of style can easily lead to a loss of the artist's popularity and artistic credibility.

Singer-songwriters – Source and voice intertwined

As the descriptions of Jewel's original author image have shown, the meanings given to musical authenticity play a special role in the singer-songwriter tradition (see e.g. Connell et al. 2003: 27–29). Jewel's music was first presented as a form of personalized storytelling. Then her artistic image was shaken with the release of the *0304*, an album that blurred her image as a confessional singer-songwriter (Smith 2003). Musicologist John Potter (2007) defines the singer-songwriter as follows:

> A term used since the late 1950s to describe those mainly American and British singing composer-performers, often with roots in folk, country and blues, whose music and lyrics are considered inseparable from their performances (Potter 2007).

Potter's definition seems to match with the image that Jewel projected at the beginning of her career, which was that of a folk-rock singer who wrote and performed her own, lyric-driven music (Ankeny 2002b: 590; Dickison 2001; Dimartino 2003).

Potter (2007) describes the relationship between singer-songwriters and their instruments, usually guitar or piano, as an almost symbiotic one; normally, a simple playing technique underpins the text, but it may sometimes trigger a new direction for the lyrics. Potter also mentions the "socially aware" character of many singer-songwriters, a characteristic that holds true for Jewel, who often comments on today's society and politics in her lyrics (cf. Rutkoski 2004).[105] According to Potter (2007), such ideas of musical authorship remind of us of "a poet reading his/her own verse, to which is added the authority of a musician". The notion of singer-songwriter is not applicable to all performing artists, even those who write their own music. For example, in the case of David Bowie and similar artists, the performed song may be seen as a supporting element of a wider agenda (Potter 2007), which in Bowie's case might include theatrical effects and shifting visual imagery (cf. Alanen 1992: 128; Frith et al. 2001: 196–198; Goodwin 1992: 111). A sense of transience may also shake the belief in an originating author, which is one of the most essential characteristics of singer-songwriters, and thus, a feature that makes comparisons between the poet and the singer-songwriter possible in the first place (Kallioniemi 1990: 129).

As David Brackett (2000) remarks, the functions of writing and performing are tightly linked in the case of singer-songwriters. Because of this tight relation, the song's lyrics are usually thought to reveal some aspects of the songwriter's inner experiences. Brackett argues, however, that despite the perceived sense of confessionalism, one can never be certain that the song *only* expresses autobiographical details about the artist's personal life; it is also possible for the music to present feelings that exceed the intentions of a single author. Members of the audience may interpret a song in a way that differs from the author's actual feelings, or from those experienced by the performing artist. Also, various musical codes and performance mannerisms may add new layers to the artist's authorial voice.[106] Brackett (2000: 14–15) therefore concludes that, even if the singer-songwriter creates the song, that does not rule out the possibility of "a multiplicity of authorial voices in the musical text". Despite the theoretical complexities involved in correlating an author's intentions with a (perceived) sense of confessionalism, the singer is still typically seen as the authorial source of the music, as well as the feelings which the songs are thought to express (Brackett 2000: 14–17; see also Middleton 2000: 13).

---

105 Keir Keightley (2001: 134) sees the singer-songwriter image as one that links notions of authorship and performance to perceptions of the artist's ethical integrity.

106 We may also refer to this as the presented author image, suggested by the musical text itself.

Collectively individual

Much of the confusion in Jewel's author image seems to derive from abrupt changes in her style of music making; with these the focus of the artist's public image was shifted, from the idea of single originating authorship to a more collective manner of authoring musical works. The songs on Jewel's *0304* album were not authored by her alone. Although Jewel was responsible for the lyrics, all fourteen songs on *0304* were written in collaboration with various songwriters, ten of them with Lester Mendez[107], the musical arranger and co-producer of the album. (Foley 2003.) One song on the album was written in collaboration with Rick Nowels (who used to work with Madonna), the remaining one with Guy Chambers (a long-time partner of Robbie Williams). Also, Anthony Bell is credited as a co-writer of one of the songs, "Fragile Heart". (Petridis 2003.)

In the following quote, Jewel describes how she and Mendez, the album's producer, shared authorial responsibility during the making of the record:

> He has an expertise in technology and sound and samples and beats. I have an expertise in melody and lyrics, so we complement each other very well. He knew how to bring dance music together with all my other influences, and he also knew how to make it sound authentic and not slick. (Jewel in a press release by *Warner Music Australasia*; Warner Music 2004.)

In her comment, Jewel describes her authorial role and Mendez's input as two separate things. The artist thus seems to suggest that the presence of Mendez – or any other member of the creative collective – in no way interfered her own musical know-how and artistic freedom. Still, several reviewers have harped on the fact that Jewel did not pen the songs on *0304* alone (Erlewine 2003; Foley 2003). With this the critics seem to hint that the input of so many different songwriters might have muffled Jewel's authorial voice and lessened her control over music making and artistic creativity.

In discussing the artist's authorial responsibility, Jewel does not linger on the collective and social aspects of her authorship:

> A lot of writers don't necessarily want to be influenced by other writers, or don't want to share credit. But I'm a writer who enjoys writing with other people, and I think when you work with people who are really talented you learn from it and you're better off for it. (Jewel in a press release by *Warner Music Australasia*; Warner Music 2004.)

Even working as part of a creative collective, Jewel stresses the importance of imposing her own imprint on all that she does, and of making sure that the music "keeps

---

107   Mendez had previously worked with artists such as Shakira, Santana and Enrique Iglesias (Foley 2003).

Picture 9. Jewel, contrasting album covers: Pieces of You (1995), down-to-earth style; 0304 (2003), polished looks. (Pictures by: West Kennerly and Peter Robathan.)

sounding like you and not your producer" (Jewel in a press release by *Warner Music Australasia*; Warner Music 2004). Jewel, then, seems to believe that she was able to inject her personal input and sound into the music, despite the fact that a number of people participated in writing and producing her album.

The musical and stylistic shifts that characterize Jewel's career have done little to divert audiences' attention from the public artist. Though more people participated in the making of the *0304* album than in the artist's previous releases, it is exclusively Jewel's public persona that is presented in the public eye. Also, the visual marketing of the album is based on the artist's celebrity power: it is Jewel's visual image and ap-pearance that are circulated in the media. As with her four previous albums, the cover of *0304* displays a picture of Jewel. The colours are richer and brighter than those on previous albums – a departure from the earth-tone ambiance of earlier covers (see *Picture 9*). The collective nature of *0304* is revealed only if the listener peers closely at the credits on the album cover, or comes across album reviews or artist interviews that highlight the collaborative efforts that went into making the album. The album's cover design and marketing strategies still rely on the artist's star power and visual looks. On the other hand, the dance pop genre of the *0304* album may in itself be seen to imply creative teamwork (in contrast to the folk-rock / singer-songwriter tradition in which the artist used to operate), while in no way subverting the artist's authorial primacy in terms of marketing.

Mediated self-expression

Mediation can be defined as that practice by which one party acts as a go-between that brings two or more others into a relationship (Mäkelä 2002: 48; Thwaites et al. 1994: 136–137). Mediation joins together technology, institutions, and cultural forms. Keir Keightley (2001) lists some ways in which mediation might interfere with musical authorship:

> [F]orms of technological mediation, the involvement of superfluous personnel or industrial procedures, monetary corruption of the performer's motives for performing, an over investment in sounding "up-to-date", the repetition of old ideas, or any number or forces which render musical expressions of the self compromised or distorted (Keightley 2001: 133–134).

For Keightley, mediation inhibits the celebration of performers as being the sole authors of their songs.[108] Another common belief is that, if the artist is not involved in originating the text that he/she performs, the artist's self becomes disposed to alienation and corruption. (Keightley 2001: 134.) Finally, the "extra" people involved in music making – such as publicists, sound engineers, art designers, and all the rest – come to be seen as mere intermediaries, whose job it is to bridge the gap between the artist and the audience (Negus 1992: 46).

Moore (2001) further questions the relationship between mediation and the idea of the artist's self-expression, when he asks if even singer-songwriters themselves can express their intentions through their songs. Moore argues that what the singer really projects in the song is a persona that is always dependent on the means of representation and on the listening process (reception). In this respect, the meanings of the lyrics represent a ground for negotiation, since the singer, despite any attempts made at encoding through performance techniques, cannot determine absolutely the meaning of his/her songs. It is the listener, instead, who bestows his/her own set of meanings on each musical work. Moore (2001: 187) concludes that any identification of meanings with the singer can be only partial, since it is always "mediated by the ephemerality of the music itself, the questionable role of the lyrics and the very fact of having to construct the persona of the individual to whom we are listening". From Moore's perspective, the communication between artist (and his/her sense of self-expression) and audience is always affected by a variety of mediating factors, such as sound produc-

---

108 Aside from the singer-songwriter tradition, Deena Weinstein (1999) connects the sense of pure mediation to the ideologies of punk. Typically, it is believed that punk music record labels allow artists to express their visions in a totally independent manner, free from the constraints of commercialism. Weinstein claims that punk music has adopted a preindustrial folk culture, in which the music is performed and applauded by the whole community, and is not viewed as the sole product of "some unique professionalized and individualized artist". (Weinstein 1999: 60–62.)

tion and technology, recording companies, and the processes by which recordings are conveyed to the ears of listeners.[109] (Moore 2001: 186–187.)

In Jewel's case, the artist still emphasizes the importance of being in direct contact with her audience, despite her involvement in collective practices of music making. For example, it is said that she enjoys writing her own album-liner notes, because doing so involves no journalists or other third party. The artist also praises the Internet for taking out the middleman, including record labels, radio stations and record stores. (DiMartino 2003.) Jewel sees the Internet as a form of direct communication, which the artist can use to nullify the mediated nature of making and marketing today's popular music:

> It's the fans who allow me to live my dream, they buy my albums. I find that very humbling. It keeps me going, even when I think the business is suffocating everything beautiful and pure. (Jewel in *Yahoo! Music*; DiMartino 1998.)

On the other hand, Jewel points out that she is grateful for opportunities to give interviews, at which she can articulate the motives and purposes behind what she does. Jewel also hints that the media have presented an overly simple, one-sided image of her – an image that she wishes to expand. Replacing it may prove difficult, as Jewel herself recognizes, since her original author image has become so well established that it constitutes something like a brand name:

> Of course, I'm branded as "the girl with acoustic guitar that lived in a car as a 19-year-old". And it's true, you know, that's who I am. But there are also a lot of other dimensions, and so it's fun for me; I've been able to build a career that's lasted 10 years. That's an accomplishment. And so now I'm able to show more facets and fill out the picture – because nothing's one-dimensional. Certainly my mind and my art aren't. And so it's fun for me now that I can start to fill things out and challenge standards more. (Jewel in *Yahoo! Music*; DiMartino 1998.)

What Jewel regards as her brand is, hence, the image by which she first became well known. The picture of her as "the girl with acoustic guitar that lived in a car as a 19-year-old" – the foundation on which her public image was originally built – will probably follow Jewel throughout her career, despite any changes in her musical style. The question remains as to whether Jewel can create a more versatile (presented) author image, and convey it to the media and the public without losing her artistic credibility.

---

109 Similarly, Keith Negus (1992: 73) links the construction of authenticity in popular music to the way in which the relationship between the artist and the audience is mediated and articulated.

Art and commerce face to face

Other negative critiques of Jewel's stylistic transformation are connected to the assumption that, with the *0304* album, her previous artistic intentions have been replaced by more commercial motives (see e.g. Smith 2003). According to these claims, Jewel is believed to have switched from her earlier folk-rock influences to dance-pop tunes because of the diminishing sales of her two previous albums. It is argued that Jewel has compromised her artistic views and become a pawn in the commercial machinery of popular music culture. To some reviewers, Jewel's *0304* album is a great letdown, because it abandons the style of her previous ones:

> Is *0304* a sell-out? Well, let's see: folk singer sells millions, sees a decline with the third and fourth albums, completely revamps her image, appearance, and style of music, suddenly becomes publicly accessible, and imitates the style of the day. It may not [be] that Jewel has sold out, but it sure feels that way. (Brian A. Smith in *Tollbooth*; Smith 2003.)

In the above quote, Jewel's stylistic change is viewed as a calculated, commercially motivated move – a step into the superficial and more accessible world of pop music.

Jewel seems to be aware of the art / commerce opposition that is often associated with popular music (cf. Frith 1983: 53; Middleton 2001: 215; Wicke 1990: 91, 112). When describing her authorial identity as a songwriter, Jewel separates her artistic motives for music making from the more commercial ones:

> You can be in this job for two reasons, basically. One is because you like art, and one is because you like fame. And you can use art as a vehicle to be famous, or you can use art as a vehicle to be a better artist. Knowing which one of those you have chosen makes things really simple. For me, it means that every time you make a decision, you ask, does this support me being a good artist? It's a daily thing. (Jewel in a press release by *Warner Music Australasia*; Warner Music 2004.)

The artist's motives for making music are also pointed out in the following comment, in which Jewel explains the hardships she experienced at the beginning of her musical career:

> My hands and my creativity were going to waste. But I never even thought I could sing and make a living because that was a hobby. A lot of us just aren't taught that something you love can make you money. (Jewel in *Yahoo! Music*; DiMartino 1998.)

The above statement suggests that Jewel makes music on her own terms and for her own reasons, not just to earn money and fame. When asked about the charge of commercialism levelled against her new image, Jewel argues that the *0304* album is actually a parody of today's pop culture, and that the sexualised images of the "Intuition" video (which presents Jewel in somewhat revealing clothing) are supposed to be interpreted as mockeries of commercialism. According to Jewel (Warner Music 2004), "The whole song's really about media and media saturation, and being able to step away from that, and get back to your instinct and your intuition". Jewel (Warner Music 2004) also questions the idea that sexiness and authenticity cannot co-exist in the author image of a single artist: "A lot of people say you can't be sexy and smart or authentic at the same time. I don't believe it." Even if *0304* is intended as a parody of today's pop culture, it can nevertheless be seen to profit from those very aspects of commercialism which it is said to target. In the end, it is up to audience members to decide whether to believe the claims of the artist (and his/her marketing machinery) or the critical writings of (some) media representatives.

Technology – Automated inauthenticity?

Other reviewers claim that the artist's increased use of new music technology on *0304* also detracts from Jewel's authentic image (Sterdan 2003). On her first three albums, Jewel became known for her charismatic live performances, in which she accompanied her singing with the acoustic guitar (Dickison 2001; Dimartino 2003). In fact, the only instruments used on Jewel's debut album *Pieces of You* (1995) are the acoustic guitar, bass, drums, piano and strings. In contrast, *0304* features a wide variety of instruments, including electric guitars and electronic keyboards – a radical departure from Jewel's original, acoustic sound (see also Sterdan 2003). Though traditional acoustic instruments, such as a violin, trumpet, accordion and trombone also appear on *0304*, the overall sound mix places the new music technology in the foreground (Erlewine 2003). With the appearance of *0304* and its changed sound, analogies likening Jewel and Joni Mitchell were replaced with those liking her with Madonna and Kylie Minogue (Foley 2003). Here is what the artist herself says about music technology and its relation to her original, acoustic sound:

> I think when you think of Jewel, you think of the acoustic guitar. But I embrace technology; I love it. I love dance music, and I love dance remixes. [...] It's opened up the world for me. If your try to deny it, it's like being a painter and saying "I'm not going to use red or yellow. I'm only going to paint with these colors". Now I can use programming, I can use sequencing, I can use synthesizers. I can use those colors to serve my goal, and it's still emotional. (Jewel in a press release by *Warner Music Australasia*; Warner Music 2004.)

As Jewel's case has shown, the means of music making can affect evaluations of the musical outcome. If Jewel's previous albums were typically regarded as authentic

114

expressions of the artist, because of the acoustic instrumentation and overall sense of "naturalness", the use of music technology takes a more central position in reviews of *0304* (Foley 2003; Smith 2003). That album, with its increase in "slick" production techniques and music technology, is a startling break from Jewel's trademark sound, as established on previous recordings. The live back-up band on *0304* may in some way recall the sound of the artist's previous albums. Nevertheless, the most salient sound characteristics of the album come from the use of dance-beats and other forms of digital manipulation (for example, the tempo of Jewel's voice is slowed down in the song "America"). As a result, the artist's image is seen as more impersonal and less sincere (cf. Frith 1986: 265; Warner 2003: 103). Also, the blurred connection between the author and her work tends to dispel any sense of a single, originating authorship.

Another change has taken place in Jewel's music making. Gone are the live recordings, like those which appeared on her first three albums. They seem to have been replaced by such things as remixes; for example, *0304* contains both the original *and* a remix version of the song "Intuition". One of the acoustic numbers, "Sometimes It Be That Way" (from the album *This Way*), even includes a false start, followed by Jewel's reattempt to perform the song. The fact that the record includes the failed beginning may be connected not only to Jewel's image as taking a "natural" attitude toward music making, but also to the live-performance tradition in general, which understands each performance as an original entity of its own (cf. Goehr 1992: 121). By contrast, the remix version on *0304* underlines the mechanistic aspect of popular music as a form of repetition and recycling of preexisting material (see also Krasnow 1995: 183; Souvignier 2003: 155).

The presumably falsifying nature of music technology can be seen to reduce an artist's aura of authenticity (see e.g. Frith 1986: 265; Schumacher 1995: 264; Warner 2003: 103). In reviews of Jewel's *0304* album, for example, some critics argue that the overwhelming presence of new music technology overrides not only Jewel's voice, but also the music and lyrics of the songs (Smith 2003). This is how one critic puts it:

> On her fourth album *0304*, the singer-songwriter [...] buries her acoustic guitar under thumping beatboxes, booty-wiggling basses and squiggly robo-synths, cops the staccato arrangements and slick production of the Backstreet Boys, and puts her angelic, crystalline voice to work on insubstantial fluff stuffed with deep and timeless sentiments (Darryl Sterdan in *The London Free Press*; Sterdan 2003).

While Jewel may view music technology as a useful resource, others see it as a waste of the artist's talent, especially her vocal skills (Sterdan 2003; see also Foley

2003; Smith 2003).[110] Yet, *0304* has received some positive reviews of the production techniques and use of technology on the album, which have been viewed as elements that distinguish Jewel's recording from others in the same genre. For example, Stephen Erlewine (2003) points out that, although the album has a polished, commercial sheen, the juxtapositions in the production endow *0304* with a more original sound than that of the average dance-pop record.

In relating the idea of authenticity to the use of music technology, Sarah Thornton (1995) examines the ways in which new authenticities are formed in today's media culture. According to Thornton, music is perceived as authentic if it *"rings true or feels real,* when it has *credibility* and comes across as *genuine"*. Thornton also notes that constructions of authenticities are not fixed and immutable, but change over time.[111] (Thornton 1995: 26.) In the light of Thornton's ideas, it may be concluded that the opposing views on Jewel's stylistic change and the *0304* album form part of the ongoing negotiations of meanings connected with musical authenticity. One might assume that those listeners and critics who quickly accepted Jewel's revised author image are adept at re-formulating their views in tempo with changes taking place in practices of music making. In contrast, those who could not understand Jewel's stylistic changeover are probably more reluctant, in general, to part with established concepts of authenticity. A solid belief in an artist's original identity may inhibit the formation of a revised image of the artist – which, in a sense, may be just as authentic as the original one. Based on the musical style of her sixth full-length album, *Goodbye Alice in Wonderland* (2006), it seems that Jewel wished to bring back her original author image (and acoustic sound) as a confessional songwriter who performs original material. The critics, too, refer to Jewel's latest release as the artist's return to her musical roots (Gardner 2006; Taylor 2006). The stylistic swerve of Jewel's *0304* album may thus be understood as a passing artistic experiment, instead of a permanent change of course in the artist's career. Jewel's return to her original image and musical style is also another indicator of the changing perceptions and evaluative criteria of musical authorship.

---

110 Mark Butler (2003) notes that certain vocal features are often taken to indicate deep personal involvement with the song. For example, the singing style of rock usually includes sighs, moans and grunts as signs that the singer is struggling when performing the song. By contrast, the singing mannerisms of dance-pop are less strenuous, indicative of ease and effortlessness. (Butler 2003: 3–4.)

111 The key concept in Thornton's view is that of *enculturation.* Thornton (1995: 29) claims that "a musical form is authentic when it is rendered essential to subculture or integral to community". Because of the process of enculturation, new technologies, which may at first seem foreign, artificial and inauthentic, eventually come to be seen as natural, organic and authentic. As an example, Thornton (1995: 29) mentions electric guitars; at first, these were said to alienate music from its folk roots, but in time the sound of the electric guitar became fully integrated into the aesthetics of (folk-)rock culture.

Conclusion

The concept of authenticity has a variety of functions in discourses on popular music authorship. First, authenticity serves as a criterion by which to evaluate musical works, artists and their author images. The notion of musical authenticity, in turn, feeds upon the widely-held notion of a single, originating author. Authenticity, coupled with (perceived) originality, work together in determining the artist's place in the critical hierarchy. Second, because of its contingent nature, authenticity means different things to different people; and opinions as to what constitutes authentic music are not only diverse, but constantly changing. The shared criteria for determining authentic musical authorship also vary according to different musical styles, genres, and performance traditions. In the case of Jewel, critiques of the artist's authenticity are largely built around the oppositions of acoustic instruments *versus* studio technology, self-sufficiency *vs.* collective authorship, creativity *vs.* commercialism, and finally, naturalness *vs.* sound effects.

Jewel's case also demonstrates of what can happen when an artist's public persona changes suddenly, as happened with her foray into dance-pop. If some media representatives and audience members were willing to revise their image of the artist, others found the "new" Jewel unacceptable, and longed for her "more original" author image. As a result, the earlier image of Jewel, as a confessional singer-songwriter, was broken down. Her increased use of music technology and reliance on the creative input of a larger collective were seen as unwelcome mediations that inhibited the free flow of artistic "purity". Notions of what constitutes an authentic music maker may change, but questions relating to musical authorship remain central to evaluations of artists, their public images, and their ways of making music.

III

MEDIATED AUTHOR CONSTRUCTIONS

Those involved in making music clearly do exercise
varying degrees of personal autonomy,
but this is always circumscribed by the available technologies
and expertise, by economics,
and by the expectations of their audience.

Roy Shuker 1995

5. Images and impressions

Implied authors and preferred readings

In this age of pervasive media technology, the messages of popular music culture seem to be everywhere. Media such as recordings, radio, TV, Internet and magazines play a crucial role in disseminating those messages with which popular music audiences construct various authorial images. Communications theorist John Fiske (1989: 24) claims that popular culture is produced by people, not by a faceless industry. In his view, members of the audience are active participants in that culture, as producers of meanings and pleasures. For Fiske, there are no consumers in popular culture, only "circulators of meanings". This brings us to the notion of *text*, which may be defined as a discursive structure of the potential meanings and pleasures that constitute a major resource of popular culture. (Fiske 1989: 27.) Fiske's ideas have met with some resistance.[112] Still, they are a good reminder that, as concerns the reception of popular music, it is important to realize that people give different meanings to each musical text, be it a song, a live performance, or a music video. Without discounting the audience's active role as a producer of meanings, we may also consider the role of the public artist. As Fiske (1989: 125) remarks, intertextual relations of popular culture are organized around the author-artist. In fact, the artist's public persona takes its place among a set of many meanings which are circulated intertextually. Extending Fiske's thought on the construction of author images, we can say that the artist's public image, too, is an intertextual construct, consisting of meanings that audience members produce based on information which they receive from various sources (see also Marshall 1997: 56–59).

The formation of meanings that make up musical authorship – and artists' author images – can, thus, be understood as a process in which each member of the audience gives his/her own meanings to each text (cf. Grossberg et al. 1998: 148–154). But are those meanings produced arbitrarily? The literary notion of *implied author*[113] would suggest otherwise; since, according to that concept, the text is believed to include within itself an image or idea of the author (Bacon 2000: 218; Bennett 2005: 13; Hietala 1992: 12). According to Lawrence Grossberg et al. (1998: 167), the implied

---

112   See Gilbert 2003: 88; McGuigan 1992: 72–75; Middleton 2000: 9; Storey 1996: 7; Strinati 1995: 256–257. For example, Jim McGuigan criticizes that Fiske's reluctance to explore the complex circuits of culture, leads to "a drastic narrowing of vision" (1992: 73–74).

113   The notion of implied author was originally introduced by Wayne C. Booth in his book *Rhetoric of Fiction* (1983). The implied author refers to a construction, created by the listener/reader, that he/she understands as the source of the meaning of a given work (Booth 1983: 71–76).

author "is the image of the author constructed from the information in the text". In a sense, then, the implied author could be seen as a *preferred reading*, or what Roy Shuker (1994: 17) calls "a dominant message set within the cultural code of established conventions and practices of the producers and transmitters of the text". Despite the ideas of implied authors and preferred meanings, however, the dominant message that a text is supposed to carry is not automatically adopted by the reader (Croteau 2003: 289; Kellner 1995: 37; McGuigan 1992: 132; Turner 1992: 91).

If musical texts include an image of the author that puts the process of interpretation into a certain frame of reference, the question arises as to whether the suggested image tells all there is to be told about a given text and its author(s). For example, the implied author may suggest that the public artist has created the music, thus ignoring the contribution of other authors involved in the music-making process. Nevertheless, a musical text may be seen to hint at the meanings that the audience should give to it. To this we should add the media biases that also affect the audience's interpretation of each work, including their construction of authorship. Contradictory readings of the same text illustrate not only the perennial struggle over "correct" meanings, but also the discursive nature of author images. As pointed out by David Croteau et al. (2003: 289), the preferred readings and dominant ideologies circulated by the media – which include what the author is said to have inserted into his/her work – are only the raw materials of signification, which are in turn revised, thus bringing forth new meanings.

Manipulated messages

In many cases, the media seem to strengthen the image that the artist (and/or the promotional machinery) wishes to present to the audience.[114] In some cases, however, the presented author image does not automatically correspond with the one constructed by the media. In sum: when drawing distinctions between image types, one should be aware of who is producing the image, while also remembering that the presented author image is part of the mediation process. In this chapter, I deal with three popular music artists – Coldplay, Britney Spears and Prince – each of which presents a different notion of musical authorship. Above all else, it is the various authorial roles and degrees of authorial responsibility that separates those artists' author images from one another. The material analysed in this chapter consists of media texts, including artist interviews and album reviews, as well as the writing credits and imagery displayed

---

114 For example, such is the case with Björk: both the artist and the media typically present Björk as a self-expressing, innovative artist.

on album covers. Beneath the diverse author images and musical styles of these three artists, there runs a common thread: all the three case studies demonstrate the fact that presented author images are not automatically confirmed by the media.

Before getting to the case studies, let us look at some well-known attempts to sway audience opinion. Andrew Goodwin (1992) discusses theories of manipulation in his analysis of star images in music television and popular culture. According to Goodwin (1992: 106), the construction of star personas "involves a massive degree of manipulation on the part of the culture industries (not just the music business, but also the media commentator and critics who collude in these constructions)". As an example, Goodwin adduces music videos in which bands are presented as more successful than they actually are. The media's manipulative power may be seen, for example, in the Guns N' Roses' video clip *Paradise City*, which shows the band performing live in front of a huge crowd at Giants Stadium in New York. Before the video came out, the band had released only one album (*Appetite for Destruction*, 1987). In the music video, they are presented as though they were already widely-known – a wildly popular group performing in front of tens of thousands of fans. When the video was shot, Guns N' Roses were in fact playing as an opening act to Aerosmith, though the clip gives the impression that the crowd had come just to see their performance. (Goodwin 1992: 106.)

Another example, mentioned by Grossberg et al. (1998), comes from the 1990s: the almost infamous case of Milli Vanilli. From the beginning of their career, the duo took no part in writing, engineering, playing or producing the songs they performed. Still, the duo appeared in the music videos and other promotional material, thereby becoming the public face of Milli Vanilli. Upon finding out that these "authors" did not even sing on the album, audiences felt betrayed. When it was discovered that the public artists had contributed nothing to the production of what was purportedly "their" musical texts, they could no longer be regarded as the authors of the works they were seen to represent. (Grossberg et al. 1998: 154.) As a result, the National Academy of Recording Arts and Sciences revoked the duo's 1990 Grammy Award for "Best New Group". The general public, too, felt that since the duo had no part in making or even performing the band's songs, the two men could claim no authorial relation to the music of Milli Vanilli. On the other hand, some fans stood by them, claiming that it was the men's presence, face, style and image that gave the music its identity and popularity, even though the duo took no part in the creative process (Grossberg et al. 1998: 154).

As the examples suggest, it is hard to give an unambiguous, generalized definition of authorship and authorial roles. It is clear, however, that to gain any credence as an author of any kind, a popular music artist is expected to contribute to the music making, in at least some capacity. Diverse author images and artist personas are used to construct and convey certain impressions to audience members – some of whom are more critical than others of the received information. Hence, in order to understand authorship in the context of popular music, it is essential to explore not only the actual processes of music making, but also the strategies by which author images are constructed by the artist, marketing machinery, and the media.

Authorship through mediated images

One writer who has explored the mediated construction of images is media theorist Erkki Karvonen. According to Karvonen (1999: 78), the construction of images is a process that involves agents, the media and citizens. In the following, I have reformulated Karvonen's thought, adapting it to explain the construction of author images in popular music (see *Table 3*):

Author (Artist)	-> <-	*Media*	-> <-	*Audience*
interpretation/ text A.		interpretation/text		interpretation/ text B.

Table 3. The mediated construction of images.

In this diagram shown in Table 3, "author" refers explicitly to the public artist, whether or not the artist has taken part in the music making. Thus, the public artist may or may not be the authorial source of the work that he/she represents in public. The table excludes some authors involved in the creative process of making music. Typically, these include producers, technicians and studio musicians whose authorial responsibilities are often ignored by the media. The notion of (presented) author image refers, then, to that public image of the artist which the audience is intended to adopt. Karvonen defines the image as an (inter)subjective structure of knowledge that people construct in their minds.[115] Images do not depend solely on the sender or receiver of the knowledge; they are also derived from cultural encounters and interactive processes. As Karvonen explains it, the image acts as something external, visual and communicative; at the same, it manifests internally, as something processed by the receiving agent. (Karvonen 1999: 39–40.) In relating this thought to the concepts

---

115 Here Karvonen draws from ideas advanced by Dan Nimmo and Robert L. Savage; see Nimmo et al. 1976.

of presented, mediated and compiled author images, we may see the first two of those to serve mostly communicative purposes. By contrast, the compiled author image is mainly an "internal" one; though constructed initially in the minds of audience members, it may later become "externalized" (for example, in clothing, fan-club membership, etc.). This is not to say that the compiled image can have no communicative significance. Quite the contrary: the functioning of popular music culture also depends on discourse about audience perceptions of artists and their public images.

In this model, each agent is seen as an active participant. For example, when interviewing an artist, a journalist formulates his/her own interpretations of the interviewee's statements. As a result, the next set of interpretations – made by readers, listeners and others – will not be based on direct observation; but rather on messages that are transmitted to the audience through a media filter. Karvonen (1999: 79) also understands the media as an active agent, which interprets source-based information on the grounds of its own structure of knowledge, and for its own purposes. The media are not passive channels, but transformers of the texts which they convey to the public, the members of which in turn produce their own texts and interpretations in response to the messages they receive. (Karvonen 1999: 78–79; see also Danesi 2002: 2–23; Grossberg et al. 1998: 18–21.) For example, consider live concerts: there the audience sees the artist face to face, so to speak, seemingly without intermediaries or mediation. Even so, the information presented in the media continues to affect the interpretation process; a live performance is, after all, just one of the texts comprising an artist's author image. Therefore, it may be difficult to draw a line between the images constructed by the audience and those produced by the media, in so far as both involve intersubjective and sociocultural practices. As Karvonen (1999: 78) points out, the aim of the public persona is to make as genuine and favorable an impression as possible. In fact, the public and the presented images are normally intended to embody the needs and desires of the target audience – not to represent some kind of "reality". As a result, the image does not necessarily tell how things are, but how people (of different interest groups) would like them to be. (Karvonen 1999: 83.)

The model presented above helps to clarify the relation between author, media, and audience members. Mediated construction of images works mainly to market music through a recognizable front figure; hence the creative input of studio musicians and other musical authors remains outside the public eye (see also Ahonen 2004: 9–13). Issues of multi-authorial input are played down, when media imagery centers on the public artist and his/her star persona. Normally, the media present popular music artists as solitary individuals, though their music making necessarily involves a variety of authors (cf. Brackett 2000: 14–17; Gracyk 1996: 94–95; Shuker 1994: 99–111).

Creative collectives

Collective authorship, though typical of popular music, does not gel with the normative concept of authorship in Western arts (Gracyk 1996: 95). Though most music making does not follow or represent the intentions of a single author, it is commonly assumed that the proper meaning of a text is the one which the author had in mind (Grossberg et al. 1998: 151). Such an assumption is faulty, because each text always constitutes a polysemic and intertextual unit of its own – the meanings of which, in turn, depend on other texts (see e.g. Barthes 1979: 77; Hartley 2002: 15). The supposition that the author determines the meaning of a text poses yet another challenge: how to determine who the author actually is. Lawrence Grossberg et al. (1998) take cinema as an example. Filmmaking is a collaborative effort in which authorial responsibility is usually shared by several persons, such as scriptwriters, directors, actors or producers (Grossberg et al. 1998: 151–153). In popular music, too, it is often difficult to single out an individual author from among the music-making collective, which consists in songwriters, producers, mixers, technicians, program agencies, managers, record companies and others (Brackett 1999: 127; Des Pres et al. 2000: 87–149; Shuker 1994: 99–100). As Grossberg et al. (1998: 153–154) conclude: "The traditional thinking that the creative artists are entirely responsible for their creations is no longer appropriate in the age of the mass media and the mass production of popular culture".

Antoine Hennion (1990) defines the creative collective involved in making popular music as "a team of professionals who simultaneously take over all aspects of a popular song's production". This team, as Hennion sees it, has replaced the individual creator. The roles traditionally assigned to the single creator are now shared among team members, each of which fulfils various duties; some of these last relate to musical know-how, others to knowledge of the public and the market, still others to technical production and artistic personality. (Hennion 1990: 186.) Even the most self-sufficient singer-songwriters must rely on the help of other professionals, at least during the recording and producing stages of album making. The result is a kind of agglomerate, claims Hennion, the instantiation of "a continuous exchange of views between the various members of the team". Last but not least, the meanings given to the "final" product consist also of individual readings constructed by each member of the audience. In sum, the meanings of a musical work may be said to derive from their relation to other signs, those of the past as well as the present (Jensen 2002: 186).

In addition to the collaborations just described, there is the issue of musical arrangements. Once a song has been written, new ideas are born during the arranging stage, and these play a great role in determining the recorded version.[116] In terms of

---

116   For more on popular music's challenge to the Romantic-Modernist notion of a (musical) work, see Fisher

copyright law, however, the most relevant question about song authorship is, Who wrote the melody and the lyrics? Other aspects of making music rarely reap any benefits when it comes to the distribution of royalties. (Des Pres et al. 2000: 141–148; Théberge 2004: 139–141.) As one illustration of the unequal sharing of credits, Theodore Gracyk (1996) mentions The Beatles' song "Come Together", a key element of which is the drum pattern invented and played by Ringo Starr. The melody and lyrics of the song, penned by John Lennon and Paul McCartney, are protected by copyright laws; however, Starr's rhythm patterns are not. Some bands (e.g. U2 and R.E.M.) distribute the writing credits between each band member, which seems to be both equitable and a good way of avoiding the disputes. (Gracyk 1996: 94.) The first case study of this chapter examines a group that view music making as a form of equal collaboration. Such a view, of course, calls into question the notion of a single originating author. Moreover, the mediated author image of the band may well differ from the group's own, egalitarian self-image.

Democracy with a front figure – Coldplay

Coldplay[117] is a four-member rock band that achieved fame soon after its formation in 1998. From the very start, the members have considered themselves coequals in the band, comprised of Chris Martin (vocals and piano), John Buckland (guitar), Will Champion (drums) and Guy Berryman (bass). (MacKenzie 2002: 234–235.) The four men share credit for all the songs, though there is no set way in which they are composed. The group's drummer, Will Champion, describes the band's creative process: "Chris might bring us an idea for a song and we just sit around and play with it and take it from there" (Will Champion in *The Inside Connection*; Rutkoski 2002). With such statements, the band members emphasize their teamwork, rather than spotlight whoever might come up with the initial idea for a song. Though vocalist/keyboardist Chris Martin is hailed as the band's front figure and driving force (Begrand 2002; Rutkoski 2002), Martin sees the band's functioning as a democratic team to be more important than squabbles over writing credits and royalties:

1998; Torvinen 2007: 146–147.

117 The four men were fellow students at the University College of London when they started making music together. One year later, and after making a couple of EP's (*The Safety* and *The Brothers and Sisters*), Coldplay signed a record deal with Parlophone. After three more EP's (*The Blue Room, Shiver*, and *Yellow*), the band released its debut album *Parachutes* in November 2000. The album gained several award nominations and was widely praised by the press. Coldplay quickly gained a firm foothold in the British rock scene and became an international success story. Since their debut album, the band has released two more: *A Rush of Blood to the Head* (2002) and *X&Y* (2005). (MacKenzie 2002: 234–235.)

I don't want any more than the others. Do I really want to spend two weeks in court some way down the line arguing with my closest mates about who wrote that? (Chris Martin in *Q*; Odell 2002: 110.)

Will Champion remarks that the band members agreed on their work principles even before entering the music business:

We were very careful when we signed a record deal. We didn't want to be taken for a ride or compromise anything. We were very careful to have total control from day one. (Will Champion in *The Inside Connection*; Rutkoski 2002.)

Based on these and other comments, it is clear that the men wish to share equally in controlling the music and artistic direction of Coldplay.

Underlining their sense of unity, the men typically refer to the band as "Coldplay" or as "we", instead of mentioning individual members (Parker 2004; Rutkoski 2002). Also by sharing the writing credits, the band signals the fact that its members have contributed equally in the making of albums. Yet despite the band's efforts to present themselves as coequals, the lead singer, Chris Martin, has been profiled as front man and lyricist of all Coldplay songs (Begrand 2002; Parker 2004; Rutkoski 2002). The following excerpt, taken from an album review, illustrates how the public figure of Martin is credited with endowing the band's songs with emotional appeal:

There is just something about Chris Martin's vocals that makes you almost melt inside. Two years in the making and it becomes apparent Martin has poured every feeling, thought and emotion into this debut album. He sings with such passion and intensity, similar to Radiohead's Thom Yorke or the late Jeff Buckley. (Wendy Currie in *The-reservoir. Music culture magazine*; Currie 2000.)

The above comment implies that Coldplay's music is especially revelatory of Martin's ideas and feelings. The reviewer pictures Martin as something like a singer-songwriter accompanied by his "back-up" band. In yet another album review, it is Martin's authorial role as the band's lyricist which is seen to set him apart from the rest of the band:

The dark, yet brilliant title track shows the most growth in both Martin's lyric writing ("He said I'm gonna buy a gun and start a war / If you can tell me something worth fighting for") and the band's songwriting, the song deftly alternating between eerie silence and disturbing crescendos. (Adrien Begrand in *PopMatters Music Review*; Begrand 2002.)

If the band itself tries to project an image of democratic authorship and equality of input, reviewers tend to regard their songs as autobiographical stories about Martin. In this way, the media can connect musical works with specific authors and performers –

without which the marketing of music would be much more difficult. With the help of a distinct leader figure, it is also possible to associate the music with a public persona, who gives the music its face. This is how Martin explains his role in the spotlight:

> [W]hen a car comes toward you, all you see is the front of the car, that's how it is with bands. There's always a front figure and a front face, but there's also the engine and the seats and the things that hang from the mirrors, all the little details that you never see when it comes past you. (Chris Martin on *Yahoo! Music*; Parker 2004.)

As the citation implies, Martin is not too surprised by the particular attention he has drawn from the media, since lead singers are commonly the most prominent figures of any band. For their part, the other members of Coldplay are not overly concerned about the media's enthralment with Martin. The band's drummer, Will Champion, says that he actually enjoys not having to be in the spotlight (Rutkoski 2002). Bassist Guy Berryman seems to agree with Champion, saying that the frontman routine is just part of Martin's role and that Martin is very good at handling the attention (Diehl 2003). In turn, Martin stresses the interdependence of the band members and their working as a unified whole. According to Martin, the band requires all four men in order to function: "Because I know I've been given a gift, and without the others I'm lost – and they're lost without me" (Chris Martin on *Yahoo! Music*; Parker 2004). Berryman echoes Martin's message by stating that "Coldplay's a complete democracy: We all have equal say. It takes only one person to disagree with something for it to be vetoed". (Guy Berryman in an interview by Matt Diehl 2003; Diehl 2003.) Despite the media's preoccupation with the lead singer, Martin says that people who are truly interested in Coldplay will recognize the creative input of each band member (Parker 2004).

Some writers do go along with the band's claims about itself as a democratic team. In the following excerpt, the reviewer acknowledges the creative contributions of all the band members:

> With more catchy piano from Mr. Martin and some excellent, understated bass from Guy Berryman it is a well-balanced song. The opening chords of Daylight have an almost sitar-like guitar sound played perfectly by Jonny Buckland. With some very strong machine gun-like drumming from Will Champion it is an excellent song. (Dian Gaffney in *Craze-wire: Music news by music listeners*; Gaffney 2002.)

Other reviewers even mention the input of Coldplay's co-producer, Ken Nelson (Lingas 2002; Tangari 2002), though the band itself downplays the importance of any creative input other than their own. Though the media have no prescribed way of treating the band members' authorial roles, the issue of authorship remains a prominent one, connecting the music to the idea of individual creation. When a band member is mentioned separately, it is almost always Chris Martin who is spotlighted as the band's figurehead (Begrand 2002; Currie 2000; Parker 2004; Rutkoski 2002). As noted earlier, the idea of single authorship, as highlighted in the isolating of a charismatic front figure, also aids in the marketing of musical products.[118] Thus, even in cases of collective authorship, the songs made and performed are usually seen as the creations of a single individual (see also Brackett 2000: 14–15; Toynbee 2000: 61).

It is not necessarily just a question of profitable marketing plans, but also of the media's and audience's need to perceive and label music makers as unique individuals.[119] According to Richard Dyer (1986: 8), the idea of "stardom" serves to concentrate attention on the individual. As argued by sociologist David Chaney (1993: 111, 146), star images present a world in which the idea of individual identity is possible, by providing various reference points with which a multitude of publics can identify themselves. We see this in the case of Coldplay: if their songs did not arouse a sense of individuality, then we would not find descriptions of them carrying the singer's every "feeling, thought and emotion". Perhaps the sense of having a unique connection with given musical (and other) celebrities helps strengthen our concept of self-hood – the conviction that, deep inside, we are all individuals.

The presented author image of Coldplay portrays the band as a collective whose members are equally responsible for the music making. In this image, the precise authorial input of each member is held to be of no consequence. Interestingly, however, the cover of their *Parachutes* (2000) album, which shows photos of the band members, introduces each one of them separately and describes their individual roles: Martin is singing into a microphone, while Champion is playing the drums, Buckland the guitar and Berryman the bass. All the four pictures are black and white, in dark lighting. There are also two other pictures (one on the back cover), these in pale colours, which present the four band members standing close to each other, as if stressing the unity of the group. Yet a closer examination shows that in both pictures, the singer Chris Martin is made to stand out from the others. In the first photograph, Martin stands a short distance from the other three men, who are shown lining up with each other. In the second picture, the four men stand side by side in a row, three of them with their elbows propped on a railing, while Martin is pictured as reaching above his fellow band members (see *Picture 10*). These two pictures hint that the band members do not play identical roles, but that Martin is the group's leading figure. The

---

118 As articulated by Graeme Turner (2004: 53–58), discourses on talent, artistic integrity and authenticity are present even in discussions surrounding *Popstars*, *Pop Idol* and other reality TV formats, the idea of which is to transform ordinary people, with no special abilities or achievements, into celebrities.

119 For example, Jeremy Gilbert (2003: 90) refers to individualization as the dominant social process of our time. See also Beck et al. 2002.

Picture 10. Coldplay, Parachutes (2000) album, back cover: Chris Martin shown standing out from fellow band members. (Photographs by: Tom Sheehan and Sarah Lee.)

composition of the pictures also seems to conflict with the band's wish (as suggested in artist interviews and through the sharing of equal credit) to be regarded as an absolutely unified whole. Rather, the cover imagery recalls Martin's comparison of the band with a car, which he made in describing his role in the spotlight. Hence visual imagery giving prominence to Martin's character may be seen to represent the way in which the band is viewed by the media, rather than the band's own image of Coldplay as a democratic foursome.

Britney Spears – Manufactured autobiography?

The degree to which the public artist takes part in the process of making and producing the music varies a great deal (Brackett 1999: 127; Shuker 1994: 99–111). Some artists aim at controlling every step of the process, whereas the authorial responsibility of other artists is limited to performing songs that someone else writes for them (see e.g. Des Pres et al. 2000: 87–149). The division of labour between star singers and songwriters may be traced back to the beginning of the last century, when professional composers were employed to write songs for stars, whose task it was to interpret the songs of certain tunesmiths (Marshall 1997: 156; see also Des Pres et al. 2000: 96–97). Until the 1950s, it was common to regard popular music as a form of manufactured entertainment, since up to that time, artists did not usually write their own material. Nor did they have control over their repertoire, but were instead told what to sing and how to sing it. (Wall 2003: 228.) The following case study of Britney Spears is meant to clarify the relation between the public artist's creative input and that of the behind-the-scenes collective that labors to endow the public figure with celebrity power. The author image of Britney Spears is typical of those performers whose main authorial responsibility is to perform songs written by others. In examining the meanings projected by her authorial image, the case study also points up certain contradictions between the author image presented by the artist herself (and/or the marketing machinery) and the one constructed by the media.

From the beginning of her career as a recording artist, Britney Spears[120] has worked with a number of well-known songwriters and producers. Her popularity is often explained as a fruitful combination of songwriters' and producers' input, with Spears's singing and star charisma (Huey 2005). As for Spears's authorial input and creative contribution, it may be noted that on her first two releases, the artist's role was to perform songs that were written by various professional songwriters.[121] A key figure on Spears's first two albums was the Swedish producer and songwriter Max Martin.[122] In fact, some credit her global celebrity status as issuing from Martin's skillful mixture of dance-pop songs and sentimental ballads. (Huey 2005.) The following discussion centers on the artist's eponymous third album, *Britney* (2001). One thing distinguishing the artist's third release from her first two albums is the new group of contributing songwriters (including The Neptunes[123]).

Though the creative signature of Max Martin is still present, the new collaborators brought novel sounds and beats to this third album (Tranter 2001; Walters 2001). For example, two hit singles from the album ("I'm a Slave 4 U" and "Boys"), both produced by The Neptunes, are influenced by genres such as hip-hop and r 'n' b, which were not associated with Spears's earlier musical style and public image. The input of the new collaborators also lends a sense of progress and inventiveness to her third album, the themes of which focus on Spears's blossoming adulthood (Erlewine 2001; Tranter 2001; Walters 2001). Spears also expanded her own area of authorial responsibility by co-writing five of the twelve songs on the record (Rutkoski 2001). The imagery of the album, too, pictures Spears as being in charge of both her music and career. The cover photos show only Spears's character, with no back-up team in sight (see *Picture 11*). Nevertheless, the album probably could not have come off as planned without the aid of a versatile and popular production team. In this sense,

---

120 Britney Spears was born on 2 December 1982 in Los Angeles. She started performing at a young age and signed her first record deal with Jive Records when she was fifteen. The success of her debut album, ... *Baby One More Time* (1999) and the second release, *Oops! ...I did It Again* (2000), made Spears an international pop phenomenon. Spears has since issued three more albums, *Britney* (2001), *In the Zone* (2003) and *Greatest Hits: My Prerogative* (2004). (Huey 2005.)
121 Except for her second album, which lists Spears as co-writer of one of the songs.
122 Martin has also worked with other popular artists, such as Ace of Base, Backstreet Boys and *NSYNC (Huey 2006).
123 The Neptunes is a well-known American producer-duo (Pharrel Williams and Chad Hugo) that has collaborated with artists such as Usher, Nelly and Justin Timberlake (Birchmaier 2006).

Picture 11. Britney Spears, Britney (2001): Cover photo shows Spears only, no acknowl-edgement of back-up team. (Art direction by: Fredrik Peterhoff.)

Spears and other members of the creative collective are dependent on the fame and skills of each other.

In speaking about her third album, Spears states that it was a big step for her to become more involved in the overall creative process (Rutkoski 2001). She describes what it meant to her to participate in writing the songs on the album:

> It's the first [album] I ever really have written on and really took my time on. When I listen to the whole album it's just that more special. I put my whole self in it. [...] When I rehearse it and get to sing songs I wrote, it means so much more when it comes from you. (Britney Spears in *The Inside Connection*; Rutkoski 2001.)

Spears claims to hear her personalized imprint on the songs she co-wrote, though without describing her actual part in writing them. In another comment, Spears acknowledges how her fellow music-makers helped put her at ease in her new role as songwriter:

> I thought, "Can I even write?" But it was a lot simpler than what I thought. I got with people who made me feel really comfortable. [...] It really wasn't that complicated, except for picking out songs. (Britney Spears in *The Inside Connection*; Rutkoski 2001.)

Paul Théberge (2004: 141) points out that musical performers are usually denied the status of artists or creators of what they record, even though they may well contribute to the authorial power of the work (Abbate 1993: 234–235). Thanks mostly to advances in audio recording technology, the performer can now become the author of a permanent creative object (Bosma 1996) – whether or not his/her input is acknowledged publicly. Reviews of *Britney* usually mention the contributions of various songwriters, but the songs and overall theme of the album are typically associated with events relating to Spears's public image (Erlewine 2001). The song titles themselves – for example, "I'm Not a Girl, Not Yet a Woman" and "What It's Like to Be Me" – signal that the songs are Spears's personal confessions. All this may imply that Spears penned the various tracks and that, with them, she is narrating personal experiences; but the liner-credits indicate that she took little part in writing the songs on the album. Ironically, most of them were not written by the public artist, even though the album is meant to reflect Spears's growing-up process and achieving artistic independence.

Spears's authorial role is, thus, typically distinguished from the input of the collective team working behind the scenes. As a result, the contributions of some who took part in writing and producing the album are played up, while the value of Spears's creative role is minimized. Here is the weight that one writer gives to Spears's input: "Britney just wants to be Britney, this self-reflexive CD reasons, even as everyone around her is feverishly constructing 'Britney' the product" (Barry Walters in *Rolling Stone*; Walters 2001). The writer is claiming that such behind-the-scenes actors as the record company, songwriters and producers, are the actual authors, whose creativity has gone to constructing Spears's public persona. On this view, the "personal imprint", of which the artist was so proud, does not even exist. According to the reviewer, the album's sense of confessionalism and purported insights into the artist's private life are merely calculated marketing strategies and mediated constructions. The writer argues also that Spears's success stems ultimately from the songwriting and the production work: "Despite Spears's five co-songwriting credits, her music is ultimately driven by producers who must work around her vocal limitations" (Walters 2001). The comment also points up something else: though Spears has been seen to prove her vocal talent on slower ballads (Tranter 2001), her singing skills are generally not mentioned in discussions of her star image, possibly because they are dimmed by the pervasive use of music technology and sound manipulation. In addition, the artist's sexualized image helps to construct a public persona that centers more on her physical attributes and dancing abilities, rather than on her singing voice. In the end, Spears's authorial responsibility lies in giving a public face to the creative efforts of those behind-the-scenes forces that create and sustain her star persona.

In control – Prince

The presented author image of some musical artists depicts them as being in total charge of their music making, career and public image. Prince[124] fits well in this category. Widely known as a singer, musician, songwriter, performer and producer who is unwilling to compromise his musical self-sufficiency, Prince insists on performing only original material, and even plays most of the instruments on his recordings. (DeCurtis 1999; Erlewine 2002b.) As a mark of authorial autonomy, the liner notes of all his albums bear the following inscription: "written, composed, performed, and recorded by Prince". In addition to his musical eclecticism – various mixtures of pop, folk, rock, funk, and rhythm and blues – Prince is also known for his virtuosic vocal abilities, (sexually) controversial lyrics and vibrant live performances. (Erlewine 2002b; Greenwood 2004; Robinson 2005.) Here are two typical descriptions of Prince's musical career and public image:

> With each album he has released, Prince has shown remarkable stylistic growth and musical diversity, constantly experimenting with different sounds, textures, and genres (Stephen Thomas Erlewine in *All Music Guide*; Erlewine 2002b: 889).

> Prince is the one who is the true visionary, a reluctant celebrity whose challenging, sometimes insular work has made him a superstar in spite of himself. Even today, Prince's 1980s albums sound fresh, inventive, and not at all dated. This is because Prince wasn't following the trends of the decade – he was inventing them. (Charlotte Robinson in *PopMatters Music Review*; Robinson 2005.)

Despite the well-deserved praise, there have been both ups and downs in Prince's extensive career. In 1978, Prince released his first album *For You*, which was succeeded by more that twenty others. His fame reached its heyday in the 1980s. The albums

---

124   Prince Rogers Nelson was born in Minneapolis on June 7, 1958. Since his first solo album *For You* (1978), Prince has released several full-length albums, including *Dirty Mind* (1980), *Purple Rain* (1984), *Diamonds and Pearls* (1985). The Revolution and The New Power Generation are the most notable bands with which Prince has toured. (Erlewine 2002b.)

1999 (1982) and *Purple Rain* (1984) were both commercial and critical successes that elevated the artist to superstar status. In the 1990s, Prince became dissatisfied with the fact that he was not in total control of his musical career, and saw his record company (Warner Brothers) as wielding too much power over his creative work. After signing a record deal in 1992, the artist proclaimed himself a slave of the music industry and refused to deliver any new records for release. (Erlewine 2002b: 889.) Rebelling against the company, Prince expressed his regret at not owning the master tapes of his early records, and sought to obtain the rights to his creations: "If you don't own your master tape, your master owns you. And you might as well write slave on your face too. It's all about ownership." (Prince on *Jet* 1997; Prince 1997.)[125] Prince eventually negotiated his way out of the record contract with Warner Brothers, and in 1996 signed with EMI, whose sole responsibility was to manufacture and distribute his recordings. The same year, the album *Emancipation* was released on Prince's own label, NPG. (Prince 1997; Sutcliffe 1998: 62.)

The underlying reason for the dispute was that Prince wished to have full command over his records. This is what Prince has to say about the constraints he felt while still under contract to Warner Brothers: "If you hold a man down and tell him what he can or cannot do, he will rebel. If they rule the artist, is it really art?" (Prince in *Ebony*; Norment 1997.) As an example, Prince argues that Warner Brothers would never have permitted him to make the song "Holy River", which is an eight-minute track featured on his *Emancipation* album. With the new record deal and a new album, Prince felt he had regained his musical freedom. Prince tells about making the album: "The whole process of this record was different. I'm a free man, I'm a happy man, I'm a married man and I'm a clear man. All the tracks on this record are free, happy and clear." (Prince in *Jet* 1997; Prince 1997.)

Throughout the 1990s, some audiences and media representatives found Prince's new musical ventures to be overly experimental (Greenwood 2004; Lundy 2004). Ironically, though Prince's "emancipation" was meant to emphasize the artist's integrity, common opinion held that his masterworks were created when the artist was working under contract with Warner Brothers. One reviewer describes the tension between the artist's musical freedom and loss of success during the 1990s:

> Following his "emancipation" from Warner Brothers Records, Prince was free to do whatever he desired – as they say in the comics, with great power comes great responsibility. Prince didn't handle this responsibility carefully; ultimately his status as an independent musician turned out to be a curse disguised as a blessing. (Zeth Lundy in *PopMatters Music Review*; Lundy 2004.)

---

125 Also, during that time, Prince only appeared in public with the word "SLAVE" written on his face. The same word can be seen on Prince's cheek, on the cover-photo of his album *Emancipation*.

Artistic independence usually draws praise. Prince, however, was accused of going too far, by prizing artistic freedom above everything else, including the expectations of his faithful audience and the media. Contrary to what one might predict, Prince's dogmatism was regarded as a selfish act. Here is how another critic viewed the situation:

> Prince's star faded not long after he won emancipation from Warner Brothers in 1995, as he abandoned the mainstream so he could follow his whims however he liked. Which meant that he effectively started making records for nobody but himself. (Stephen Thomas Erlewine in *All Music Guide*; Erlewine 2004.)

Prince's determination was not, in itself, automatically seen in a good light. Instead of being admired for his self-sufficiency and inventiveness, Prince drew criticism as a whimsical and moody artist who had taken his musical experiments too far. The following excerpt, from an album review, serves as another typical comment on Prince's moodiness:

> Prince has made a curious debacle of his career for the past fifteen years. He's been foolishly stubborn (suing his own fanzines) and eccentric beyond belief (changing his name back and forth, releasing an instrumental album of new age jazz, rebuffing commercial distribution), never once choosing the easy way out. (Eric Greenwood in *DrawerB*; Greenwood 2004.)

When in 1993 Prince changed his name to a cryptic symbol, it did little to improve the situation (DeCurtis 1999; Prince 1997).[126] Eventually, in 2004, Prince released the album *Musicology*, which is often referred to as the artist's comeback record (DeCurtis 2004; Greenwood 2004). This is how one writer views the different phases of Prince's musical career:

> Starting somewhere in the early Nineties, he seemed to disappear into his own bizarre obsessions – the muddled jazz-fusion spirituality of *The Rainbow Children* (2001) and the instrumental meanderings of *N.E.W.S.* (2003) being only the most recent accesses. But then, late last year, his election to the Rock & Roll Hall of Fame made you remember just how potent, irresistible and groundbreaking a force he once was. (Anthony DeCurtis in *Rolling Stone*; DeCurtis 2004.)

---

126 Because the symbol – an ankh-like cipher with added flourishes – was unpronounceable, Prince was also referred to as "The artist formerly known as Prince", or simply "The Artist" (see e.g. Norment 1997). Even though Prince reverted to his original name in 2000, he occasionally still uses the symbol as a logo and on album artwork. It may be added that the name "Prince" does not appear on the front of his two most recent albums, *Musicology* (2004) and *3121* (2006). This toying with names might be seen as another way in which Prince underlines his wish to remain in charge of his career and creative activities: if he cannot control the music industry, he can at least determine by what name (or symbol) he wishes to be called.

Picture 12. Prince, Musicology (2004), album cover: Artist presented as solitary, contemplative genius. (Picture by: Afsin Shahidi and Armour Photography.)

The photographs on the cover of *Musicology* present Prince as a multi-talented and self-sufficient artist who is the master of his music. One of the pictures shows Prince playing the guitar, thus pointing up his talent as a skillful instrumentalist. Another photograph captures the artist's showmanship during a live performance. In this picture, Prince, wearing a bright red suit, executes his dance moves, while the crowd is dancing in the background. Three other photographs present the artist in a contemplative state of mind (see *Picture 12*). In two of the pictures, Prince's eyes are fully or partially shut; in the third one, Prince is looking straight at the camera. The artist is even shown with his hands lifted next to his face, as if to emphasize the intense mental efforts that went into making the album. In sum, these three pictures are clearly intended to strengthen Prince's image as an independent artist and a gifted composer. Two more photographs introduce some members of Prince's backing team. In the first picture, two saxophonists and one trombone player are shown playing on stage. Unlike Prince's photos, however, this picture was probably not intended to popularize the players individually: the lighting is dim, and their faces are pointed downwards. The picture can rather be seen to underscore the highly charged, energetic atmosphere of the artist's live concerts. In the second photograph, Prince is standing in the middle of a group consisting of seven persons. All of them are looking straight at the camera – including Prince, who stands in a domineering posture with his hands in the pockets of a pinstripe jacket. This picture, showing Prince surrounded by the backing group, supports his author image as a leader who gives the orders and whose visions the team must follow.

Though never questioning his musical talent and creative gifts, both audiences and the media have expressed various reactions towards the artist during his career. Prince himself, however, claims that his attitude toward music making has never changed. In fact, when asked about the various stages of his success, Prince characterizes the 1990s as being no different from his commercial heyday of the mid 1980s (DeCurtis 1999). Prince's case demonstrates that there is a fine line between the idea of single, originating authorship and a musical author whose public persona comes across as petulant or self-indulgent. Nevertheless, Prince has made, and continues to make, an indelible mark on popular music. Though some of his albums are valued more highly than others, and though the general public has not always agreed with Prince's choices, no one has doubted his musical prowess. As one critic puts it: "No one questions his ability, but his taste is another matter" (Greenwood 2001b). Both the media and the general public have, from time to time, seen Prince's uncompromising attitude towards music making as being a detrimental, rather than edifying, artistic quality.

Team undercover

The foregoing analyses of media texts have demonstrated that an artist's presented author image may not correspond with the mediated one. We have also seen that construction of an artist's public persona normally involves the creative and authorial input of other participants in the music-making process. In the following, I examine that process more closely, and how authorial credits are shared on one album by each artist under discussion. The discussion examines the distribution of authorial responsibility between the artist and his/her backing team, as well as the question of authorship in relation to the artists' public images.

First under consideration is Coldplay's debut album, *Parachutes* (2000). According to the album credits, the band wrote and produced all the songs on the record. The band is also credited with participation in the design and photography of the album cover. The names of individual band members are mentioned, but each one's responsibility is not specified more closely. Counting the band and producer-engineer Ken Nelson, there are altogether eleven persons mentioned as having contributed to making of album. These include a computer consultant, a sound master, two photographers, four (assistant) engineers, a manager, an artist-repertoire representative and another producer-engineer-mixer. Neither these people nor their authorial inputs receive mention in the album reviews and artist interviews cited earlier. In this manner, the public image is constructed around the artist's star persona, while the media largely ignores the input of others in the creative collective. The manner in which attention is focused on the band's contribution also highlights what is usually most respected with regard to the making of popular music: the work of songwriters and performers – those whose public images are used for marketing purposes – is valued more highly than the input of sound engineers or other members of the creative collective.[127]

Next to be examined is an album by Britney Spears entitled *Britney* (2001). In addition to performing vocals, Spears is credited with co-writing five of the album's twelve songs. Another contributor to the album is Max Martin, whose input also received mention in media texts concerning *Britney*. The liner notes list Martin as producing, engineering and mixing four songs on the album, on two of which he also plays guitar and sings background vocals. Media texts mention only Martin's role as a producer, and pass over his other areas of responsibility. In fact, if audiences were to judge only from the reviews, artist interviews and other material presented in the media, they might easily get the impression that "Spears the artist" and "Martin the producer" made the album all by themselves. That impression would be wrong, however, since the liner notes show fifty-nine persons as having contributed to making the album. Listed are nineteen (assistant) engineers, seventeen background vocalists, seven producers and four mixers. Also mentioned is the input of four guitarists, a bassist, two (string) arrangers, a sound master, a person responsible for LP "scratching" and another for turntables. The members of the production duo The Neptunes are referred to separately as "musicians". Many of the producers also participated in the songwriting, engineering, mixing and arranging on the album and/or played an instrument on the record. In addition to this mixed group, three other people receive album-credits for songwriting. Finally, and listed separately, are eight persons credited with the cover design and styling.

A large and varied group of people took part in the making of Spears's album, but few of them are mentioned in album reviews and artist interviews. Instead, mention is made only of contributions by the public performer and by famous producers, such as Max Martin and The Neptunes. Album reviews and other media texts obscure the fact that over sixty people contributed to the making of the *Britney* album. By focusing attention only on the public artist and on celebrated producers, it is easier to present the album as a product of Spears's personal storytelling. If reviewers had mentioned the input of everyone involved in making the album, attention would have been drawn away from the artist's star power, around which Spears's author image is constructed.

---

127 There is an abundance of music technology publications, such as *Electronic Musician*, *Future Music*, *Remix*, *Sound on Sound* and *Keyboard*, which focus on music production and recording technology, electronic musical instruments, and music production hardware and software. Nevertheless, the popular media make little mention of engineering and production work – probably because it is easier to market music that can be clearly linked with one primary author. By contrast, music technology magazines are used primarily by the music software industry, as forums for marketing home-studio technoculture (Sirppiniemi 2005: 178–182).

Despite her extensive back-up team working behind the scenes, as well as the manu-factured nature of her overall star image, Spears's public identity as an artist aligns itself, in the end, with traditional representations of single authorship,

The third album under scrutiny is Prince's *Musicology* (2004). According to the album credits, the artist is the composer, performer, arranger, producer and engineer of the record. He is moreover credited with playing all the instruments and singing all the vocals on four of the twelve songs on the album. Yet even Prince, notorious for seeking total control over his music making, required outside help in making of the album. Nineteen names are mentioned in the album credits. The collective consists of six background vocalists (one of whom is also a saxophonist), two (assistant) en-gineers, and six instrumentalists, these last consisting of two horn players, a bassist, a drummer, a percussionist (playing shaker), and keyboardist (on Fender Rhodes). Receiving separate mention is the creator of string samples on one of the songs. The remaining four members of the team were in charge of photography and album-cover design. These acknowledgements of the backing team in no way obscure the fact that Prince is the primary author of the album.

Suggested images and multiple meanings

These three case studies have shown that the presented author image and the mediated author image do not always tally with each other. The authorial role of the artist has been shown to differ in each of the three case studies. As shown above, the presented author image of Coldplay typically presents the band as a four-man democracy. In the case of Spears, her self-entitled album *Britney* gives the impression that all songs on the album are autobiographical. Finally, Prince's presented author image – on the discussed album and throughout his career – powerfully and consistently emphasizes the notion of single authorship. It has been shown that, in all three case studies, the media-constructed image diverges from the presented author image. *Table 4* summa-rizes the conflicting relations between the artist's presented images and the mediated author images, as revealed by the three case studies.

Artist	Presented author image	Mediated author image
Coldplay	*Democratic foursome: band members portrayed as taking equal part in the music making.*	*The music is seen as a form of personal expression, that of lead-singer Chris Martin.*
Britney Spears	*Autobiographical confessionalism: the songs are made to seem like autobiographical revelations of the artist's private life.*	*Most of the attention goes to the authorial input of the songwriting and production team; the sense of the artist's confessionalism is referred to as a marketing strategy.*
Prince	*Autonomous creator and single, originating author who wishes to control all aspects of the music making.*	*A whimsical and self-indulgent person, whose output of the 1990s is viewed as too experimental.*

Table 4. Contradictory readings of the images of Coldplay, Britney Spears and Prince.

In all three cases, the media representations seem not to conflict with the image that the artist (and/or his/her marketing machinery) wishes to express, as indicated in interviews and other presented author images. In the case of Coldplay, the media focus on Chris Martin and his role as the band's front man; however, the band describes itself as something like a (socialist) democracy, whose members share equally in all writing credits. A similar dissonance shows up in Spears's case: album reviewers emphasize the role of the songwriting and production team, whereas both her comments and the song lyrics suggest that the music is based on the feelings and emotional experiences of the public artist. A similar conflict obtains in Prince's case. The presented author image portrays the artist as the sole author, who exerts total creative control and fights to establish his rights to ownership. By contrast, the media tend to represent Prince as a whimsical, selfish artist, who sometimes goes too far with his musical experiments.

The remaining question has to do with the *compiled author image*, i.e. the image constructed by audiences. What kinds of meanings does the audience link to the artist in cases where the presented and mediated author images conflict with each other? Should we assume that the compiled author image consists equally of both the presented author image and the mediated one? To recall the comment made by Coldplay's Chris Martin: the band believes that those audience members who are deeply interested in the group will be aware of the authorial equality between band members. From Martin's comment we may infer that in these kinds of conflicting situations, the (competent) audience is likely to choose the information that he/she believes to be coming from the artist, over that disseminated by the media. It is, then, up to audience members to arrive at their own interpretation of the artist's public persona, which is based on a group of ideas that are always inadequate and, sometimes, contradictory.

Conclusion

The construction of author images is connected not only to makers and performers of music; the media and the audience also play an active role in the process. Because of the mediated nature of image construction, it is not a matter of direct communication between sender and receiver; rather, the meanings given to musical texts are influenced by a number of intermediary forces. The images and impressions constructed by the public artist and the media also affect the ways in which the audience perceives the artist, his/her authorial role and artistic capabilities. The meanings given to each text are constantly in flux, hence the artist's author image, too, is never permanent. There is more than one way of interpreting artists and their works, since a variety of meanings may be linked with the same artist and his/her public image.

In the foregoing case studies, the perceived tension between the presented author image and the mediated one may be seen to differ from artist to artist. What is common to all of them, however, is the media's insistence on isolating a front figure that will give the music its face. Nevertheless, the media often point out how much authorial responsibility each artist has in the process of music making. Whether or not it is the artist's (presented) authorial voice that the listener pays most attention to in compiling his/her own reading, the artist's public persona plays a crucial role in constructing the author image. Either way, by promoting the idea of single authorship, it is possible both to increase the sales of a given publication and to underline the artist's creative integrity and musical capabilities.

If mediated author images of Coldplay attribute the weightiest authorial contribution to the band's singer, Chris Martin, reviews of Britney Spears underscore the significance of the songwriting and production team, at the expense of Spears's creative input. In Prince's case, the media present the artist as an egotistical and moody character; this is somewhat discordant with the presented author image, which vaunts single-authorship and artistic control. Authorial images are constructed around the most varied ideas and assumptions, the meanings and importance of which may vary from case to case. Still, it is the artist and his/her status as an author and a public artist around which those readings, even contradictory ones, are constructed.

6. Genre-based author images online

Theorizing genre

One of the most common ways of classifying popular music is according to genre. Genre-based categories are used by music makers, marketers, and listeners alike (Kemp 2004: 21, 28; Negus 2001: 42; Shuker 1994: 147). For example, in record stores, albums are usually classified under different labels, such as pop, rock, heavy metal and dance. Also most music magazines and radio stations concentrate on one specific genre, and thus, define the audience based on readers' and listeners' musical preferences. Similarly, the typical album or concert review usually starts with defining the artist's generic location in comparison with other artists and musical traditions. Listeners, too, commonly use generic and/or stylistic terms in describing their popular-music preferences. (Straw 2001b: 53–73.) Genre categories, such as rock and pop, not only point out musical differences, but also indicate differences in lifestyle (see e.g. Frith 1996: 95; Kemp 2004: 21–22; Shuker 1994: 146; Straw 2001b: 63–71).

Theoretically speaking, musical genres are often understood as social agreements that create expectations and rules about each style of music (Negus 1998: 362–363; Shuker 1994: 145–147; Wall 2003: 145–146). Genre-specific expectations also delimit the types of authorship available to different kinds of music making. The authorship of each artist is not a matter of chance; rather, it is constructed within genre-specific categories (Negus 1998: 362–363; Shuker 1994: 145–147; see also Herman 2006: 24). In this chapter, the construction of author images is examined in relation to the genres represented in the present study: rock, pop and electronic dance music. I concentrate on three popular music artists and their author images, as presented on the artists' "official" Internet homepages. Each of these artists – Bruce Springsteen (representing rock), Kylie Minogue (pop) and Kraftwerk (electronic dance music) – has a long and established career, and may thus be considered as typical representatives of their respective genre-classifications. Before examining the author images of the mentioned artists, it is important first to understand the notion of genre and its functioning within the field of popular music.

Fluid, dynamic and codified

Genres are usually defined as codes that are used in categorizing music (Negus 2001: 37; Wall 2003: 145). Established, genre-specific codes set the rules by which music is produced, distributed and consumed (Kemp 2004: 28). Genres also offer us a vocabulary that makes a given phenomenon appear more coherent and contained, or less random and disordered (Phillips 1999: 166). Simon Frith (1996: 95) claims that all discourse about popular music is constructed according to generic vocabularies:

> It is genre rules which determine how musical forms are taken to convey meaning and value, which determine the aptness of different sorts of judgment, which determine the competence of different people to make assessments. It is through genres that we experience music and musical relations, that we bring together the aesthetic and the ethical. (Frith 1996: 95.)

According to Frith, the classification of popular music relies heavily on generic conventions that are socially constructed. Genres are learnt categories; they are not absolutes. Moreover, they should not be viewed as permanent conventions, but as constantly changing agreements (Kemp 2004: 20; Negus 1999: 26; Walser 1993: 27). Genres, then, are dynamic patterns that develop over time and consist of interrelated elements (Kemp 2004: 26). Generic codes also guide both audience and media reactions to different styles of music. Says Jason Toynbee (2000: 115): "the industry needs to make music knowable, to place that which cannot be seen and which has not yet been heard in the realm of the familiar". Toynbee (2000: 115) is arguing that the generic codes must be made clear at the very start of a song, so that listeners can immediately classify it in terms of musical style and tradition. Socially learnt codes also determine the kinds of meanings that are given to artists who operate within certain musical categories – how their music is heard, how their images are constructed, and their performances perceived.

Generic distinctions are never clear-cut and absolute. They are constantly changing, as influences from a number of musical styles mix and blend with each other (Kemp 2004: 20). Genre is also a matter of perspective, as Keith Negus (1999: 26) concludes, since "what from one perspective are perceived as codes, rules and conventions are from another point of view heard as dynamic and changing musical characteristics". Adding to this ambiguity is the fact that some artists incorporate a variety of musical styles into their music, which makes it difficult to classify them into just one category (Kemp 2004: 27; Shuker 1994: 146). This might explain why the musical styles of some artists require closer specification in terms of *subgenres*, such as "album rock", "experimental rock", "dance pop" or "Euro dance". In the comparison of subgenres, the slightest differences among them may count, such as the knowledge of instruments, performance context, vocal traits, or the opinion of media commentators (Kemp 2004: 25). It is also possible for the genre category linked with a certain artist to differ, depending on the point in time in the artist's career.[128] In addition, the overall construction of the artist's public image takes place over time, as the artist's music and image come to be associated with certain values, beliefs and identities (Negus 1992: 70; Negus 2001: 42; Shuker 1994: 147). In this way, the media and audience members also help to determine how musical categories are defined and promoted.

Genre shaping

As market regulators, genres are also essential to the economics of popular music (Frith 1996: 75; Negus 2001). The film industry clearly demonstrates the economic importance of genres. According to film theorist Dudley Andrew (1984), cinematic genres construct their own consumers, since the viewer's taste and behaviour are largely the result of exposure to certain generic norms. These last trigger certain viewer expectations, and regulate the spectators' relation to images and narratives that are constructed especially for them (Andrew 1984: 110). We may ask if genres have an equally decisive role in the functioning of popular music. Are the choices of the audience determined by existing genre classifications? Or can listeners create their own musical taste without any such guidance by popular music culture? Instead of situating the power of decision in the marketing machinery, it might be more realistic to see genre classifications as resulting from relations between various agents, whose independent actions shape our conceptions of each musical style.

Though genres are contingent, socially constructed and constantly changing, we should not forget the role of the market place. According to Negus (1999: 30), whose writings focus on interrelations between industrial tactics and genre classification, the latter has to do with the tension between the products of industry and those of culture. Frith (1996: 75), too, remarks on how genre categories are used in organizing sales. Frith concludes that genres provide a way of combining the question of music (what does it sound like?) with that of its market (who will buy it?). Through genre market-ing with distinctly ideological designs, the choice of one style of music over some other may work as both a mark of individuality and of collective identity. (Frith 1996: 76; Frith 2001: 38–39.) Hence genres are not usually regarded simply as formal codes, rules and constraints, but as socially operating categories.[129] With the notion of *genre*

---

128   For example, the style of Depeche Mode has over the years changed from pop to harder rock (Goodwin 1992: 113).

129   In a landmark essay, Franco Fabbri (1982) defines a musical genre as "a set of musical events (real of pos-

culture, Negus (1999: 28) wishes to underline that sociological aspect of genres. Negus is trying to say that genre issues are not only linked with ongoing debates between artists, media and audiences, but extend to wider social contexts.

Because of their social aspects, the genres with which artists are associated cannot be determined merely by musical features (Frith 1996: 95; Kemp 2004: 21–22; Shuker 1994: 146). Visual elements also come into play. These, like all other generically determined codes, are connected with certain attitudes, values and beliefs. The visual image of an artist also informs the audience as to what the music of a certain artist is supposed to sound like (Goodwin 1992: 51; Negus 1992: 67). Based on the artist's clothing alone, it is easy to distinguish an artist who performs heavy rock from one who performs rap music (see also Connell et al. 2003: 84–88). Shared generic conventions also strengthen the sense of togetherness that binds listeners and music makers to a given style of music. To illustrate the importance of visual material and its linkage with genre classifications, Andrew Goodwin (1992) investigates the visual designs of album covers. According to Goodwin (1992: 51), the album cover imagery is the site where "the genre is often established". Other visual material shares a similar function, by suggesting certain ways of decoding generic rules and codes. As an example, Negus (1992) discusses the manner in which different artists are presented in photographs. According to Negus (1992: 67), rock artists are usually photographed on location, for example, on a hillside or a street, whereas most dance and pop artists are typically pictured in a studio environment, with the focus on the artist's clothes, hairstyle, make-up and overall visual appearance. By taking into account the issue of visuality, my aim is to draw attention to the fact that musical authorship is not only a question of how the music sounds, but also what it looks like.

The presented author image online

Visual elements and other genre-specific codes also play an essential role in the construction of artists' author images. In the following, I analyse the author image of three popular music artists, each of whose authorship is based on different generic rules. Since the material analysed in this chapter comes from artists' official Internet homepages, the discussed images may also be referred to as their *online author images*. At the same time, the material on those homepages is produced by the artist and/or his/her marketing machinery, and is therefore also part of the artist's presented author image. In *Table 5*, I have divided the elements of the presented author image

sible) whose course is governed by a definite set of socially accepted rules". Fabbri (1982: 52–81) groups generic rules into five categories: formal and technical rules, semiotic rules, behavioural rules, social and ideological rules, and finally, economical and juridical rules.

into three main categories: music, biography and visual imagery.[130] First, based on musical elements (e.g. instrumentation, rhythm, melody and sound quality), we may recognize the musical genre with which these elements are commonly associated. The music can often contain a wide range of influences from a number of musical traditions, but the main genre, such as rock or pop, is usually quite easy to identify. Also, the artist's voice quality and singing technique can evoke generic associations. Thus apart from the story recounted in the lyrics, the sense of personal storytelling may also derive from the artist's singing voice. In addition, the lyrics can include messages (e.g. political, ethical, and so on) that link the song to a certain time period, social context or tradition (cf. Brackett 1999: 134–139).

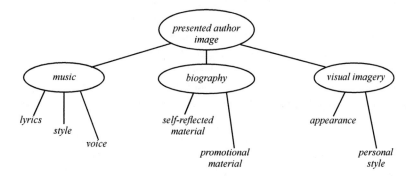

Table 5. The presented author image and its elements on artist websites.

The second main category, biography, refers to the history that is linked with the artist's public image. The story may consist of comments made by the artist (or those presented as such) – in interviews, on web blogs, album liner notes etc. – as well as those expressed by marketing representatives and/or by the media. The biography consists of those events which are construed as the most important turning points in the artist's life and musical career. These events also explain the artist's socio-cultural background and connect the music to his/her personal history (see also Hennion 1990: 199–202). The link between artists and their biographical details also explains why musical works are often assumed to tell about artists' personal experiences (Reynolds et al. 1995: 249–275).

130   The mediated and compiled author images can be said to consist of similar elements, but in this examination, and throughout this study, primary attention is paid to the one producing the image. For that reason, the *presented author image* is relevant in this context.

The third category consists of the artist's visual imagery. This category is composed of (official) visual material that is made public, mostly music videos and artist photographs (taken at public appearances or for promotional purposes such as cover art, for posting on websites etc.). The visual imagery, which consists in the artist's clothing, makeup, hairstyle and facial expressions, often projects certain genre-specific codes. In determining the kinds of material shown publicly, the artist and/or the marketing machinery can further specify the generic codes to be associated with the presented author image.[131]

In the following, I analyse the presented online author images of Bruce Springsteen, Kylie Minogue and Kraftwerk by examining the material presented on their homepages. The artist websites are an effective means of making the artist better-known, through the distribution of various artist-related materials, including sound and video clips, photographs and artist biographies. Apart from the official sites, one can usually find several other websites dedicated to each artist. These are maintained by fans who have gathered information about their idols.[132] These "fansites" present images constructed by the audience; by contrast, the material on the official homepages is controlled by the artist and/or the marketing strategists. Some fansites present the artist in a way that differs from the one presented on the official website.[133] The fansites of artists with high celebrity value may also include visual material (e.g. photos taken by paparazzi) that is not available on the artist's official homepage, and which may not have been intended for publication at all (see also Turner 2004: 20).[134] In contrast to fansites, then, the official homepages may be seen as a form of the artist's self-presentation (Chan 2000: 271–272); even though it remains unclear to what extent the public artist has affected the content and format of his/her own website, the homepages offer material that is used for constructing the artist's presented author image. We should also keep in mind that both the content and the format of websites may change as the pages are updated. The updates typically occur when new albums are released or new concerts are organized.[135] In most cases, however, the artist's public

---

131 It is also possible for the artist's image to be guided in an unwanted direction; for example, when a live performance does not go as planned or when some secretly taken photographs are made public.

132 The fansites usually tend to imitate the artist's official homepage, at least in terms of their visual style. For example, the appearance of several Kraftwerk fansites (such as www.keepwerking.co.uk, as accessed 8 November 2006) repeats the black and neon green colour combination displayed on the band's official site.

133 For example, a site called The Kraftwerk Influence (www.cuug.ab.ca/~lapierrs/creative/kraftwerk, as accessed 8 November 2006) explores Kraftwerk-inspired works made by other artists, who may, for example, use digital samples of the band's recordings.

134 For example, some Britney Spears fansites (such as www.gobritney.com and www.britneyzone.com, as accessed 8 November 2006) are dedicated to compiling all artist-related visual material that is available in the media.

135 The importance of updating is also mentioned in Christian Hall's (2005) guide to promoting an artist's music on the web (published on The Musician's Union website). According to Hall (2005), daily or weekly updates provide the website with "current interest" value, which brings visitors back for more.

image and overall sense of style stays relatively fixed, while minor changes may take place within the rules of one specific genre and its shared codes.

The material available on artist homepages often covers all the main categories of the artist's presented author image (see *Table 5*). Audio clips exemplify the music; biographical details, tour information, and other written material tell about the artist's history and current activities; photographs and video clips reveal the artist's appearance and visual style. Not all homepages include all the mentioned material; still, most of them lay out a detailed conception of the artist, his/her music and career. Like other channels of marketing popular music, artist websites are constructed mainly around the public artist and his/her star value. As a result, the websites function as a public forum where different material is collected and presented so as to offer an all-around image of the artist and his/her musical career. Artist websites also inform the public about the artist's future plans, including concert tours and upcoming releases.

The wide variety of materials presented on websites serves as a valuable resource for comparing and contrasting the author images of artists who are taken to represent different musical styles. The following examination scrutinizes the *genre-specific codes* that define the tradition to which the chosen artists are seen to belong. The analysis focuses on artists' presented online author images, and their connections with the codes and conventions that may be seen as typical of the genres of rock, pop and electronic dance music. In the latter part of the chapter, comparison is made between the presented author images of the three case studies, in terms of their music (both written descriptions and sound clips), artist biography and visual imagery.

Bruce Springsteen – Telling stories

First, I examine the online author image of Bruce Springsteen[136]. The main page of Springsteen's homepage (www.brucespringsteen.net[137]), titled "News", reports on the most recent activities related to the artist. In addition to brief newspieces, the page presents interviews with Springsteen, either partial or in full, that have been published in various music magazines and newspapers. These interviews are the only writings on the homepage in which Springsteen speaks in his own words. A unifying theme among the articles is their focus on Springsteen's live performances. As the following

---

136 Springsteen was born in New Jersey in 1949 and started his musical career in the 1960s in various line-ups. Several years and two albums later, Springsteen managed to establish his status as a recognized artist, with his album *Born to Run* (1975). From those days on, Springsteen has been regarded as the saviour of rock 'n' roll, and artist who prefers basic rock values over short-term trends and passing fashions. Springsteen has released more than ten full-length albums, including *The River* (1980) and *Born in the U.S.A.* (1984), which altogether constitute one of the most famous careers in the history of rock music. (Ruhlmann 2002: 1062.)

137 The description refers to the homepage as accessed on 3 October 2005.

quote demonstrates, Springsteen himself places live performances at the centre of his authorship:

> That's the job. As you go along, you're bringing the music and all these characters to life every night. [...] I'm not going to come out and just run through some songs, or play favorites. I'm in search of some life essence. That's why people come. (Bruce Springsteen in *Associated Press*; McShane 2005.)

According to the presented author image of Springsteen, a distinct line separates the artist's role from that of the audience; he is the one who searches for truth in his music, and the one who can touch people with his creations. Springsteen analyses his authorial role more thoroughly in another interview:

> The audiences are there as a result of my history with the band but also as a result of my being able to reach people with a tune. I have my ideas, I have my music and I also just enjoy showing off. (Bruce Springsteen in *Guardian*; Hornby 2005.)

Springsteen seems, then, to be well aware of his long career and his influence on the history of popular music. The homepage also gives out the impression that Springsteen regards his musical talent as something rare, which people in the audience admire. Music has the power to touch people and to make them forget about everything else. Springsteen's awareness of that power may be inferred from the following comment, made just minutes before the start of a show:

> That first step onstage is an unusual feeling. [...] You're taking a risk, which is the essence of all live performance. It's not an entirely comfortable feeling, but it's a necessary one. It happens every time, and it tends to stop the minute I put my hands on any instrument. (Bruce Springsteen in *Esquire*; Fussman 2005.)

Springsteen's monumental status as a live performer is emphasized on the opening page of his website. A separate section, called "Live", contains detailed information about the artist's live concerts, performance dates, cities, venues and set lists. From there a link is provided to a discussion forum, where fans can share about their experiences and give their opinions of each concert in question. Writer after writer describes the concerts as amazing, all of them heaping praises on Springsteen's showmanship. Here is a typical review, written about the show in Trenton, New Jersey on November 22, 2005:

150

Last night I was transformed.... Other words fail me to adequately describe this perform-ance. NO song was a disappointment or throw away last night. The set list speaks for itself and he left nothing on the stage last night.... He put it all out there.... (Username sbeltle on *Sony Music Forums – Bruce Springsteen*[138].)

Another user hails Springsteen as a sincere and exceptional performer:

This tour has to go down as one of the best, by any performer, ever. I'd dare any other per-former out there to do a "Solo Acoustic" tour such as this one and perform 138 songs over the course of a tour, let alone successfully pull it off. From what I've seen there is only one performer out there that can successfully pull something like this off night after night over seven months – pouring his heart and soul into every show – The Boss. Thank you sir for a great tour. (Username jgaulke on *Sony Music Forums – Bruce Springsteen*[139].)

In addition to presenting Springsteen as a talented live performer, the pages focus on the artist's long and impressive career. For example, the section named "Devils&Dust" introduces Springsteen's album of that title, released on April 26, 2005. On the page is a list of songs, a sound clip of each one, and a link to the lyrics. The next page, "Songs", lists all of Springsteen's songs in alphabetical order, and the "Album" page contains pictures of all Springsteen's album covers, from *Greetings from Asbury Park, N.J.* (1973) to *Devils & Dust* (2005).

With respect to the categories presented in *Table 5*, the material on Springsteen's website is clearly weighted toward the music. The sound clips allow users to hear Springsteen's voice and get familiar with his singing technique. They may also access the song lyrics, which can be used to construct and reconstruct their images of the art-ist. As yet there is no separate section, such as a blog or diary, where Springsteen tells (at least supposedly) more about his own experiences in his own words. Nor does the website display a biography or brief vita, to inform the visitor about the highlights of the artist's career. Rather, the pages focus almost exclusively on the music. In a sense, then, the song lyrics substitute for stories about Springsteen's personal life. Moreover, Springsteen maintains that the songwriter is always writing about personal experienc-es, since through music making the artist can try to capture a piece of the world as he or she sees it (Hagen et al. 1999: 78). The following comment by Springsteen, made early in his career (1974), supports the artist's image as a songwriter whose songs are based on personal experience, and hence, motivated by the pursuit of self-discovery:

138 Username sbeltle, http://forums1.sonymusic.com/groupee/forums/a/tpc/f/404103162/m/3481090025 (23 November 2005).
139 Username jgaulke, http://forums1.sonymusic.com/groupee/forums/a/tpc/f/404103162/m/3481090025 (23 November 2005).

Picture 13. Bruce Springsteen, shown performing before live audience (homepage photo, as accessed 3 October 2005).

> I had to write about me all the time, every song, 'cause in a way you're trying to find out what that "me" is. That's why I choose where I grew up, and when I live, and I take situations I'm in, and people I know, and take 'em to the limits. (Bruce Springsteen in *Melody Maker*, Watts 1994: 55.)

The omission of a website biography suggests that everyone already is, or at least should be, familiar with Springsteen's career. Any information about the artist's life is presented in terms of his musical development. The top of each page shows pictures of Springsteen's album covers in chronological order. These remind the reader, at first glance, of the artist's long and impressive career.

The visual imagery of Springsteen's pages consists mostly in the reproductions of album covers. A few photographs show Springsteen either posing for the camera or performing in front of a huge audience (see *Picture 13*). Another picture shows Springsteen, alone and playing guitar in an empty concert hall, among the bare seats, a shot that reaffirms the artist's image as a talented live performer. Also many of the album covers display the artist with guitar in hand, in order to emphasize his playing and songwriting skills. In most of the photographs, Springsteen is wearing jeans and a plain T-shirt – a casual outfit that can be seen to support the artist's image as a down-to-earth workingman (see also Negus 1992: 73–75). Hair ruffled and chin unshaven, the artist comes across as an authentic musician, one who is so absorbed in his craft that he pays scant attention to exterior features.

Kylie Minogue – A dancing pop queen

The second case study concerns the online author image of Kylie Minogue[140]. Through the opening page of Minogue's homepage (www.kylie.com[141]), the user has access to the actual homepage of Minogue's website, called "News". As the title promises, that page offers the latest news about the artist, with headings such as "Kylie nominated for two ARIA awards!" and "The official Kylie Calender 2006 has arrived". Since the announcement of Minogue's breast cancer in May 2005, the news section has also followed her recovery. Besides the news, there is a small window that shows video clips from popular videos by Minogue. Also, a virtual audio device plays clips from Minogue's hits. Finally, on the top of the main page, a menu appears through which to access other sections of the website. The sections are called "Kylie", "Music", "Media", "bLA bLA bLA", "Shop Kylie", "Showgirl", and "Exhibition". The menu reveals that all but the last two sections consist of several subsections.

The "Kylie" section contains an extensive artist biography, which starts with a reference to the artist as "a phenomenon of truly international proportions" (see *Picture 14*). The extensive presentation of her background and musical career gives the user a large amount of information with which to build up one's conception of the artist. A timeline lays out the main events of Minogue's musical career – a testimony to the artist's versatility and achievements. In the section called "Ask Kylie", the artist herself (or so it is claimed) tells about herself in her own words, by answering questions sent in by fans. When asked what she considers the biggest achievement of her career, Minogue replies as follows:

> The point of my job is to entertain and make it look easy, so I guess it's the parts you don't often see which make me feel proud. All the behind the scenes work, the fears and insecurities I have to face and overcome to improve myself as a person and performer, all of the people who believe in me and encourage me. (Kylie Minogue on www.kylie.com.)

---

140 Kylie Minogue was born on May 8, 1968 in Melbourne Australia. Minogue first gained recognition as an actor on a TV soap opera called *Neighbours*. After Minogue's performance at a charity event, a local record company, Mushroom Records, released her version of "Loco-Motion" as a single in 1987. The single was well-received, and Minogue travelled to London in order to work with the three-men hit factory, Stock, Aitkin and Waterman. The trio had full control over Minogue's music at that time: they wrote the songs, produced the records, and controlled the visual imagery of her music videos. Since the 1990s, Minogue has played a more active role, for example, by writing song lyrics and taking charge of her visual style and public appearance. After her fourth album, *Let's Go to It* (1991), Minogue signed a recording contract with a London dance label, Deconstruction, which resulted in the albums *Kylie Minogue* (1994) and *Impossible Princess* (1997). In 2000, Minogue again switched labels, this time to Parlophone, and again succeeded in renewing her musical style and artistic image. With a number of hit releases and changes of personal image to her credit, Minogue has carved out a long and impressive career as a performer of dance pop. (Nimmervoll 2002: 739–740.)
141 The description refers to the homepage as accessed on 3 October 2005.

Picture 14. Kylie Minogue: Artist homepage features information about her personal background and private life (as accessed 3 October 2005).

Next, the "Music" page offers detailed information about the artist's albums, singles, remix albums, videos and DVDs. There are pictures of the album covers of each Minogue album. By clicking on the cover, the user calls up track listings, release date, release summary, highest chart position and the label of each recording. The release summary also contains information about the making of each album, the writers involved, and the impact each recording has had on Minogue's career. In the summary of *Fever* (2001), for example, the album is said to have "confirmed Kylie's status as an international superstar and icon". The reader is also informed that the public artist took part in authoring the album: "Kylie co-wrote five of the tracks on the album including the singles 'Love at First Sight' and 'In Your Eyes'". The summary also describes the album's musical style, with the reference to Minogue's "oozing sensuous vocals over a backdrop of techno/electronica beats and classic disco influences". The release summaries provide users of the homepage with hints about the style, history and commercial success of each album. By contrast, the "Media" pages focus on Minogue's visual image. First, there is a gallery of photographs and video clips made at different stages of Minogue's career. There is also "behind the scenes" material, taken during the making of videos and during preparations for live shows; with these, the user has access to material that is shown nowhere else. With this material, users can deepen their knowledge of the artist by observing the off-stage persona, which as a rule is intentionally hidden from the public eye (Holmes 2004: 158–162). Even though the effect is rather illusory, Minogue's website gives out the impression that the artist is allowing her fans to follow her career up close, despite the fact that this sense of intimacy is itself a kind of consumer good, purveyed by marketers who retain tight control over the material shown on the webpages (cf. Sibilla 2006: 152).

The next section, "bLA bLA bLA", is a mixed bag, containing pages such as "Competitions", "Links", "Privacy" and "Credits". There is also a "Message board" which includes an official Kylie forum, where users may discuss anything concerning the artist, from her music and live performances to TV appearances and press interviews. On the page dedicated to Kylie's Showgirl Tour[142], the user can view photographs taken during the tour, and read comments by the musical director, choreographer and other team members involved in the making of the show. Each interviewed member of the backing team discusses what it is like to work with Minogue. They mention the qualities which they find laudable about the artist's performing skills, and around which the artist's public image is constructed. The choreographer of the tour, Michael Rooney, speaks to Minogue's performing and singing skills:

> Kylie sings live.... did you hear me? I said Kylie sings LIVE! That's almost unheard these days. She holds onto that microphone and switches it back and forth while doing these incredible movements and lifts.

In another comment, tour manager Sean Fitzpatrick emphasizes Minogue's grateful attitude towards her co-workers: "She appreciates and respects the job that everyone around her does. She is the ultimate professional. Her standards are high and she brings out the best in people." Another comment, made by choreographer Rafael Bonachela, focuses on the artist's commitment and talent as a dancer: "She is an incredible performer, a natural mover with a great sense of rhythm. Her commitment and professionalism is [sic] what I truly admire about her." Overall, such comments present Minogue as a versatile and talented performer who is willing to work hard for her success. Besides Minogue's talent and skills, the comments point to her reliance on, and collegiality toward, each member of the backing team, as well as to her need of constant practice so as to make the shows work properly. In a comment about touring and performing, Minogue stresses the importance of her loyal fans:

---

142 The name of the show was later altered to The Showgirl Homecoming Tour after being rescheduled because of Minogue's battle against breast cancer.

Showgirl is not only a celebration of pop songs and my career, but of a long time relationship with my audience. This is my way to say thank you and to share some of the most important moments of my journey so far, a trip down memory lane. (Kylie Minogue on www.kylie.com.)

The comments published on the homepage, by members of the backing team and by Minogue herself, present the artist as a member of a social and creative collective instead of an autonomous individual. The website also gives out the impression that Minogue's skills are not inborn, but rather the result of hard work and long hours of practice.

The last section, called "Kylie exhibition", displays the costumes that Minogue has collected over the years. On these pages, one can carefully examine what the artist has worn on tours, at performances and red-carpet events, in her music videos, and in the photographs on album covers. Visual images of the artist and her ever-changing looks have played an important role throughout Minogue's career (Nimmervoll 2002: 739–740). Introductory texts on the homepage also play up the importance of the artist's visual appearance, asserting that Minogue's "videos have helped define her status as a pop star, creating her most iconic moments". As the following comment suggests, tours and live shows also form an essential part of the artist's public image: "For Kylie, a live tour offers immense creative freedom. It is the ultimate in performance, a direct dialogue between the audience and herself, a pure transaction of artistic endeavour and appreciation".

The material available on Minogue's homepage covers all the categories presented in the *Table 5*. Audio and video clips provide the user with samples of Minogue's music. The presented biography, chronology, and Kylie's replies to questions serve up information about the artist's personal background and private life. Using this information, visitors to the website can (re)build their image of Minogue. Throughout the pages, one hears the artist's own voice (or what is presented as such), giving the user a sense of getting closer to the artist and sharing in her experiences. Minogue tells users about her tours, about her thrill at being nominated for awards, and about what she does in her spare time. By presenting the artist as speaking for herself, the pages make visitors feel as if they were having a private conversation with Minogue. The website also makes it possible for fans to participate in the structure and content of the pages. Finally, users may gain an extensive idea of the artist's visual image and sense of style, from the website's photographs, album covers, magazine pictures, costumes and video material. The music, biography, and visual material work together toward constructing Minogue's presented online author image.

Kraftwerk – Robotic man machines

As a third case study, I examine the online author image of Kraftwerk[143] – a band that is often regarded as one of the pioneers in the genre of electronic dance music (Bogdanov et al. 2001: ix; Poschardt 1995: 224–225; Reynolds 2000: 33–34; Sicko 1999: 27). The opening page of Kraftwerk's website is quite plain in appearance (www. kraftwerk.com[144]). On the top of the page, the text "Kraftwerk" is written in neon green against a black background, while in the middle of the page, a radio transmitter is shown emitting a circular signal. One hears an audio of monotonous, mechanical sounds, but the band members' faces are nowhere in sight. When one clicks on the page, a new window opens, containing a menu. The green and black colouring is also present on the menu page, but the only visible figure is now that of a sine wave, which may be viewed as an indicator of the band's robotic sound and use of technology. First, there is a link to the "Info" page, which displays information about Kraftwerk's tours and albums; a second subpage focuses on the live record, *Minimum-maximum*, released in 2005. The page shows a picture of the album cover, the names of the band members, and a brief listing of the formats in which the album has been released. No information is given about the making of the album or about the division of authorial responsibility among band members. No data are given about the album's reception, either in the media or by audiences; nor is one told how the album fared commercially. Similar to the previous one, the third subpage shows information about the album *Tour de France Soundtracks*, released in 2003. The content of the album is listed, and by clicking on a track title, the user may hear a sound clip of each song. Some songs lyrics are cited, but the identity of the artist remains more or less a mystery.

On Kraftwerk's "Photo" pages one finds a small gallery of photographs. Seven of the ten pictures were taken during Kraftwerk's live concerts. Though the lighting and background varies from photo to photo, all these pictures show the four men on stage, standing in a straight line behind their instruments: computers. In the two other pictures, the men have been replaced by robotic replicas (see *Picture 15*). In the last photograph, the band members are wearing striped, full-length bodywear, reminiscent of diving suits. Their faces are painted over with white colorant, their eyes covered

---

143 The roots of the band date back to 1970, when Kraftwerk was formed in Düsseldorf. Florian Schneider and Ralf Hütter met originally at the local Conservatory, where they both studied classical music. In the beginning, they called their band Organisation, but soon renamed it Kraftwerk and began working in their own Kling Klang studio. With their first two albums, *Kraftwerk 1* (1971) and *Kraftwerk 2* (1972), the band introduced listeners to an uncanny world of robotic and technological sounds. The *Autobahn* (1974) album brought Kraftwerk international fame and established a permanent position for electronic music among the mainstream audience. (Ankeny 2002a: 632.) The band's line-up has changed several times over the years; at present, the members of Kraftwerk are Ralf Hütter, Florian Schneider, Fritz Hilpert and Henning Schmitz (www.kraftwerk.com, as accessed 3 October 2005).

144 The description refers to the homepage as accessed on 3 October 2005.

Picture 15. Kraftwerk, sample photo from band's homepage, as promoting the band's alienated, robotic public image (as accessed 3 October 2005).

with what appear to be swim goggles. The suit-stripes glow neon green, matching the horizontal striping of the background; everything else on the stage is obscured in darkness. No emphasis is given to characteristics of individual members. Rather, the visual imagery presents the band as a single, homogeneous unit.

In addition to "Info" and "Photo" sections, there are ten subpages named with a title of one of Kraftwerk's songs; among those presented are "Autobahn" (from *Autobahn,* 1974), "Radioactivity" (from *Radio-Activity,* 1975) and "The Robots" (from *The Man Machine,* 1978). The user is presented with a picture from an album cover or an animated video clip, each representing a theme linked with each song. A couple of the pages do not feature the original recording of the song, but rather a version in which the user may participate, and thus take part in the (re)making of the song. The pages for "Numbers" and "Pocketcalculator" are animated websites that remind one of computer games. On these pages, users may create their own piece of music, either by combining figures that stand for robotic sounds (pronounced in German) or by clicking calculator buttons with one's mouse. This emphasis on user-participation in creating the music calls into question the concept of a musical work as something permanent and unchanging. The webpages under discussion point up the fact that a number of parallel versions of the same song may exist simultaneously. Also problematised is the concept of the author as an authoritarian figure and an exceptional individual, since every user of the website gets the opportunity to test, or perhaps to develop further, his/her own skills as a music maker. By treating the listener as an active agent, electronic dance music diverts attention from the author and his/her creation, and instead lays emphasis on the active reception of musical works (cf. Krasnow 1995: 181–182).

Kraftwerk's homepage includes very little information about the band and its members. There is no biography, no mention of different stages in the band's history, no reference to the group's success or popularity. There are no pictures of individual band members. As noted earlier, all pictures have the four men striking similar poses and wearing the same kind of clothing; hence, no emphasis is given to an individual member. Kraftwerk's image, then, provides a sharp contrast to that of pop bands, in which each member is presented as a unique personality and made distinguishable through such means as clothing and styling (cf. Turner 2004: 57).[145] The band's homepage underlines Kraftwerk's mysterious visual image, by not revealing any information about the members' personal lives or backgrounds. In the following comment, Ralf Hütter indicates that fame was something which the band wished to avoid from the beginning:

> The importance of our secrecy was necessary for our privacy and work. We never wanted to be the idols for other people. We only wanted to make our music and, of course, we hoped to reach the people with our messages and melodies. (Ralf Hütter on *BBC Radio 1*, July 1996; Barr 1998: 193.)

The band's distanced or alienated author image remains that way on their website, which offers no information which visitors might use to deepen their idea of the artist. The dissociated, depersonalized look of Kraftwerk's visual imagery seems to echo the robotic sound of the band's music, as well as the strong role of technology in their music making. Also, many of the song titles – "The Man Machine", "The Robots", "Autobahn", "Transistor", "The Computer World – refer to the world of machines, vehicles and materiality, in contrast to that of the human, the personal, or the spiritual. By presenting "man" and "machine" are presented as opposing categories, Kraftwerk's author image – like that of many other techno-driven dance groups – comes across as an "anti-man" construction, in parallel with the depersonalized, technology-based nature of its music (see also Ahonen 2006a; Den Tandt 2004; Herman 2006; McLeod 2003: 352). Through the several sound clips, the user is able to form a picture

---

145   Graeme Turner (2004: 57) mentions Spice Girls, an English all-female pop group, as an example of a band whose members were known for their individual identities.

of Kraftwerk's long musical career. Primary attention is given to the sonic material; even the visual animations are based on the sound clips.

Comparing three sets of generic rules

This examination of homepages has brought to light several great differences among the author images presented on artist websites. Those differences may be explained in terms of the generic conventions linked with each genre under discussion: rock, pop and electronic dance music. Many of the generic conventions relate to musical authorship, aspects of which have already been discussed in this study; these include the notion of single originating authorship, auteurism, authenticity, authorial contribution, singer-songwriter tradition and the use of disguised imagery (see also Ahonen 2006b: 170–171). Bearing those themes in mind, I next analyse the online author images of the chosen artists, and the ways in which those images are connected with genre-specific aspects of musical authorship.

All three homepages share a basic format: an opening page containing links to subpages. All the websites include sound clips, pictures of album covers, and a track list (at least of the artist's latest album). Thus, all the three homepages include information about the music. Based on this material, the user gets to know the musical characteristics – such as instrumentation, timbre, rhythm and melody – on the basis of which genre classifications are made. At the same time, the sound clips serve as sonic glimpses of the artist's voice, the pitch and nuances of which are also relevant in the construction of author images. The low-pitched growl of Springsteen's voice can be seen to support his author image as a rough and masculine singer-songwriter of rock. Minogue's high and delicate singing may be associated with that mix of girlish charm and mature seductiveness which identify the artist's image as that of an attractive pop singer. On Kraftwerk's recordings, the alienated, robotic voices distance themselves from human sounds, connecting the band's image to the rich use of music technology and anti-human identities typical of electronic dance music acts (see e.g. Herman 2006: 24). Also, the acts in question differ from one another in terms of their song lyrics and storytelling values. For instance, in his song "Born to Run", Springsteen speaks in his capacity as the seasoned singer-songwriter, about "the day we sweat it out in the streets of a runaway American dream". Compare that with the mood and message of Minogue's relatively superficial thoughts on "Slow": "Knew you'd be here tonight, so I put my best dress on, boy I was so right". By contrast, Kraftwerk's songs do not usually tell an actual story; rather, the lyrics often consist of short, unrelated verbal phrases, which are repeated robotically, in automated, assembly-line fashion, as occurs in the song, "Music Non Stop": "Music non stop, techno-pop / Music non stop, techno-pop / Synthetic electronic sounds / Industrial rhythms all around".

We come now to the remaining category: biography. Minogue is the only artist of the three whose homepage features a separate biography and chronology. There the user may view a detailed, year by year history of major events in the artist's life – from her adolescence to the highpoints of her musical career, from the release of "Locomotion" in 1987 to her present, ongoing popularity. Minogue's website is also the only to carry information about the sales-chart positions of her recordings. Neither Springsteen's nor Kraftwerk's homepage offers any data about the commercial success of their releases; this is not surprising, given the artists' author images as independent, self-governing music makers (cf. Frith 1983: 52–55; Middleton 2001: 215).[146]

Both Springsteen's and Kraftwerk's websites omit biographical details, but each for different reasons. The references to Springsteen's long and impressive career are made in a way that presumed visitors to the site are already familiar with such things; these references are presented matter-of-factly, as if to say: "The man is a legend and if you are not aware of his personal history, please go and find the information somewhere else. These pages only focus on the essential, his music". The author image presented on the homepage suggests that Springsteen's songs relate personal experiences, which in turn may be seen as part of the artist's private history. In this respect, Springsteen is presented as the archetypal singer-songwriter of rock music, who is expected to perform original material that reflects or recounts the artist's personal experiences (see e.g. Straw 1999: 2002). Unlike the other two, this site presents song lyrics, which in turn may encourage autobiographical readings of Springsteen's work.

An artist biography is also missing from Kraftwerk's homepage, but in this case a different set of generic rules are needed to explain the lack of personal data. The website photographs do show Kraftwerk performing live, but no information appears about the personalities of band members. The absence of biographical data may suggest that the band members' on-stage personas should be kept separate from what the men are like in real life. As Hanna Järvinen[147] (2003: 105) notes, one normally expects the image of all authors, be they star performers or singer-songwriters, to be verified by his or her personal, off-stage history.[148] Kraftwerk's faceless author image can be seen to present a rather opposite notion of musical authorship than that of Springsteen's image as a single, originating author of rock music (cf. Keightley 2001: 134).

---

146 In addition to the link between genres and certain ideologies, there are economic factors that might explain the various attitudes toward exposing or hiding sales figures. That is to say, whereas Minogue's career has been dependent on hit singles and chart positions, the economic success of Springsteen and Kraftwerk perhaps relies more on such things as solid albums, loyal fan bases, and extensive live tours.
147 In this regard, Järvinen discusses myths surrounding the Russian dancer Vaslav Nijinsky.
148 When comparing musical stars to cinematic ones, one finds that the blurring between on-stage and off-stage personas is often more evident in musical stardom, since in the latter the public artist is not playing a fictional role (Holmes 2004: 153; see also Dickinson 2003: 77–78).

If Springsteen's image derives from the belief that "Springsteen the artist" and "Bruce the private person" are one and the same person, there is a mysterious gap between Kraftwerk's robotic on-stage personas and the private lives of the band members. As a result of Kraftwerk's distanced and faceless author image, the band identifies itself with the genre of electronic dance music, as created by similarly "unknown" artists (see also McLeod 2003: 352).

The third category presented in *Table 5* addresses the visual imagery. In this category, Minogue's website features more varied and abundant visual materials than do the homepages of the two other artists. Minogue's homepage is filled with pictures of the artist's face, changing looks and glamorous costumes, thus supporting the artist's image as a pop singer, as well as the pop music genre in general, which embraces the superficiality and rank commercialism of show business and the entertainment world (Butler 2003: 14–15; Fornäs 1995: 99, 102–103; Middleton 2007b). All the pictures, including the imagery on album covers, were taken in a studio environment or during a live show. The photo backgrounds show nothing that might capture the viewer's attention, which should be fixed solely on the artist's looks, clothing and poses. Minogue varies her look with each album, presenting herself with images that are tooled to match the sound and atmosphere of the given recording. Despite her changing looks, the presented biography and information on the artist's private life are a constant reminder of Minogue's history – something that cannot be changed, no matter how many times her visual style is revised. These revisions of visual appearance, then, have become something of an artistic trademark, which, apart from the website, is also stamped on magazine covers. While Minogue is known for her changing looks, the visual images of both Springsteen and Kraftwerk have remained relatively constant throughout their careers. With his down to earth style, Springsteen gives the impression that visual appearance has nothing to do with his fame, just as his "innate desire for making music" (linked with the notion of originating authorship) is not dependent on the popularity of his songs. Also, the lack of visual material channels the user's attention toward the music, thereby linking the artist's image to notions of originality and creativity.

In comparison with the homepages of Minogue and Springsteen, the visual appearance of Kraftwerk's website is severely minimalistic, a quality that accords well with the band's musical sound. The animations and graphics are brightly coloured, and written text is sparse. In the photos, the men's faces show no hint of emotion, and the formal, controlled expressions lead the viewer to wonder: "Are they humans, robots, or what?" In fact, it is sometimes hard to tell the difference between the men and their look-alike dummies. In addition, the individual features of each band member are obscured by photo-brushing, which goes even further in making all the men look

162

the same. In sum: the band's author image is not constructed around the artist's bio-graphical details; nor does it project the single originating authorship, as commonly occurs with the rock and pop genres (Ahonen 2006b: 170; Straw 1999: 202). Rather, the band's author image is one of mystery, due to the sense of facelessness emitted by the disguised identities of band members. This image also produces some confusion about the artists' gender. If masculinity and femininity are richly exploited in the con-struction of Springsteen's and Minogue's imagery, respectively, the gender identity of Kraftwerk appears much less obvious. The imagery projects the band's gender status as one of androgynous neutrality, deriving from the combination of masculine themes relating to technology with visuals of non-human, mechanical creatures – characteris-tic of many electronic dance music artists.

These artist websites also differ from each other according to the roles assigned to users of each homepage. On Springsteen's homepage, the conversation forum is the only way in which the user may affect the content of the website. In this way, the user's role is decisively separated from that of the artist, who takes the part of a skil-ful and independent rock auteur (see e.g. Keightley 2001: 134; Shuker 1994: 114). Visitors can participate more actively on Minogue's webpage. In addition to getting involved in the conversation forum, the user can send in questions for Minogue to answer. The questions and Minogue's personal replies present the artist-audience re-lation as an interactive, dialogical one. Even though Minogue's visual looks are all about glamorous costumes and having a good time, such dialogue takes the artist off her pedestal, and brings her closer to the audience. On Kraftwerk's homepage, the user plays an even more active role, despite the absence of a discussion forum. By taking part in the music making on some of the animated pages, users themselves become performers and creators, some of whom may possibly be the next Kraftwerk. Displacing the concept of a single originating author, the roles of artist and audience are conflated and fused together.

Conclusion

Genre-specific rules, codes and conventions are connected with beliefs and assump-tions relating to each style of music. In this chapter, I have examined the construction of author images through the analysis of material presented on artist official homepag-es. As the examination has shown, there are differences between the presented online author images of artists representing rock, pop and electronic dance music. Apart from differences in personal looks and backgrounds, distinctions between these artists can be explained in terms of the generic codes associated with the musical genres they represent. These codes include common conceptions – shared by the artists, the media and the public – relating to the visual imagery and musical sounds expected of each artist. Generic rules also help shape the musical authorship that each artist is supposed to represent, in terms of authorial responsibility and artistic identity.

The material presented on artist websites may be grouped into three categories: music, biography and visual imagery. Audience members use online materials – along with other mediated information – to create and revise their conceptions of each artist. The author images presented on artist homepages vary according to different musical genres. The material on Springsteen's official homepage is linked with the artist's image as a uniquely talented rock auteur and storyteller. By contrast, Minogue's website content seems to strengthen the artist's image as a charismatic pop singer, by emphasizing her showmanship and glamorous looks. Kraftwerk's homepage shifts the focus, away from the private lives of the band members, toward the non-personalized artist image and robotic sounds that typify electronic dance music artists. The official homepages do not simply present an author image of the artist in question; the content, or lack thereof, of the website material informs the user of practices and values attached to various genres of music. The author images of popular music artists are also dependent on genre-specific codes. Like the codes, the shared criteria for assessing values are not universal and fixed, but consist in fluid, adaptable rules and beliefs.

IV

RETHINKING MUSICAL CREATIVITY

What's startling here is that just as it seems that a "self"
can no longer possibly be expressed in the ever more socially
and technically complex processes of pop production,
so artistic authority is rediscovered – in the person of the producer,
the engineer, the image maker, the deejay. We're not only desperate
but still successful in finding voices in the machine.

Simon Frith 1996

7. Expanding notions of authorship

The poststructuralist shift

Despite the fact that popular music is usually marketed in the names of its authors and performers, there are some musical phenomena that leave the public uncertain of the artist's authorial identity (Buxton 1990: 437; McLeod 2003: 346). The purpose of this chapter is to examine some of the changes in music-making practices that have forced us to expand our conception of musical authorship (see e.g. Buckley 2007; Sanjek 1994; Théberge 2004: 139). The points of departure for the examination are those ways of authoring music which seem to question the notion of single, originating authorship. In reference to such ways, I use the term diffused authorship in to designate both the coexistence of a number of parallel authorial constructions and the active reception of musical works. This variety in ways of constructing musical authorship derives in large part from innovations in music technology that have transformed the process of music making (Goodwin 1998; Théberge 1997; Warner 2003). The implications of music technology, especially the practice of sampling, will be discussed more thoroughly in chapter 8. In the present chapter, the "rethinking of musical creativity" is related to the concept of diffused authorship, the practice of DJing[149], and the authorial profile of Finnish electronic-music artist, Jori Hulkkonen.

The DJ's authorial status is examined in relation to music making as a form of communication. In Hulkkonen's case, the analysed material consists of written media texts, including artist interviews and album reviews. The theoretical starting point for the examination lies in poststructuralist thought, particularly in regards to the "death of the author" (see Barthes 1990: 142–148). Poststructuralist notions of intertextual and social authorship have made their way into cultural musicology, which understands musical works as part of the field of cultural meanings (see e.g. Leppänen et al. 2003; Williams 2001). From the poststructuralist point of view, the author's biography, which is always present in the work, ultimately becomes another text, to be deconstructed in its turn (Eagleton 1983: 138; see also Hartley 2002: 14–15). Rather than describing the genius and uniqueness of individual authors, poststructuralists at-

---

149   Here I am referring to club and rave DJs – in contrast to radio DJs, for example – many of whom have achieved a considerable reputation; for more on the (pre)history of DJing, see Killmeier 2001; Poschardt 1995: 40–96. Electronic dance music is not the only musical genre in which DJs operate. Yet because the focus of this study is limited to the genres of rock, pop and electronic dance music, I am treating DJing as an authorial form that especially typifies electronic dance music. Mention of DJs immediately calls to mind the genre of rap, discussion of which must be excluded here, as lying outside the scope of this study.

tempt to explain the social and intertextual processes through which texts are created (McClary 1991: 21–23; Scott 1998: 142; Spivey 1997: 213).

Nancy Spivey (1997: 213), voicing a constructivist point of view, aptly describes the poststructuralist idea of authorship: "authors are also readers who transform others' texts and that authors are social beings who produce their work in a social fashion". Also from the perspective of constructionism and cultural studies, musical authorship refers to a constant, ongoing process of producing meanings (Leppänen et al. 2003: 71; McClary 1991: 21–23), instead of seeing creativity to inhere in the isolated acts of individuals. In contrast to the idea of stable subjectivity, works and texts are no longer understood as conscious products of their authors; instead, the author is regarded as a changing subject, who does not possess a ready-made consciousness before his/her confrontations with reality. (Pulkkinen 1991: 138; Tiainen 2005: 29.) The poststructuralist subject is not a unified, coherent or rational agent, but a product of language and discursive interaction (Burr 1995: 40; Tiainen 2005: 29–36). Hence the text "contains" no codes that would stabilize the process of interpretation (Williams 2001: 35). Textual meanings are instead dependent on the subject position of each audience member (see also Scott 1998: 142).

From isolation to intertextuality

Two poststructuralist writers receive frequent mention in discussions about the author's "death". These writers, Michel Foucault (1926–1984) and Roland Barthes (1915–1980), take a critical stance towards the concept of a gifted individual who creates a univocal text that carries the author's intended meanings directly to the reader (Bauman 2001: 127–128; Krasnow 1995: 183; Murray 1989: 2; Spivey 1997: 215). Literary theorist Seán Burke (1998: 23) argues that the author-figure traditionally serves to ensure meaning in the absence of metaphysical certainties[150], whereas poststructuralism departs from any belief in the subject's authority, presence, intention, omniscience and creativity.

---

150 Pertinent here is the notion of "musical work". Since the close of the eighteenth century, music has been packaged as "works", in the sense of enduring musical products (Goehr 1992: 121; Leppänen 1996: 28; see also Houni et al. 2005: 12–13; Torvinen 2007: 140–143). From Romanticism there emerged the work-concept, which, according to art philosopher Lydia Goehr (1992: 123), involved "everything that concerns musical practice – aesthetic theory about music; the music produced; the social status of musicians, be they composers, performers, or listeners; the rules, manners, codes, and mores". As the principle of art as imitation (mimesis) was replaced by the compound principle of expression and embodiment, music was no longer seen to serve social, religious, or any other extra-musical purposes. Instrumental music especially soon gained respectability as a fine art, which served no outside purpose but constituted an end in itself. (Goehr 1992: 141, 147.)

In his essay "What Is an Author?" ("Qu'est-ce qu'un auteur?"), Michel Foucault (1979: 141) examines the relationship between the text and its author, and the manner in which the text points to the latter. With the notion of *author-function* (*la fonction-auteur*), Foucault refers to viewing the author's name as a classificatory item, always present in the text, and characterizing a certain mode of being. According to Foucault (1979: 147), the author's name "permits one to group together a certain number of texts, define them, differentiate them from and contrast them to others". Foucault (1979: 159) continues: "the author is not an indefinite source of significations which fill a work; the author does not precede the works, he is a certain functional principle by which, in our culture, one limits, excludes, and chooses". The image of the author as the one who generates the text is thus replaced by a conception of the author as an ideological product, a figure, and a principle that is implemented in the process of reading (see also Houni et al. 2005: 9–10; Stam 2000: 124).

Also in popular music, the author's name is employed to create a sense of the artist's personal imprint on works/products that are marketed in the name of the public figure (Coombe 1994: 104; Wall 2003: 155–157). By promoting the author as the originator of his/her works, the author-function creates a sense of unity and coherence (Heath 1981: 217). Hanna Järvinen (2003) describes the author's role as a means of endowing everyday life with meaning:

> In discourse, the "author" is a functional element, not a natural category or a real person. It helps us to group the incoherent fragments of the past into understandable segments, to rearrange the life of an individual into a narrative that can have meaning for our lives. (Järvinen 2003: 13.)

In addition to grouping texts together into understandable narratives, the author's role is to differentiate one set of texts from all the other texts created by someone else. The author's name also regulates what can be said and perceived within a certain type of speech and recognized bounds (Mills 1997: 75). When a group of texts is placed under the same category, a relationship between the texts emerges, so that on the basis of the emerged connections, the works explicate one another. As Foucault (1979: 147) points out, the fact that a text bears its author's name indicates a certain permanence, such that the text should not be considered as everyday, transient speech, which merely comes and goes. The personification of texts also helps readers/audiences to differentiate one text from another.

Right here, right now – Instant reception

When questioning the author's predominant role as the sole source of meanings, Barthes (1990: 143) concludes that every text is written *here and now* – even though the *explanation* of each work is usually sought in the author who produced it. Barthes (1990: 142–143, 145) claims that the author's voice loses its originary status at the moment writing begins, as the author simultaneously enters into his/her own death. Here is how Barthes phrases his central claim:

> The reader is the space on which all the quotations that make up a writing are inscribed without any of them being lost; a text's unity lies not in its origin but in its destination. [...] [T]he birth of the reader must be at the cost of the death of the Author. (Barthes 1990: 148.)

Barthes argues that a text no longer proffers a single, "theological" meaning, that is, a message from the Author-God. In his view, the text is "a multi-dimensional space in which a variety of writings, none of them original, blend and clash". (Barthes 1990: 146.) In equating the theory of text with writing, Barthes (1979: 77–81) concludes that it is the reader who *executes* the work. What Barthes is claiming is that the author comes into being simultaneously with the work. The cultural meanings of the author are no longer seen as a pre-existent category; rather, they are born during reception. What is more, the reader's task is not to look for the meanings implanted by the author, since until the reader makes a text signify through his/her own prejudices and beliefs, it is merely a group of marks (Harland 1999: 242; Lehtonen 1994: 218–219). The author is no longer regarded as the point of origin, but as a site where writing takes place (Beadle 1993: 18; Houni et al. 2005: 8–9; Silverman 1994: 29; Stam 2000: 124; Zurbrugg 2000: 18).

One of the first critics of conceiving the author as a self-expressive agent and guarantor of the meaning of his/her works was philosopher of art, Monroe C. Beardsley. According to Beardsley's (1982: 188) theory of the intentional fallacy[151], information about the author's intentions should not serve as a basis for interpreting and evaluating his/her work. Readers need not seek the author's intentions in order to interpret a given text (Grossberg et al. 1998: 239; Hietala 1992: 10). All texts, including musical ones, are seen as collective, intertextual forms of playful rhetoric (Butler 2002: 24; Williams 2001: 35). As a result of this "liberation of the text", the audience member is believed to give meanings to each work, independently of the author's intentions.

---

151 Beardley's and William Wimsatt's essay, "The Intentional Fallacy", was originally published in 1945.

Author God and the anti-author

To clarify the relation between the author-function and the question of gender, Marcia J. Citron (1993: 117) adopts Barthes's thought in her approach to the issue of authorship. Citron refers to Barthes's method as "the elimination of the author". In Citron's opinion: "[for] Barthes, [...] it is the reader, not the author, who creates literary meanings and thus the reader is the more important element". (Citron 1993: 117.) With the author-function, Citron refers to the author's persona and mythical status, both of which are linked with the notion of a single originating author, who is shrouded in an aura of timelessness. Barthes seems to argue for a replacement of the author-function, and Citron suggests that another option would be a structure grounded in community. (Citron 1993: 113–116.)

Jason Toynbee's (2000) critique of originary authorship addresses the idea of a self-expressing artist. Toynbee echoes the poststructuralist arguments about the author's supposed death and the liberation of the text. Though structuralist and poststructuralist criticism grew out of literary modernism, the theses articulated by Foucault, Barthes and other poststructuralists also seem applicable to musicians and musical texts. Toynbee is not yet willing to side with the kind of anti-authorism that opposes any notion of agency.[152] In his opinion, authors are mediators in the intertextual process of exchanging sounds, styles, musical ideas and forms. (Toynbee 2000: xiii.) Thus, in contrast to the expressionist mode, Toynbee favours the so-called *transformative mode* of performance, which takes the social aspect of authorship into account. In this mode, the authorial origin is not seen simply as an individual subject, but possibly as a collective, a historical moment, or geographical place. The transformative mode also acknowledges the active role of the audience. (Toynbee 2000: 63; see also Toynbee 2006: 76–77.) Because of the poststructuralist critique, it has become more common to take the social and cultural context of music making into account, rather than see musical authorship as simply a linear process where music is communicated from "left to right", from music maker to listener (cf. Grossberg et al. 1998: 17–22).

By questioning the link between the author's intentions and his/her works, Foucault and Barthes aim at shifting the focus towards the reader and the parallel interpretations of each text. Still, as Carolyn Krasnow (1995: 181) points out, neither Foucault nor Barthes argues for a nihilistic post-world in which there is no possibility of communication or meaning; rather, it is a matter of directing more attention to the ways in which texts are used and circulated. From the poststructuralist point of view, texts

---

152 Musical works and styles that tend to oppose the notion of author are, then, still made by someone and include the idea of author – whether or not they wish to do so. It has also been argued that those who criticize the notion of author do no more than echo the author-based way of thinking (cf. Rojola 2001: 95–96; Stam 2000: 125).

are never whole, complete units, but works-in-progress (Krasnow 1995: 183). Another musicologist, Carolyn Abbate (1993: 229), sees the poststructuralist program as a means of disentangling authority and meaning from the historical author, which would permit alternative ways of hearing all musical artworks. According to Abbate (1993: 232), Barthes actually proposes the rebirth of an author "inside" the artwork. Or as art philosopher Anita Seppä (2003: 44) puts it: "With his emphasis on the importance of the *context* of each artwork, Foucault [as well as Barthes] challenged the more traditional ideas of the author as intending to represent some specified thoughts or personal emotion in his or her work". By casting doubt on genius- and work-centred aesthetics (Seppä 2003: 44–45), Foucault and Barthes aimed to reformulate the author-concept and to focus greater attention on the reader.

Musical authorship through communication models

Another way to conceive of the audience as the producer of meanings is to examine musical authorship as a form of communication. In doing so, we may gain a better understanding of the processes through which musical texts are produced. Because such musical production requires input from multiple parties, it is hard to view the composer alone as dictating the meanings of each work. In addition to producers, engineers and DJs, the audience members, as active interpreters, project their own meanings onto musical texts (see e.g. Moore 2002: 210; Scott 1998: 142).

We may start by comparing two models that have been central in communication studies. First is the *transmission model*, which envisions messages as moving from a sender, through a medium, to a receiver. The transmission model, known also as the "bull's-eye model" (Danesi 2002: 20), is illustrated in *Table 6*.

| *Sender* | -> | *Message* | -> | *Receiver* |

Table 6. The transmission model of communication.

The transmission model recalls the notion of single originating authorship, in which the author, as sender, is believed to determine the meanings of the work.[153]

---

153 In today's popular music, the artist's authorial voice does not issue only from his/her musical works (recordings, live performances etc.). As noted in earlier chapters, a variety of other mediated texts – such as press releases, commercials, reviews, interviews, website resources – play into shaping an artist's public (presented) author image, as well as the meanings that listeners attribute to the artist and his/her works (see *Table 2*).

According to this model, the work is seen as a permanent object, through which the author's intended meanings are conveyed to the audience (see *Table 7*).

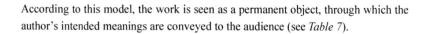

| Author | -> | Music | -> | Audience |

Table 7. Musical authorship presented in terms of the transmission model of communication.

Second, there is the *cultural model of communication*. Here "communication" is understood as a space or map of meanings that is shared by given groups of people (Grossberg et al. 1998: 17–22). In the cultural model, communication is regarded as a constant process "of producing new shared meanings out of the interaction of historically given shared meanings and individually created meanings" (Grossberg et al. 1998: 20). Today, in this age of mass media and mass production of popular culture, the author is usually a group of people – instead of a self-sufficient individual. If works are seen as polysemic and intertextual, it is no longer plausible to argue that a text should have only one meaning, i.e. the meaning encoded by its author. (Grossberg et al. 1998: 153–155.)

Stuart Hall (1980) notes that the interpretation of messages consists of two distinct modes of articulation, i.e. *encoding* and *decoding*.[154] By stressing the discursive aspect of the message and the active nature of interpretation, Hall's model seems to accord with poststructuralist theory and its focus on active reception; namely, when interpreting texts, the audience articulates messages into its own codes. The process of decoding is also dependent on the social positioning of each audience member. A certain asymmetry obtains in the encoding/decoding of messages, if we assume that the decoded meaning of each audience member will differ from the meaning encoded by the author. Textual determinism crumbles in the face of active interpretation and variant readings of the same text. (Hall 1980: 131; see also Grossberg et al. 1998: 16.)

The so-called source-message-channel-receiver (SMCR) model of communication[155] is an expansion of the simple transmission model. The SMCR model has four major components: (1) a source (S) or originator of the communication; (2) a mes-

---

154 Hall discusses the communication model mostly in the context of mass communication and TV spectatorship. For an analytic model of the communication process in music, see Tagg 1982: 39–41.
155 The model was introduced in the early 1980s by American communications theorist Wilbur Schramm (Danesi 2002: 21).

sage (M) and its information content; (3) a channel (C) through which the message is transmitted from one place to another; and (4) a receiver (R) to whom the message is directed (Danesi 2002: 21). In the diagram shown in *Table 8*, musical authorship-as-communication is explained in terms of the SMCR model.

Source		Message		Channel		Receiver
Author	->	Music	->	Media	->	Audience
		(sounds, words, images)		(TV, radio, press, Internet...)		

Table 8. Musical authorship presented by means of the SMCR model of communication.

On the basis of the diagram presented above, the primary originators in popular music are shown to be the artist and his/her works, and most importantly, the artist's public persona and recordings. Various media transmit the artist's public image and musical works – with their attendant sounds, words, visual imagery etc. – to receivers of the message, i.e. to audience members. As applied in *Table 8*, the SMCR model shows itself to be somewhat limited, in that it does not account for some important aspects of the production and reception of musical works. For example, because of the intertextual nature of author images, an artist's star persona and previous output will affect the ways in which his/her works are interpreted (see also Marshall 1997: 56–59). Further, it is not certain that the media or audience members will automatically construct the image which the public artist and/or the marketing machinery wish to imply.

DJing – Producing and reproducing

Critical emphasis on reception has also affected the ways in which the notion of musical author is understood in popular music (Buckley 2007; Hesmondhalgh 2000: 291; Sanjek 1994: 344; Schumacher 1995: 264). Musical works that are based on material originally put out by other artists also destabilize the belief in an originating author. As argued by Richard Middleton (2006: 228), however, despite the supposed death of the author and the changing ways of music making within the culture of digital technology, "new forms of author-function continue to circulate". Similarly, Lev Manovich (2001: 124) points out that users of new media technology, including music makers, are still seen as authors, whose task is to select from a library or menu of predefined elements or choices. In this way, Manovich (2001: 124) stresses, users of technology may feel that they are not mere consumers, but authors of new media objects or experiences. On this view, authorship does not descend to the level of "mechanized" activity, a mere slinging together of pre-existing material. Rather, such authorship is seen to display a certain creative expression, related to the choice of pre-existing materials and the skill with which they are assembled into "new" works.

The applied model of communication would indicate that the DJ's authorship lies in mediating between the recorded music and those who hear it. Nevertheless, by combining recordings originally made by two or more different artists, the DJ also encodes his/her own meanings into the music. The DJ's authorship, then, is a combination of creating and reproducing. Though the DJ works with materials made by other artists, his or her performance still requires creative and individual choices. (Fikentscher 1998: 91; Herman 2006: 25–27; Thornton 1995: 58–66.) One writer describes the DJ as at once both composer and listener (Poschardt 1995: 378–380). If seen as a composer, the DJ is certainly not one of those who are seen to create *ex nihilo*. The essence of DJ authorship rather lies in "the ability to mix selected elements in rich and sophisticated ways" (Manovitch 2001: 135). In addition to selecting and combining materials, DJs authorship also involves performance, in the form of active participation and individual expression (see also Brewster et al. 1999: 361; Herman 2006: 21–25; Thornton 1995: 63).

It may be asked whether the DJ's role is most analogous to that of a performing artist, or if the DJ should be considered more as an encoder/decoder of musical messages. As to the latter: the encoding performed by DJs is of a different nature than that of the traditional composer. DJs do not begin with music or other materials that they created; rather, their raw materials for composition consist in recordings made by other artists. As a performer, the DJ departs from the type most prevalent in popular music: DJs are usually known by their names rather than their faces. (Thornton 1995: 63, 65.) If the DJ imposes his/her own meanings into a musical text during a performance, it would seem inadequate to refer to the DJ as simply a decoder – this last having a passive connotation, as one who merely interprets or receives, that is, as one who neither inserts meanings into texts, nor exerts any power over the way a musical work turns out. An increased respect for DJing is evidenced by the fact that, since the 1990s, many famous club or rave DJs, including Paul Oakenfold, Paul Van Dyk and John Digweed, have become stars in their own right.[156] Thanks to the achievements of such stars, the practice of DJing has risen from the status of mere job to that of a

---

156 As further pointed out by Christophe Den Tandt (2004: 155), the DJ's fame is often associated with specific clubs, raves and house parties at which he/she performs. Audience members, too, can define their musical tastes by reference to particular DJs (Brewster et al. 1999: 361).

valued skill.[157] (Brewster et al. 1999: 361; Herman 2006: 21.) DJs with celebrity value have come to represent yet another type of musical authorship through which works of popular music can be marketed.[158]

The nature of DJ authorship is made more complex by the fact that artists who work as DJs often work also in other areas of music making or production. For example, many DJs, such as Fatboy Slim and DJ Shadow, make remix versions and produce albums for other artists (Souvignier 2003: 158). From a socio-musicological standpoint, Andy Bennett (2001: 121) argues that the DJ's authorial identity may consist in playing several roles that used to be narrowly defined and given separate consideration, such as composing, arranging, producing and performing. Similarly, Bill Brewster and Frank Broughton (1999: 335) link together the roles of DJ, remixer and producer, noting that, in addition to their live performances, most DJs are also known for their remix work. Many DJs also serve as important sources of information for record companies, by reporting on the success or failure of the records they play in various venues (Straw 2001a: 168). In the following case study, I examine closely the authorship of Jori Hulkkonen, who is known as a performing DJ as well as a solo artist.

The authorial profile of Jori Hulkkonen

Jori Hulkkonen[159] is one of the pioneers of electronic (dance) music in Finland. Pursuing his interest in electronic music, Hulkkonen built a home studio and by the end of the 1980s had started making house-influenced recordings. Hulkkonen began sending demo tapes to various record companies, of one which was F-Communications, a French organization that in 1996 released the artist's debut album, *Selkäsaari Tracks*. (Grönholm 1997: 31; Klemola 1996; Potts 2006.) Besides making his own music, Hulkkonen has performed as a DJ in dance clubs and radio stations around the globe. He has also made remix versions and produced albums for various artists. (Aine G.

---

157 Changes in DJ authorship recall similar developments in the authorial status of record producers. If in the mid-1960s the producer's main task was to document a performance, the introduction of multitrack recording technology turned the studio into a means by which producers could prove their artistic skills and creative capabilities. As sound recording technology became an integral part of musical making, the producer's name might carry a commercial value of its own. (See e.g. Des Pres et al. 2000: 138; Muikku 1988: 35; Negus 1992: 88; Poschardt 1995: 278–279; Théberge 2004: 141.)

158 Bill D. Herman (2006: 21) argues that the music industry instilled the DJ with authorship to compensate the increasing anonymity of dance-music producers.

159 Jori Hulkkonen was born in 1973 in a small town called Kemi, in the north of Finland. Together with Ari Ruokamo and Jukka Hautamäki, Hulkkonen formed Lumi Records in 1993. According to Hulkkonen, the foundation of the record label was a reasonable decision, because at that time there was no Finnish record label dedicated to the genre of electronic music. (Grönholm 1997: 31; Klemola 1996; Potts 2006.) Other highlights of Hulkkonen's musical career are the albums *The Spirits Inside Me* (1998), *When No One is Watching, We Are Invisible* (2000) *Different* (2002), and *Dualizm* (2005). (Potts 2006; www.jorihulkkonen. com/disco, as accessed 8 November 2006).

2002; Dax-DJ 2004; Potts 2006; Silas 2002.) Though he refers to himself as a producer-DJ-remixer, the most important area of authorship for Hulkkonen is the making of his own albums (Silas 2002: 22). In fact, according to Hulkkonen, many artists engage in remixing and producing simply for the purpose of becoming more famous (Klemetti 1999: 13; Silas 2002: 22), while making and performing self-written material gives them greater control over their music and their careers. Hulkkonen, too, admits that he has always aimed at making music on his own, so that he would have to make no compromises as to its content. This is how the artist explains his idea of musical authorship:

> I have a very romantic view of techno and house [music]. The guy sits at home in the corner making music with his own equipment without having to listen to anyone else's opinions, but he may do exactly what he wants. That is why I have collaborated so little with other artists. In cases where I need a vocalist, I write a melody and lyrics and then find a suitable singer.[160] (Jori Hulkkonen in *Rumba*; Juhala 2000: 28.)

Although Hulkkonen has made several remix versions of songs by other artists, he is unwilling to put his own music at the disposal of others. As an exception, Hulkkonen mentions remixes of some of his songs by Nigel Hays (on "Let Me Luv U") and Dan Electro (on "Whisper"), which, in the artist's view, present something new and take the songs in an interesting direction (Silas 2002: 22). Hulkkonen's wish to have full control over his music may also explain his signing with the French label, F-Communications. As Hulkkonen points out:

> If I recorded with some major company, it would probably mean that my activities would be interfered with, and attempts would be made to direct my music into a more commercial format (Jori Hulkkonen in *Rumba*; Juhala 2000: 28).

As a DJ, Hulkkonen is known for regarding the audience members as active participants (see also Krasnow 1995: 181–183). Concerning his performance at Notting Hill Arts Club in London, for example, the artist remarks that he wished to stir "the arrogant snobs" in the place by playing music by Clifters and Scorpions. Hulkkonen's repertoire also features songs by some Finnish artists, such as Matti Nykänen and Trio Erectus, which usually are intended for more or less humorous effect. It has been said that the artist, by mixing the humorous pieces with other songs, is testing to what extent that Finns in the audience will "get the joke". (Sirén 2004.) Hulkkonen, like other DJs, does not intend the played material to be taken as a form of self-expression.

160 Hulkkonen's quotes, as published in Finnish music magazines *Rumba* and *Rytmi*, have been translated into English by Ahonen.

Rather, his particular manner of combining and mixing other artists' material is what constitutes the central attraction of Hulkkonen's performances. In his role as composer, however, Hulkkonen argues that originality and distinctive sound are the most important things for an artist of electronic music. Here is a piece of advice he gives to young electronic artists on how to become successful:

> Be original. Obviously you need to take influences and follow trends, but only to a certain degree. The only way to get noticed nowadays is to make records with high quality production, original ideas and a personal sound. (Jori Hulkkonen in *Family House*; Dax-DJ 2004.)

The authorship of Hulkkonen and similar artists, thus, stands on their ability to create unique soundscapes, whether the music is self-written or was originally made by someone else. The use of other artists' material, however, does not necessarily signify a lessening of artistic originality. Rather, the notion of musical creativity has been redefined.

Hulkkonen's conception of music making accords well with the idea of socially constructed authorship (see e.g. Toynbee 2000: 63). In addition to creating original ideas and distinctive sounds, artists in this field are expected to be familiar with the history of electronic music and with the musical creations of their forerunners. When asked about his musical influences, Hulkkonen mentions artists such as Depeche Mode, The Pet Shop Boys, The Cure and Kraftwerk (Grönholm 1997: 31). On his website, Hulkkonen describes his experience upon first hearing a song by one of his idols:

> I can still recall the first time I heard *West End Girls* by the Pet Shop Boys on radio, and the sensation it gave me. Those chord changes in the intro and when that bass-line comes in ... magic. It was basically then that I started seriously thinking about making electronic music. (Jori Hulkkonen on www.jorihulkkonen.com/bio[161].)

Hulkkonen is forthright about certain production ideas that he borrowed in making the album *Different* (2002). For example, the artist notes that the fake ending in the song "Latin Taiga" was inspired by "That Joke Isn't Funny Anymore" by The Smiths. Also, in "We Are Rising Sun", the opening street noises and trumpet at the end are meant as a tribute to the Pet Shop Boys' "West End Girls". (Aine G. 2002.) Though adopted influences may signal an artist's lack of creativity, such allusions can serve equally as a mark of respect for the original artist. In this regard, Hulkkonen remains loyal to certain artists that he got to know in the early years of his career. He remarks: "It is important to stick to those musical influences that you've used before. It is not

---

161   As accessed 8 January 2006.

Picture 16. Jori Hulkkonen, When No One Is Watching, We Are Invisible (2000): Album cover highlighting the artist's geographical background. (Design: Hotspot.)

necessarily a good thing to jump into something new and completely mix one's routines." (Hulkkonen in *Rytmi*; Grönholm 1997: 32.)

The fact that Hulkkonen comes from a small town in northern Finland has become a key narrative in the construction of his public image (see *Picture 16*). It is the story of "small-town boy makes good"; in this case, a self-taught artist of electronic music evolves his own style in solitude, until an international record contract opens doors for him to enter the "wide-wide" world (Klemola 1996; see also www.jorihulkkonen. com/bio[162]). Nevertheless, Hulkkonen's author image remains somewhat incoherent and diffused, probably because he engages in so many different areas of music making – writing and recording his own music, performing as a DJ, and producing albums for other artists (Klemetti 1999: 13; Silas 2002: 22). In addition to those activities, Hulkkonen writes columns and works as editor and host of his own radio program.[163] Factually speaking, his authorial profile combines so many different roles that it can hardly be said to exemplify the aesthetic concept of a single, originating authorship. Nevertheless, the artist's presented author image conveys a recognizable author-figure, through which the artist's works can be marketed.

Hulkkonen's author image is complicated even further by his use of various pseudonyms, such as Bobby Forrester and Jii Hoo. Hulkkonen finds pseudonyms appropriate for albums released outside the F-Communications label, for instance, or for cases in which a recording does not sufficiently embody the original "Jori Hulkkonen sound". For example, the recording *Sunglasses at Night* (2001/2002) was released

---

162 As accessed 8 January 2006.
163 On Finnish radio channel YleX since 1998; see www.jorihulkkonen.com/bio, as accessed 8 January 2006.

under one of Hulkkonen's pseudonyms, Zyntherius. (Aine G. 2002.) Hence the author image of "Jori Hulkkonen the artist", as purveyed by his recordings, is based on a recognizable "Jori-sound". By contrast, at DJ gigs Hulkkonen combines elements from the different authorial roles that he has created under a group of pseudonyms. By adopting various artistic identities, Hulkkonen can employ a number of authorial roles, as well as a broader selection of sounds. Tim Wall (2003: 157) sees the DJ's use of aliases as a way of intentionally depersonalizing the individual, i.e. the author.[164] The author images of Hulkkonen and other DJs thus diverge widely from those of popular music stardom, in which the artist's public image is made to seem as coherent and solid as possible. At the same time, the diffusion and ambiguity of author images, in such practices as DJing and electronic music making, may be seen to disturb the notion of artistic self-expression, along with that of uniform identity (Ahonen 2005: 38–40; Frith 1986: 265; Schumacher 1995: 264; Warner 2003: 103). It may be added that the diffusion of author images, as occurs with Hulkkonen and similar artists, mirrors the reception of musical works as an active, multifaceted process that cannot be adequately theorized apart from its social surroundings.

Conclusion

In this chapter, I have discussed some ways of constructing authorship that seem to question the image of popular music artists as self-sufficient and originating authors. From a poststructuralist standpoint, musical works are seen as socially constructed objects, whose meanings are not proscribed only by their titular authors. In fact, the making of popular music usually involves several authors, including producers, engineers and DJs, who take part in encoding and decoding the meanings given to each musical work. Poststructuralist theory also sees interpretation as an intertextual and active process, wherein audience members assign their own meanings to musical works. As a result, a shift has occurred, away from seeing the artist's work and identity as a unified whole, towards understanding music making as a social and collective process. It has also become possible for artists to adopt parallel authorial identities and various creative roles, as the case of Jori Hulkkonen has shown. These alternative ways of constructing artists' author images offer proof that the Author-God concept

---

164 Will Straw (1999: 207) explains the blurred author images of electronic dance music artists as arising from the fact that "[w]ithin the dance music community, little value is attached to the idea of a creator retaining a consistent identity through ongoing changes of style and genre". As an example, Straw mentions the British DJ, producer and artist Norman Cook, who changes his stage name according to whatever musical style in which he is operating. Cook is known as Fatboy Slim when working in the "big beat" genre, and as Pizzaman when making house music. (Straw 1999: 207.)

is no longer the only frame of reference for understanding musical authors and their creative activities.

In addition to shifts of emphasis, from work to text and from author to audience, changes in digital music technologies have affected the ways in which musical works are created and perceived. Shifts in practice and ideology have emerged with the advent of digital music technologies, and with the DJ's attainment of superstar status in the 1990s. Evolving technological possibilities have also forced music makers to find new ways of constructing their author images. The question remains as to whether the new, more diffused ways of authoring popular music can continue as primary means of bolstering the figure of the author-subject. That figure shows no sign of retiring any time soon, but at most undergoing renovations of image and changes in mode of operation.

8. Sampling – Authorial voices in collision

Defining sampling

The ways in which popular music is made, distributed and consumed have been changed radically by new music technology (Buckley 2007; Goodwin 1998; Théberge 1997; Warner 2003). In the following, I examine one use of such technology, which has forced us to redefine our views on musical authorship. *Sampling* refers to the process in which a sound is taken directly from one recorded medium and transferred onto a new recording (Fulford-Jones 2007b). Samplers are employed for encoding, storing, manipulating and reproducing any sound, in ways that result in essentially no loss of sound quality (Goodwin 1990: 261; Théberge 1999: 218). Sampling and other new music technologies have not only impacted recording studios; they have also brought forth redefinitions of musical authorship (Buckley 2007; Sanjek 1994; Théberge 2004: 139). In the following discussion, I examine how some notions linked with musical authorship, such as those of creativity and originality, have changed because of technological developments. Should an artist who constructs music based on other people's compositions be regarded as an author? Has the idea of a complete musical work lost its meaning, when recorded music is understood as mere sound material to be reused and recycled? One may also ask, Whose voice is heard in a musical work in which the authorial signatures of various artists intertwine? Before trying to answer these questions, let us first get acquainted with the brief history of sampling.

The early practices of sampling may be traced back to the early 1960s, to Jamaica, where a group of local DJs were experimenting with a type of music called "dub". The dubbing DJs combined instrumental reggae recordings with other styles of music. The DJs would also rap over the musical backgrounds. In the early 1970s, these practices spread to the United States, especially to New York City and environs. Dub soon adapted to the new environment, and reggae quickly made its way into soul music, Motown, gospel, disco and funk. In 1979, a hip-hop trio called The Sugarhill Gang released the single, "Rapper's Delight", in which the song lyrics are rapped over the instrumental track of a disco hit, Chic's "Good Times". (Bush 2002: 1100; Souvignier 2003: 139–140.) This single introduced the rap genre and sampling to a worldwide audience. At that time, sampling was made directly from the original, vinyl sources (LPs). At first, the DJs mixed various songs together on recordings be played during their sets; later on, the mixing would take place during live performances. By the mid-1980s, sampling had become a common technique in the making of rap and hip-hop music. With the invention and marketing of inexpensive computer technologies, such as the first affordable digital sampler, Ensoniq Mirage (1985), sampling made its way into other kinds of popular musics. (Fulford-Jones 2007b.) Nowadays it is difficult to find any form of contemporary musical production that has remained untouched by digital sampling. In today's recording studios, digital samplers are as common as microphones, or other standard equipment used by composers, musicians, engineers or producers. (Porcello 1991: 69.) In addition to professional music production, sampling technology has been used in playback-only forms in digital synthesizers, drum machines, organs and pianos, and also in the creation of music and sound effects for film and television (Théberge 1999: 218).

Samplers were initially designed to emulate the sounds of conventional instruments. In this way, production costs could be reduced by employing samplers in place of session musicians, especially string sections, horn players and drummers (Théberge 1999: 218; see also Théberge 2001: 15). Samplers are still used to save money; but more and more producers and engineers have come to regard sampling as a sophisticated technique that promises new levels of innovation and creativity (Bennett 2001: 121). Nowadays the sampler is often viewed as a compositional resource rather than a simple performance tool (Porcello 1991: 83). The aesthetic desire to create new and unique sounds is another reason for the increase in sampling and other studio technology. Such distinctive sounds can serve as emblems or identifying marks, thereby aiding in the promotion and marketing of certain artists and genres. (Théberge 1997: 195.)

When describing the influence of samplers and other digital equipment, David Sanjek (1994: 344) argues that the roles of programmer and composer are now synonymous, since if one can type, one can compose. Studio technology has not only transformed the artist's role; by "democratising" musical production, it has also brought performers and audiences closer together. Nowadays the affordable costs of building and equipping home recording studios have made them accessible to almost anyone. The availability of studio technology has turned consumers into potential creators; this phenomenon has, in turn, triggered a rethinking of creativity, aura and autonomy.[165] (Sanjek 1994: 348.) As a result, the lines between art and craft or inspiration and technique have become blurred (Reynolds 1998: 376; see also Théberge 2004: 152–154).

Ulf Poschardt (1995: 282) argues that sampling, with its new kinds of sonic architecture, requires a more complex idea of musical authorship.[166] As an example of how

---

[165] The rejection of these notions may also be associated with the poststructuralist tendency to see musical texts as open-ended and collective processes, instead of closed entities stocked with definite meanings by their authors (Eagleton 1983: 138–139).

[166] According to Georgina Born (2005: 26), digital music media afford entirely new modes of collaborative

new music technologies can problematise the notion of originality, David Buckley (2007) mentions the case of Natalie Cole, who in 1991 recorded a cover version of the standard "Unforgettable" with her long-dead father Nat "King" Cole. Similarly, on his album *Swing When You're Winning* (2001), Robbie Williams sings a duet of the song "It Was a Very Good Year", together with Frank Sinatra, who had passed away some years earlier. Such recordings can disturb conceptions of popular-music history as a linear category. The "resurrection" of earlier artists on contemporary recordings turns back the traditional timeline, in which new artists are seen to follow successively in the footsteps of previous ones. Such uses of music technology also complicate ideas of musical authorship, by joining in one space or recording the authorial inputs of several artists.

Sampling has also aroused concerns of a moral, legal and artistic nature. Most of the debates in this regard are linked with ideas of artistic freedom, musicianship and property rights. (Théberge 1999: 219–220; see also Bennett 2001: 121.) Some critics see no difference between sampling and stealing; they simply regard the technique as a way of taking over the work of other artists. It has also been claimed that practitioners of sampling are incapable of creating anything on their own (Sanjek 1994: 351). Some ethical and legal aspects of sampling, as well as the claimed (non)creativity of sampling artists, are discussed in the latter part of this chapter. Another concern has to do with the question of the identity of a composition (Middleton 2007c), in cases where a recording no longer represents something final or complete, but acts rather as a storage place for sounds that can be continuously recycled and reconstructed. In the age of sampling, the recording is an object that captures sounds only temporarily. As Buckley (2007) has stated, it seems that the main goal of music making is no longer to create highly individual pieces of art; nowadays, the artists are expected to treasure older musical forms, and to assemble aural collages that exhibit both historical awareness and musical know-how.

From home studios to MTV – The Avalanches

In the following, I analyse some of the ideological, artistic and ethical questions that sampling has raised. As a case study, I examine the music making and author image of an Australian group, The Avalanches, whose album *Since I Left You* (2000) is estimated to include over 900 samples drawn from some 600 different musical sources (DeVito 2001; LeMay 2000; Wade 2001). The Avalanches thus represent a rather ex-

authorship, since "digitalized music, distributed via MP3s, CDs and the Internet, is continually, immanently open to re-creation".

183

treme example of artists who use samples as part of their music. In addition to the band's debut album, the analysed material consists of written media texts, including artist interviews and album reviews. Also considered is the manner in which their music-making procedures are reflected in the band's author image. As an individual case, the reception of Madonna's hit single "Hung Up" (2005) will be examined, to illustrate some of the attitudes taken toward sampling artists and their music making.

The Avalanches were formed in Melbourne in the mid-1990s. The initial stages of the band rehearse the familiar story of fans who set out to make their own music. Robbie Chater and Darren Seltmann, former members of various garage-rock bands, became interested in samplers and shared the idea of making electronic music. The duo turned into a six-member group that included Darren Seltmann, Robbie Chater, Gordon McQuilten, Tony Diblasi, Dexter Fabay and James De La Cruz. The men acquired turntables and then started to wonder how they might take advantage of the newer studio technology. They acquired the most affordable sampler available and began experimenting with it.[167] The group practiced with studio technology, including sampling technique, in two home studios, which later became their main workplace.[168] (Kellman 2001; Sullivan 2001.) Through trial and error, these former music consumers turned into composers. Darren Seltmann tells how it happened:

> We'd bought the cheapest sampler that money could buy and started knocking stuff together. There was a lot going on at first but thankfully we found DJs like Dexter [Fabay] and James [De La Cruz] who were so technical and they helped us whittle it down. (Darren Seltmann in *Amazon*; Sullivan 2001.)

Chater and Seltmann, who work in the studio, are usually presented as the band's driving force (DeVito 2001; Sullivan 2001), whereas during live performances, the number of band members varies between six and ten. This is how Robbie Chater describes the band's somewhat mutable membership:

---

167 Despite the random learning methods of many artists, the ease of sampling should not be exaggerated, since the creation of samples is still usually supposed to require a large amount of flair and skill (Frith 1993a: 9; Jones 1993: 76).
168 The Avalanches' first single, "Rock City", was issued by Trifekta Records in 1997. In the same year, another record label (Modular) published the *El Producto* EP, which was followed in 1998 by an EP called *Undersea Community*, released by Rex (a subsidiary of a bigger record label, XL). The band has also made remix versions for well-known bands. For example, for Manic Street Preachers, The Avalanches remixed a song by the Manic Street Preachers, called "So Why So Sad", which appears on the album *Know Your Enemy* (2001). The band has also done a remix version of the Belle & Sebastian single, "I'm a Cuckoo" (2004). Through such revised versions of material first popularized by well-known artists, the audience get to know both the song's original performer as well as the artist(s) behind the remix version. Remixing may also be seen as another means by which sampling artists can prove their musical skills and artistic capabilities. (Kellman 2001; Sullivan 2001.)

I guess there's Darren and I who are in the studio all the time. And there's just this big group of people. When we do shows, there's six, but sometimes as many as ten. (Robbie Chater in *Plan9music*; DeVito 2001.)

The Avalanches' live shows differ a great deal from the music heard on their albums. When performing live, the band uses a drum kit, bass guitar, analogue synthesizers, two pairs of decks and samplers. The band members regard the album and the live shows as two separate entities, and have no wish to reproduce their album live. Instead, they prefer traditional live shows, packed with high volume, energy and chaos. (Teilmann 2001.) Chater says that, in live shows, The Avalanches become a kind of garage rock band that is performing cover versions of their album cuts (DeVito 2001). The band also writes new songs to be performed live, some of which may contain elements of songs first released on an album. As such, the Avalanches' live shows are a combination of more traditional forms of music making with the use of new music technologies. The idea of the musical work as a fixed category is called into question by the band's different ways of performing live versions of songs originally released on an album. (See e.g. DeVito 2001; Teilmann 2001.)

From sonic fragments to album

The Avalanches are best known for their full-length album *Since I Left You*, first released in Australia in November 2000. The record achieved platinum sales and critical acclaim across the country. The band quickly gained international fame when the title song, "Since I Left You", came out as a single. In March 2001, the single entered the UK top 20 and a month later, the album was heralded as "Album of the Month" by all major UK music publications. The band continued to make name for itself, when in the following year the album was released in the United States.[169] (Kellman 2001.)

It took two years for the band to assemble the *Since I Left You* album (Sullivan 2001; Wade 2001). It is a danceable, concept album constructed almost entirely of sonic fragments which have been detached from their original contexts. Though it consists in countless fragments, the album was intended as a coherent whole that listeners could easily apprehend. The samples are woven together in intricate ways, making the album like a seamless and continuous piece of work. If some of the melodies are somewhat melancholy, the album is predominantly a positive, energetic dance record. Melodies, however, are not the most crucial element in the album; the general

---

169 The band has been working on their second album since 2001 (DeVito 2001). The album was actually completed in 2006, but the record company, Modular, rejected it for sounding "too rushed" (Zugna 2006).

mood and overall atmosphere are what matter most. (Kellman 2001; LeMay 2001; Sullivan 2001; Wade 2001.) Seltmann comments on the creative process:

> We do try to create lively music. It's such a frustrating process the way we make records using samples. It's so time consuming that you lose perspective and the initial fresh atmosphere. Those kinds of things are very hard to maintain and we are conscious of it so we spend a lot of time trying to recreate the atmosphere. (Darren Seltmann in *X-Press Magazine*; Wildy 2000.)

The band wanted the record to represent a sad voyage that takes listeners on a journey around the world. The hour-long trip takes place on the open sea – sonic references to which are heard on the album (for example, boat noises). The nautical theme comes from Seltmann's and Chater's grandfathers, both of whom were sailors, who told the boys exciting tales about their seafaring adventures around the world. (Wildy 2000; see also Sullivan 2001.)

In addition to fragments of music, the samples on the album consist in other noises and sounds. After all, one can sample any kind of sound that can be recorded. Timothy Warner (2003) mentions four characteristics by which samples can be qualified. First, samples may carry pitch, rhythmic or timbral information, or some combination thereof. Second, samples may include sounds that suggest a particular physical environment or a situation. Third, sampled sounds can relate to a particular time and place; and finally, there are samples that are derived from the process of audio recording and production. Warner concludes that the use of samples inevitably gives rise to a conflict between musical and extra-musical elements. (Warner 2003: 95–96.) With his classification, Warner brings out the blatantly intertextual nature of sample-based music (see e.g. Gracyk 2001: 63). Clearly, The Avalanches aim at arousing extra-musical connotations, by telling about the nautical theme around which the songs are constructed (Wildy 2000). After identifying the boat noises on the album, listeners may further relate those sounds to a previous voyage or to a seaport they once visited. Although each audience member will interpret the album in his/her own way, it is still possible that listeners will associate the music with the "nautical" childhood memories which the band members have recounted in the media.

Since I Left You also includes samples of disco, strings, piano, beats, animal noises, whistles, vocoders and film dialogue, to name a few. The music samples are mainly taken from fairly unknown or forgotten (especially from the point of view of today's youth) pop music artists, such as The Osmonds, Bert Kaempfert and Kid Creole. Some of the fragments feature the sounds of better-known artists, including Madonna, Boney M, Wu-Tang Clan, the Isley Brothers and De La Soul. (Kellman 2001; LeMay 2001; Sullivan 2001; Wade 2001.) The diverse spectrum of the samples also demonstrates the band's keen awareness of the history of popular music. Spending long hours in second-hand record stores, the band members have built up large record collections to serve as resources for musical samples. (To facilitate his search for specific musical styles, Chater categorizes his massive collection according to the instruments played on the records.) The record collections serve, then, as a sort of sound library, from which the band members select certain sounds to fit into specific tracks. (Sullivan 2001.)

Ulf Poschardt (1995: 386) points out that many artists use their knowledge of music history, along with earlier recordings, as the "raw materials" of their own production. Sampling techniques serve also to conflate even more the roles of artist and listener. As Warner (2003: 96) remarks, sampling empowers the artist to explore those parts of his/her musical imagination which developed as a result of listening to records originally made by other artists. The Avalanches, too, were first fascinated by specific records and sounds, then came to use sampling as a means of exploring, refining, and focusing their musical enthralment (LeMay 2001; Sullivan 2001).

Lost origins

Whiles some samples on *Since I Left You* are easily recognized, others leave the listener wondering about their origins (see also Kellman 2001). The samples used, and their original contexts, have prompted many questions from audience members. Like most bands of today, The Avalanches have their own Internet homepage (www.theavalanches.com[170]). On the website, users can share their views on a discussion forum that consists of two sections: "music", which includes discussions relating to The Avalanches or to other musical interests; and "general", to which all non-music-related comments should be directed. In addition to talk about The Avalanches and their music, some of the discussions focus on dance music in general. These online discussions serve as valuable resources for determining the kinds of author images that audience members have compiled of a given artist.

The origins of the samples used in *Since I Left You* are a major topic of discussion on the website. Among the talking points is a thread called "The Sample Thread", in which discussants can share their discoveries concerning samples used by The Avalanches. Thread users try to identify both the album on which a given sample originally appeared, and the original artist behind each sample. Combining their efforts, users have detected and identified the sources of many samples used on the album.

---

170   As accessed in 2 October 2004. In 2005 the website was hacked into, and posts of the original forum were lost.

The online discussions show that some of the samples are easily recognized, where-as identification of other samples requires extensive knowledge of various musical styles. None of the discussions center on ethical aspects of sampling; rather, users tend to evaluate the band's authorship in terms of the choice and manipulation of sonic fragments.

Some issues related to sampling are ethical in nature. For example, Should the sampling artist try to raise awareness about the artist(s) from whose music he/she takes samples? (Hesmondhalgh 2000; Schumacher 1995). This question is especially pertinent with regard to the sampling of more arcane sources. In such cases, the identity of the sampled artist usually remains unknown, either because the sampling artist does not bring out the history behind the used samples, or because the audience is unwilling or unable to find information about the original artist(s). As David Hesmondhalgh (2000: 280) asks: "To what extent does the act of recontextualization, the placing of a sample next to other sounds, mean that authorship [...] should be attributed to those sampling, rather than those sampled?" Hesmondhalgh (2000: 66) mentions artists like The Rolling Stones and The Animals as examples of bands who worked in the 1960s to raise awareness of the musics and the original artists from which they borrowed. By contrast, Moby offers little, if any, information about the borrowed musics on his album *Play* (1999), which makes use of samples originally recorded by musicologist-folklorist, Alan Lomax (Hesmondhalgh 2000: 57). The Avalanches, too, hesitate to speak of their creative process, nor do they tell about the histories related to their use of certain samples. For copyright reasons, there is a list of the used samples on the album cover. It is, however, left to the audience to obtain more information about the used samples, their historical origins, and original performers. By revealing so little about the artists sampled or about their motives for borrowing from certain pieces of music, The Avalanches continue to contribute to their somewhat mysterious public image.

Proving creativity or lacking imagination?

As in other areas of music making, the evaluation of an artist's musical creativity is based on established hierarchies, acknowledged by musicians, media, and audiences, that dictate the common criteria for such assessment. As Andrew Goodwin (1998: 127) points out, the *creative* use of sampling was at first seen to require some *changing* or transformation of the original sample; later on, creativity in sampling was determined by how well the sampling artist could display his/her knowledge of various musical traditions and styles. As a result, a new set of criteria emerged, by which a line could be drawn between amateur and professional sampling artists (Goodwin 1988; Porcello 1991; Sanjek 1994). In evaluations of creativity, the ability to mix different genres and styles of music together is usually seen as an indication of the sampling artist's musical expertise and skill.[171] The artist is also supposed to have carefully chosen the samples used in the music making. (Goodwin 1998: 127; Schumacher 1995: 259–266; Théberge 2004: 147–152.) Therefore, the technique of sampling can be regarded, on the one hand, as a creative and demanding process, or on the other hand, as a relatively shallow enterprise, in which the sampling artist randomly mixes sonic fragments together, without taking any interest in their origins.

In response to those who view sampling as mere cut-and-paste, and in no way comparable to composing, Chater underlines the band's talent for putting samples together in a creative manner:

> We consider ourselves writers, you know, and we have a predetermined goal that we want to get to and we find the piece that we need to help us [to] get there. The samples are just what we happen to use. (Robbie Chater in *Synthesis*; Teilmann 2001.)

Hence, when cast in a positive light, the band members are usually presented as composers who make use of carefully chosen samples in their music making. The band's use of samples is often described by reviewers as exceptionally creative and skilful. Here are some extracts from positive commentaries:

> There's more imagination in this hour-long odyssey than most sample-based artists manage in their entire career (Ian Wade in *Yahoo! Music*; Wade 2001).

> The source material is almost entirely other people's records, but the ideas are all The Avalanches'. [...] forgotten disco, lounge, tropicalia, soundtrack, funk and hip-hop serve a new master and work together to produce a coherent, original whole. (Jesse Fahnestock in *Ink Blot Magazine*; Fahnestock 2001.)

> But what really makes this album brilliant is not as much the volume or quality of the samples used as the way that they're employed. The Avalanches have managed to build a totally unique context for all these sounds, while still allowing each to retain its own distinct flavor. (Matt LeMay in *Pitchfork Media*; LeMay 2000.)

> Although the Avalanches perhaps haven't done anything revolutionary technically speaking – hip-hop producers have been cutting and pasting samples for decades – their work is a genius of its context. The manner and order in which they splice and dice disparate pieces creates totally new meanings, melodies, and beats. (Simon Rabinovitch in *Remix*; Rabinovitch 2001.)

In the foregoing and other such reviews, the band's music is praised in the same terms one uses when reviewing any other style of music, even though the concept of a single originating author plays no part in the evaluation. Instead of the "original

---

171   The eclectic use of a myriad of styles has further linked sampling with postmodern collage (Kallioniemi 1990: 148). Other discourses on postmodernism also show the influence of sampling; for example, in the way quotations are used and in the blurring of distinctions between traditional, popular and avant-gardist art (Théberge 1999: 220).

author" criterion, emphasis is placed on the artist's adroitness in conjoining disparate samples into a coherent whole. The sampling artist – rather than the original author(s) of the sampled fragments – is viewed as the one responsible for the ideas and choices that make the music sound as it does (LeMay 2000; Rabinovitch 2001). In sum: the authorship of a sampling artist may be regarded as a creative and innovative practice, then, even though authorial creativity is assessed apart from the idea of single authorship (see also Goodwin 1998: 127; Schumacher 1995: 259–266; Warner 2003: 97–98).

A similar question relating to the sampling artist's artistic abilities was raised when Madonna released her single "Hung Up" (from the album *Confessions on a Dance Floor*, 2005). The song includes a sample from ABBA's 1979 hit, "Gimme Gimme Gimme". As one might expect, ABBA fans threw themselves into ensuing discussions of Madonna's motives for using bits of this famous song (www.abbasite.com/forum[172]). Some ABBA fans considered "Hung Up" as Madonna's way of paying homage to ABBA, whereas others thought Madonna was just trying to make money by capitalizing on ABBA's creativity. Here are two comments that illustrate contrasting attitudes towards Madonna's use of sampling:

> I don't understand the people who criticize Madonna for doing this. She's paying homage to ABBA and putting them in the spotlight again. [...] And don't forget she asked for permission and paid for it. (Username carlos850 on www.abbasite.com/forum[173].)

> [S]he totally copied the whole idea, used the same melody line and took those lyrics. [...] She copied a sure hit and the whole "concept" of ABBA's "Gimme! Gimme! Gimme!", but without the novelty that it had back in 1979. (Username Dani79 on www.abbasite.com/forum[174].)

The first writer finds the use of ABBA's sample to be totally acceptable, because Madonna obtained permission to use the sample, and moreover because Madonna's sampling drew attention to the original artist ABBA and its music. Some of the positive comments also note that, in the media, Madonna has openly discussed her use of the sample and its origins. The latter writer, by contrast, sees Madonna as simply copying ABBA's musical ideas, and introducing no creative input of her own. As some discussants point out, however, that view may be countered by recalling Madonna's early career, when she proved her talents as a songwriter. In fact, Madonna's long career also seems to be the main reason she was permitted to use the sample. Benny Anderson, who with band member Björn Ulvaeus co-wrote ABBA's songs, tells us his reason for letting Madonna sample their music:

172   As accessed: 29 January 2006.
173   http://www.abbasite.com/forum/thread.php?t=34993; as accessed 29 January 2006.
174   http://www.abbasite.com/forum/thread.php?t=34993; as accessed 29 January 2006.

We get so many requests from people wanting to use our tracks but we normally say "no". This is only the second time we have given permission. We said "yes" this time because we admire Madonna so much and always have done. She has got guts and has been around for 21 years. That is not bad going. (Benny Anderson in *Telegraph*; Hastings 2005.)

Anderson's interviewer goes on to point out that the agreement between the group and Madonna stipulates that ABBA will receive a significant share of royalties gained from the airplay of Madonna's single (Hastings 2005). In the end, both artists benefit financially from combining their respective authorial inputs.[175] Many commentators on Madonna's use of the ABBA sample feel strongly that the sampling artist should acknowledge the input of the original artist, so that both artists would receive recognition for the song's potential success. What Madonna's case also brings out is that, even though some artists have developed unique and original styles in their usage of sampling, they may still be subject to ethical censure, in this case, the charge of theft.

Imitation, quotation, recognition

The intertextual nature of sample-based music making comes to light in the ways artists sample a number of musical ideas drawn from a wide range of musical styles (Gracyk 1996, Sanjek 1994: 344–345; Schumacher 1995: 264–266). In fact, the same principle seems to describe the making of popular music in general. As Simon Frith (1993a: 6) asks: "Haven't pop writers and producers always used musical elements eclectically, taken sounds and ideas from wherever they could find them?" What seems to make the difference here is the fact that the sampled music is reproduced, not imitated (see also Porcello 1991: 69–70; Théberge 2004: 144–147). Though imitation might be regarded as a typical characteristic of all musical works, sampling is based exclusively on "borrowing" from other people's creations. Thus, the interpretation of sample-based music is not dependent just on the meanings of each sample; rather, new meanings emerge when samples are transferred from one context to another. As a result, the meanings given to a song comprised of samples are not reducible to the meanings of constituent samples.

In connection with the construction of meanings, sampling techniques may be compared with the use of montage in film, in which the relations among scenes determine the meaning of given to each scene in question.[176] When two pieces of film are

---

175 As another indication of the artists' mutual respect, ABBA's *ABBA Gold: Greatest Hits* album was available for sale at Madonna's official merchandise stands during her Confessions tour in 2006.

176 Montage theory was initiated in the 1920s by a group of Soviet filmmakers, including Lev Kuleshov, Sergei Eisenstein and Vsevolod Pudovkin, inter al. (see e.g. Joyce 1999: 417–450).

placed side by side, the viewer is led to conclude that the shots must be related to each other (Joyce 1999: 422). However, as the Russian film director and theorist Sergei Eisenstein (1985) remarks, sequential elements are not perceived as being *next* to each other, but rather on *top* of each other. The superimposition of two elements always produces a new, higher dimension, with a new meaning of its own. (Eisenstein 1985: 107.) Another film theorist, André Bazin (1985: 27), defines the montage technique as follows: "[T]he creation of a sense of meaning not proper to the images themselves but derived exclusively from their juxtaposition". Similarly, the supposed meaning of a sample-based piece of music does not lie in the individual samples, but in the ways in which the samples are brought together. The meanings given to the music may thus be seen to arise from the juxtaposition of samples, as the listener perceives links between the individual samples during the process of interpretation.

Cinematic montage and musical sampling used in sound edition are, in a sense, based on a similar principle. As montage enables viewers to join disparate and unrelated visual material into coherent sequences (Joyce 1999: 23), samplers allow the artist (as well as the audience) to weave unrelated bits of sound into a continuous sonic palette.[177] In the case of *Since I Left You*, for example, audiences are likely to take in the songs as complete units, instead of examining each sample and its distinctive meaning separately. In this respect, the nautical theme employed by The Avalanches may be seen as a way to give meaning to the album as whole, as well as to the individual songs. Whether or not listeners recognize the samples used, they are still likely to hear the sonic fragments as parts of a larger whole, since the identification of each sample is affected by its relation to the rest of the musical text (cf. Warner 2003: 30).

For example, at the beginning of a song called "Stay Another Season", there is a sample of the bass line to "Holiday" by Madonna. Upon identifying the sample, it is possible that the listener can never hear the song again without thinking of Madonna and everything associated with the artist, her public image and musical career. On the other hand, listeners may reformulate their interpretation over and over again, each time they identify a new sample used in the music. The number of meanings and the extra-musical connotations associated with the music then grow in pace with the recognition of new samples. In the end, the network of the meanings given to a certain musical text may become just as complex and eclectic as the piece of music itself. Also, each audience member will interpret the album in a different way, since

---

177 When discussing the process of selection, Lev Manovich (2001) draws a line between the montage technique and DJ authorship. According to Manovich, what defines the DJ as an anti-montage artist, is the ability to create a perfect temporal transition from very different musical layers, and yet move seamlessly from one track to another. (Manovich 2001: 144.) Even though both DJs and sampling artists select from pre-existing material, it seems that montage describes the authorship of the sampling artist better than it does the DJ's practice. This is because the making of sample-based music is based more on the dissonances between different elements, though it is also possible to create complete musical works by means of sampling.

the listener's past and personal relations, evoked during the act of listening, will vary from person to person. Some listeners may pay more attention to specific samples and sounds, whereas other audience members might find the album's general mood to be the most important element. Finally, the meanings given to the album consist not only of the meanings given to each sample and its origins, but also of the meanings that emerge when all the samples are collocated within the frame of the album, or more broadly, within the band and its overall public image.

Ethical and legal concerns

As briefly noted above, sampling and other digital music techniques have also raised ethical questions (Sanjek 1994; Schumacher 1995). Mostly, as Frith (1993b) points out, such issues are connected with the use of new music technologies and their legal definitions.[178] Another factor that has increased interest in copyright law is the globalisation of culture and its goal to produce international norms in the area of copyright regulation. (Frith 1993b: ix.) As a result, the relationship between art and copyright has become more complex (Théberge 2004). On the one hand, there is a tendency to continue the belief that a musical work can express the artist's individuality, even if the musical text was produced collectively (Brackett 1999: 127; Woodmansee 1994b: 28). On the other hand, the laws of intellectual property, which work as a means of protecting something abstract and owned by its creator, need to be brought in balance with the practice of intellectual commodity.

In making their album, The Avalanches took no account of the legal ramifications of using samples.[179] First, the band members had pictured the album as a project only for themselves; they would worry about obtaining clearances for samples only when a record label showed interest in releasing their songs. When the band members found out that the album was actually going to be released, they hired an American lawyer

---

178 As Martha Woodmansee (1994b: 28) remarks: "[I]t would seem that as creative production becomes more corporate, collective, and collaborative, the law invokes the Romantic author all the more insistently". Woodmansee (1994b: 28) also points out that the copyright law has not yet been affected by the critique of authorship initiated by poststructuralist thinkers. Therefore, the law should be revised to better account for all kinds of authors operating within the field.

179 One of the first exemplars of illegal sampling is the case of a British band called M/A/R/R/S. In 1987, the band released a single titled "Pump Up the Volume", which was constructed of samples from about thirty other records. The samples were overlaid on a drum-machine track and a bass line (Fulford-Jones 2007b). When the single became an international hit, several record companies sued the band for illegal use of samples taken from their artists. The original writer of the song is, then, justified in demanding a fee for letting someone sample his/her work. As a result, the use of samples is legal if the sampling artist has secured the approval of the original artist; otherwise, the original writer has the right to claim copyright infringement. Dodging the rights of the original artists, some think it is safe to sample sounds from old, obscure tracks or from world music albums, since the authors of those kinds of recordings unlikely to take legal action. (Frith 1993a: 8.)

to take care of the sample clearance. (Sullivan 2001.) This is Seltmann's view of what the lawyer did to clear the samples used on the album:

> She's known as "the detective" and she tracks down the owner or the original song and also the owner of the actual recording itself. It could mean tracking down two or three people for each sample, even more in some cases, and then you work out a deal to licence that track and they also get credited as a songwriter for the tracks. For some of the songs we put together we didn't retain any of the song writing in the end. (Darren Seltmann in *X-Press Magazine*; Wildy 2000.)

Because of the band's reverse marketing plan, it took a whole year to clear the samples. The samples for which the band got clearance are listed on the album liner notes; the fragments of music for which the band did not obtain permission to use had to be erased from the album. (Sullivan 2001; Wildy 2000.) The right to use only certain samples thus determined the kind of an album *Since I Left You* finally turned out to be, even though the mandated changes were based on the band members' artistic decisions. The original version of the album was about two hours long, but the editing and sample-clearance changed both the duration and the make-up of the recording. For example, The Rodgers and Hammerstein Organization did not give permission for the band to use a sample that was originally placed at the beginning of the album (DeVito 2001). Instead of the initially planned harps and singing girls, the released version of the record starts with sounds of crying and talking combined with sounds of guitars and flutes. The band was nevertheless lucky in being the first artist ever to get clearance to use a sample of Madonna (Kellman 2001; Sullivan 2001).

Hidden creators

The practices of music making are also reflected in the way the artist's author image is presented to the public. Because of the reuse of material, sample-based works are not necessarily marketed in the name of the artist and his/her celebrity power. In the case of The Avalanches, the band's public image is both faceless and distant. The published photographs of the band usually present six men, their picture taken from a distance. In the pictures, the band members wear casual clothes that do not stick out in any way. Some of the men also wear sunglasses or caps, in order to make identification even more difficult. Because of the band's distant image, it is probable that not too many audience members, though aware of the band's background, know what the band members look like. As made clear in a comment by Seltmann, it was a calculated decision by the band members not to present themselves in public:

Picture 17. The Avalanches, Since I Left You (2000), album cover: Nautical painting sub-stitutes for group photo of band, emphasizing "depersonalized" artist image.

[T]his album was more about giving it the feeling of it coming from somewhere else or an-other time. And that was like to be anonymous, it didn't feel right exposing ourselves when we didn't want to sing on the record. (Darren Seltmann in *Turntable2k*; Garrido 2002.)

Based on Seltmann's statement, the underlying reason for the men to keep their personal appearance undercover is that the sounds on the album do not originate from the band members as such. After realizing that it is not the authorial mark of the band members alone that is heard on the album, they decided that it was needless to appear in public as well. The public image of The Avalanches recalls the disguised identities typical of electronic dance music artists, such as Daft Punk and Kraftwerk, discussed earlier in this study. In the case of The Avalanches and other sampling artists, what makes it even more difficult to pick out only one source or author to be presented in public, is the fact that their music is full of countless authors and voices. The men are absent also from the cover of *Since I Left You*, which features a painting of a sinking ship, with the band's name and title of the album written in small white print (see *Picture 17*). No clues appear that would help audiences to figure out what kind of music the album contains or what sort of band The Avalanches are. Still, one may conclude that the album is not likely the work of a pop star or singer-songwriter, whose public image is typically built around the artist's personal appearance and star power. The music on this album must come from a different kind of artist indeed.

When discussing the influence of sound technologies on music, Timothy Taylor (2001) pays attention to the obscure images of some artists. According to Taylor, the tendency to hide, rather than reveal, works to counteract celebration of the individual musician. Because of their obscure names and faceless images, such artists are believed to draw attention to themselves, not as individuals, but as hidden, mysterious creators. (Taylor 2001: 140.) Also, the use of sampling challenges the idea of music as the artist's personal storytelling (Hesmondhalgh 2000: 291; Schumacher 1995: 264). Since it is usually expected that there is an author who links the voice together with its authorial source, the lack of an artist's direct contribution to the music making sets aside the idea of self-expression (see e.g. Keightley 2001: 133–134; Schumacher 1995: 264; Shuker 1994: 111–114). The notion of single originating authorship seems to lie in the background of Seltmann's reasoning, quoted above. Seltmann observes that the creative input of band members is not comparable with that of a singer, even though it was those men who put the album together. In spite of their contribution, the band members do not regard themselves as the real authors of the album, but as hidden creators, as Taylor noted above.[180] The mysterious construction of artists' public images also illustrates the effects of redefining musical authorship and the new practices of music making to which they have led.

Conclusion

The practice of sampling has caused a great deal of confusion in the making, production and reception of music during the past few decades. Samplers are used not only for economic reasons, but also for creating new and distinctive aesthetics. Besides the technological changes, sampling has forced us to redefine the notion of musical authorship, especially in terms of musical creativity. Use of this technique has produced new kinds of evaluative hierarchies that, on the one hand, emphasize the differences between so-called traditional music and that which is digitally composed one, and on

---

180   The lack of self-expression may also be related to the use of music technology, which is often believed to lead to the absence of individual feel or touch (see e.g. Frith 1986: 265; Warner 2003: 103).

the other hand, draw a distinction between creative and non-proficient sampling practices. Second, in sample-based music, several authorial voices are entangled. Sampling has also brought confusion to notions of originality and authorship, since the blending of authorial voices by a number of artists makes it more difficult to link the used sounds and samples with their origins. Third, because of the intertextual quality of sampling, listening to such music often seems to be more distracted, in comparison with the ways one listens to more conventional forms of music making. Because of the ongoing recognition of samples, interpretation relies on the listener's knowledge of different genres and styles of music. Depending on their earlier listening experiences and musical background, audience members may identify familiar samples and situate them properly within the history of popular music.

Notions of musical authorship, creativity and originality have been reformulated to correspond current ways of making, distributing and consuming popular music. The music by The Avalanches and similar artists, in making their music, include authorial voices from a number of artists, instead of relying on the idea of single authorship. As yet, changing ideas of musical authorship are applicable only to some areas of popular music, since the effects of digital music technology do not automatically supersede earlier ideologies, including the celebration of stardom. It remains to be seen whether the tranquil coexistence of contradictory concepts will continue in the future, and in what ways popular music culture may change, as new ways of making popular music are introduced. To judge from the authorship of sampling artists, the notion of musical authorship is not about to lose its pertinence. New forms and functions emerge as ideas about authorship are adjusted, so as to accommodate the changes in music-making practices.

CLOSING WORDS –
POST-AUTHORSHIP AND AFTER

The author – Front and center

In popular music culture, the author is placed front and center. It is the author who is typically seen as the point of origin of musical texts and who is believed to be responsible for songs' emotional charge. It is the author's star persona and public image that are used in the marketing of musical products and in giving the music a recognizable face. It is also the author's celebrity value that makes the field of popular music a fascinating phenomenon – and a theme for research alike. At the same time, this study has not dealt with authors as such, but with their public images and mediated constructions.

In this study, I have examined the mediated construction of author images of several artists, whose music is categorized under the genres of contemporary rock, pop and electronic dance music. In reference to the concept of *author image*, I have explored processes by which artists' public images are constructed in a set of media texts. Using the notions of *presented, mediated* and *compiled* author images, I have theorized the construction of images as an ongoing activity, as negotiations between the public artist, the media, and the audience. Most of the examined case studies have clarified at length the construction of presented and mediated author images; less attention has been paid to the standpoint of the listener. My emphasis on the artist's and the media's perspectives should not be taken to imply that the audience's role is less essential. Rather, the analysed material has proved more suitable for studying the first two types of images. Nevertheless, the views of some individual listeners have been taken into account, to illustrate ways in which the compiled author image can be constructed by audience members. Based just on the narrow examination of compiled author images included in this study, I believe that online discussion forums and other web communities provide interesting material that can serve as new points of departure for future studies on musical authorship.

My purpose in examining author images has been to shed light on the changing authorial roles and areas of responsibility of the various agents operating within popular music culture. In the latter, musical works are typically personified by their public performers; however, the artist with celebrity value is usually not the only author involved in the process of music making. Instead, authorial responsibility and artistic control are often divided among members of a larger creative collective. To these collective practices should be added the roles of the media and the marketing machinery, which further complicate attempts to specify the ways in which authorial contribution is shared. In this respect, the aim of this study has been to examine practices of music making as they relate to mediated processes of constructing the images through which public artists and their authorial status are presented in a certain light. The image presented in public, which is often built around the artist's star persona, usually provides a rather limited picture of musical authorship as it arises within the complex functioning of popular music culture.

In addition to musical texts and written publications in different media, the artist's author image consists of visual imagery, including album cover photography and music videos. These fragments of the artist's public image are scattered and recycled throughout different media, while the "complete" author image is still typically seen as a fixed and permanent category – and as another object to be consumed. Thus, the construction of author images may be seen as an intertextual process that centers around the public artist and his/her celebrity power. Due to the media's power as an intermediary force, however, neither the public artist nor the marketing machinery can fully control how the artist's image is presented. Ultimately, the meanings given to artists' public personas are dependent on the individual subject position of each audience member and his/her competence as a musical connoisseur.

Mediated stardom, constructed images

Given the way that works are normally associated with authorial sources, musical texts are personified by those who perform them in public. Based on mediated information, it often remains unclear as to how the public artist actually participates in the music making. When media attention is directed to the public artist and his/her star persona, the creative input of other music makers involved in the process is easily ignored. The compiled image is always a subjective interpretation; moreover, because of the mediated construction of images, the audience may never see the whole picture. The author images suggested by the artist, the marketing machinery, and the media can also be mutually contradicting, further underlining the fact that the "reality" under investigation is always a matter of mediated images and preferred readings.

Though the construction of images is an active and intertextual process, it is still common to treat the public artist as the point of origin. The belief in single originating authorship also explains why artists are typically presented as innovative and creative individuals whose works are to be interpreted against their real-life stories. The idea of a single creative individual also sets expectations as to the kinds of qualities the artist should have, these qualities serving as criteria by which to measure his/her creativity and originality. This study has shown that the concepts of *auteurism* and *authenticity* have been used as criteria by which to evaluate artists and their works. Those concepts embrace such notions as self-sufficiency, originality, and pursuit of control; those three characteristics are commonly used in descriptions and assessments of an artist's authorial role and public image. The auteur is expected to be in charge of his/ her music making, especially songwriting. The belief in single originating authorship also explains why the creative skills of covering and sampling artists are often called into question. And yet, as the case of Tori Amos has shown, an artist who has attained auteur status, as an innovative and original music maker, may experiment rather freely – for example, with covering – without losing his/her place in the authorial hierarchy of popular music.

Author images also work as a means of classification, in as much as they group together certain texts, thereby distinguishing them from other texts. Through a distinctive public image, the artist's star persona is presented as a unique and original figure. Some musical artists use their looks or personal appearance in constructing their public image, whereas others prefer to hide their personal identities, often behind carefully calculated disguises. The imagery presented in photographs, music videos, official homepages and other promotional material – all these aid in establishing an artist's public identity. Though it may be seen to oppose an artist's celebrity status, even disguised imagery can be used in the marketing of musical products.

Bringing the cases together

Concentrating on the public images of selected artists, I have explored some ways in which author images are constructed in popular music. The examination has revealed that, despite the many differences between the selected artists and their public images, all of these are connected by certain underlying similarities. Many of these similarities appear to derive from genres and generic codes, which define the kinds of authorship that are typically valued in different styles of music.

The belief in single originating authorship unites the author images and star personas of Björk, Tori Amos, Prince, Jewel and Bruce Springsteen. All these artists fall under the category of "singer-songwriters", who mostly perform self-written material. Many singer-songwriter types also meet the criteria for *auteur*, an especially celebrated position in the genre of rock. Artists of this stature are often presented as pioneering figures who have full control over their career and music making, and their music is seen as the artist's personal storytelling. Even when they participate in collaborative music making, it is usually assumed that such artists have chosen

200

those with whom they wish to collaborate, such that the final outcome is believed to present the artistic vision of the *auteur* in charge. Still, as the example of Jewel has demonstrated, when changes in an artist's public image and musical style are too drastic, doubts may arise as to the artist's authenticity and sincerity (in Jewel's case, the changes involved a shift to blatantly collective music making and an increased use of music technology). The notion of single authorship was also evident in the case of Coldplay: the public persona of the lead singer is highlighted in the media, which present him as the authorial source of Coldplay's songs, and disregard the creative input of the rest of the band.

In contrast to artists whose author images are based on notions of self-sufficiency and originality, the images of Kylie Minogue and Britney Spears project the artists as skilful performers and charismatic entertainers. Although their creative contributions may vary, the main authorial responsibility of these types of pop artists normally lies in performing songs written by others. Consequently, the authorial focus of such artists is typically diverted to their vocal performance, showmanship and glamorous looks, with less attention paid to the artist's contributions (e.g. songwriting) in the actual process of music making. Even when a large backing team is involved, however, the music is marketed in the name of the public artist and his/her celebrity power.

By contrast, the cases of Daft Punk, Kraftwerk, Jori Hulkkonen and The Avalanches serve as examples of artists with more diffused public images. Faceless imagery, logos, and pseudonyms are typically used in manufacturing the public personas of such artists – as representatives of electronic (dance) music. Despite the masked and distant author images, many of these artists seek to retain control over their careers, visual imagery, and music making (hence many of them build and make their recordings in home studios). In addition to its highly technological nature, the music made by electronic dance music artists often includes pre-existing material, much of it originally made by other artists. The phenomena of diffused authorship and parallel authorial voices, as embodied in the music making of such artists, serve to bolster the poststructuralist agenda, which questions the author's status as the guarantor of meaning, and emphasizes the reception of musical texts as an active, socially determined process.

Updated authorship

The boundaries that once separated the role of musical author from that of the listener, or the professional music maker from the amateur, are becoming more and more indistinct. One reason for this blurring of authorial roles has to do with the possibilities – such as digital sampling – that new music technologies hold out to aspiring music makers. The examination of DJ authorship and sampling artists has shown, among other things, that those artists who make use of pre-existing sonic material must sometimes adopt the listener's point of view. In the case of DJs and sampling artists, authorship is no longer a question of whether the artist is the originating source of each sample and sound. Rather, authorship in such cases is viewed in terms of the artist's skill at choosing and manipulating the borrowed material. Through the creative use of borrowed material, artists may also evidence their knowledge of popular music history and/or pay homage to their musical idols. In addition to sampling, other developments in studio technology have made it possible for practically anyone to make and record his or her own music. Thanks to the Internet, music makers now have more direct access to channels by which to distribute their creations and build up their reputations as artists and authors.

New ways of music making, and the increased possibilities for distributing musical products, have necessitated concomitant changes and expansions in the criteria by which musical authorship is defined. The increased importance of music technology has made the process of music making more "transparent" than ever before; home-studio artists, especially, are eager to share information about their favourite equipment and working techniques. Juxtaposed against this increased transparency are those musical artists who prefer shrouded secrecy, and wish to present themselves as "mysterious" creators. This preference is evidenced in the figure of the automaton-artist, as both representative and denizen of the world of music technology. Whether one approves or disapproves of such artist representations, they demand a rethinking of our views and definitions of music making and, by extension, musical authorship. New music technologies have also raised issues concerning gender. If throughout the study I have referred to the musical author equitably, as both male and female figure, it is clear that certain musical practices, such as DJing, remain male-dominated. In this study I have not engaged with gender issues as they might concern authorship, save for brief mention of them with regard to Tori Amos. Admittedly and most obviously, an author's gender cannot help but affect how his/her author image is constructed and perceived. The same can be said of other factors, such as ethnicity, race, age, and more. Such factors, as well as gender issues, as they relate to conceptions of musical authorship, can perhaps be addressed at more length in future studies.

As noted above, new ways of music making have raised new questions relating to musical authorship. Some of these have to do with whether or not a musical author should be the creator of every single sound in the musical text, or if artists who use samplers and other digital technologies should receive equal value as authors. In addition to questions relating to the artist's authorial status and artistic identity, technological changes have raised legal, ethical, and proprietary (ownership) issues pertaining to musical authorship. Should an artist benefit from a piece of music that was originally made by someone else? How should authorial credit be apportioned in the case of musical texts made up of multiple authorial inputs? Do new music technologies represent a threat to musical creativity? Or should they instead be regarded as new grounds by which to assess musical versatility? Those are some of the questions, touched on in this study, that force a reconsideration of how musical authorship is defined. Because of technological and ideological changes, new meanings have been given to the notion of musical author, in terms of his/her creative input and authorial role. All this points to the fact that the very concept of "musical authorship" remains in a state of perpetual flux and, thus, calls for endless redefinition.

The author remains

Despite the fluid and contingent nature of the meanings attached to it, the concept of musical authorship remains a powerful, normative criterion by which the public artist is adjudged an auteur, star, performer, DJ or "mysterious" creator. No matter how one defines authorial status, it is still the artist's public persona around which the author image is constructed. Apart from their role in constructing author images, stars and star images sustain popular music culture by bringing predictability to the market place. One might also venture to say that the author's role, as a uniting factor, has become even more essential in the era of fragmented (post-)authorship, when various authorial constructions are struggling to coexist.

Can the concepts of collective and single authorship be brought closer together? Is it possible for an artist to work in a creative and innovative fashion, in light of the fact that music making is a collective process, one that is dependent on social context and available resources? At least for now, the music, live performances, visual imagery, media propaganda – all of it gets back to the individual music maker and his/her creative talents. At least so far, the "individual author" is still credited as being the source from which everything else springs. Though it has become more common (and fashionable) to regard musical authorship as a collective and social process, the concept of single authorship persists. It is almost an "ontological given", to judge from the ways in which popular music is marketed and perceived, whether by celebrations of the artist's exceptional creativity or by praise of his/her role-playing or penchant for masked identities and cryptic pseudonyms. In the end, author images are not only aids to describing and interpreting popular music authorship. They help us to formulate the fundamental concepts with which we comprehend popular culture in general.

REFERENCES

Research literature

Abbate, Carolyn (1993) "Opera; or the Envoicing of Women". *Musicology and Difference*. Ed. Ruth A. Solie. Berkeley: University of California Press. Pp. 225–258.

Abrams, M. H. (1953) *The Mirror and the Lamp. Romantic Theory and the Critical Tradition.* New York: The Norton Library.

Aho, Marko (2003) *Iskelmäkuninkaan tuho. Suomi-iskelmän sortuvat tähdet ja myyttinen sankaruus.* Helsinki: Suomalaisen Kirjallisuuden Seura.

Aho, Marko (2004) "Fenolaulu, genolaulu ja Reijo Kallion kadenssi. Lauluäänen kehollisesta kokemuksesta". *Musiikki* 2/2004, pp. 23–38.

Ahonen, Laura (2004) "Populaarimusiikin tekijäkenttä, media ja mielikuvat. Näkökulmia median roolin populaarimusiikin tekijyyden rakentajana". *Musiikki* 2/2004, pp. 5–22.

Ahonen, Laura (2005) "Uutta ilmaa populaarimusiikin tekijäsubjektin ruumiiseen. Poststrukturalismin teesit ja tekijyyden rakentuminen elektronisessa tanssimusiikissa". *Etnomusikologian vuosikirja 17*, pp. 32–47.

Ahonen, Laura (2006a) "Piilossa tähteydeltä – Daft Punk ja tekijäkuvan kasvottomuus". *Lähikuva* 3/2006, pp. 19–32.

Ahonen, Laura (2006b) "Mediated Stardom, Constructed Images: The Value and Functioning of Authorship in Popular Music". *Music, Meaning and Media*. Eds. Richard Littlefield, Erkki Pekkilä & David Neumeyer. Helsinki: Acta Semiotica Fennica. Pp. 163–173.

Alanen, Antti (1992) *Sähköiset unet. Musiikkivideot: miten taiteesta tuli pop.* Production Design Ilpo Pohjola. Helsinki: VAPK.

Anderson, Linda (2001) *Autobiography*. London & New York: Routledge.

Anderson, Tim (2006) "For the Record: Interdisciplinarity, Cultural Studies, and the Search for Method in Popular Music Studies". *Questions of Method in Cultural Studies*. Eds. Mimi White & James Schwoch. Malden & Oxford: Blackwell Publishing. Pp. 285–307.

Andrew, Dudley (1984) *Concepts in Film Theory*. Oxford, New York, Toronto & Melbourne: Oxford University Press.

Armstrong, Edward G. (2004) "Eminem's Construction of Authenticity". *Popular Music and Society* 27/3, pp. 335–355.

Bacon, Henry (2000) *Audiovisuaalisen kerronnan teoria*. Helsinki: Suomalaisen Kirjallisuuden Seura.

Bauman, Zygmunt (2001) *The Bauman Reader*. Ed. Peter Beilharz. Malden & Oxford: Blackwell.

Bazin, André (1985) "The Evolution of the Language of Cinema". *Film Theory and Criticism. Introductory Readings*. 3rd edition. Eds. Gerald Mast & Marshall Cohen. New York & Oxford: Oxford University Press. Pp. 124–138.

Barthes, Roland (1973) [1957] *Mythologies*. Trans. Annette Lavers. London: Granada Publishing Ltd.

Barthes, Roland (1979) "From Work to Text". *Textual Strategies. Perspectives in Post-structuralist Criticism*. Ed. Josué V. Harari. London: Methuen. Pp. 73–81.

Barthes, Roland (1990) [1977] *Image – Music – Text*. Trans. Stephen Heath. London: Fontana Press.

Battersby, Christine (1989) *Gender and Genius: Towards a Feminist Aesthetics*. London: The Woman's Press.

Beardsley, Monroe C. (1982) *The Aesthetic Point of View. Selected Essays*. Eds. Michael J. Wreen & Donald M. Callen. Ithaca, New York & London: Cornell University Press.

Beck, Ulrich and Beck-Gernsheim, Elisabeth (2002) *Individualization. Institutionalized Individualism and Its Social and Political Consequences*. London: Sage Publications.

Benjamin, Walter (1992) "The Work of Art in the Age of Mechanical Reproduction". *Illuminations*. Ed. Hannah Arendt. Trans. Harry Zohn. London: Fontana Press. 211–244.

Bennett, Andrew (2004) "The Idea of the Author". *Romanticism. An Oxford Guide*. Ed. Nicholas Roe. Oxford: Oxford University Press. Pp. 654–664.

Bennett, Andrew (2005) *The Author*. London & New York: Routledge.

Bennett, Andy (2001) *Cultures of Popular Music*. Maidenhead: Open University Press.

Bennett, Andy; Shank, Barry; Toynbee, Jason (2006) "Introduction". *The Popular Music Studies Reader*. Eds. Andy Bennett, Barry Shank & Jason Toynbee. London & New York: Routledge. Pp. 1–7.

Björnberg, Alf (2000) "Structural Relationships of Music and Images in Music Videos". *Reading Pop. Approaches to Textual Analysis in Popular Music*. Ed. Richard Middleton. Oxford: Oxford University Press. Pp. 347–378.

Booth, Wayne C. (1983) [1961] *The Rhetoric of Fiction*. 2nd edition. Chicago & London: University of Chicago Press.

Bordwell, David (1996) "Film Studies and Grand Theory". *Post-theory. Reconstructing Film Studies*. Eds. David Bordwell & Noël Carroll. Madison: University of Wisconsin Press. Pp. 3–36.

Born, Georgina (2005) "On Musical Mediation: Ontology, Technology and Creativity". *Twentieth Century Music* 2/1, pp. 7–36.

Bosma, Hannah (1996) "Authorship and Female Voices In Electrovocal Music". Proceedings of the 1996 International Computer Music Conference in Hong Kong, http://www.hannahbosma.nl/icmc96.htm (3 July 2007).

Bosma, Hannah (2000) "Who Creates Electro-vocal Music? (Authors, Composers, Vocalists and Gender)". Published in *Ctrl+Shift Art – Ctrl+Shift Gender*, http://www.hannahbosma.nl/readaxHB.html (3 July 2007).

Brackett, David (1999) "Music". *Key Terms in Popular Music and Culture*. Eds. Bruce Horner & Thomas Swiss. Malden & Oxford: Blackwell. Pp. 124–140.

Brackett, David (2000) *Interpreting Popular Music*. Berkeley, Los Angeles & London: University of California Press.

Buckley, David (2007) "Pop. Implications of Technology". *Grove Music Online*. Ed. L. Macy, http://www.grove-music.com/shared/views/article.html?section=music.46845.2 (29 May 2007).

Burke, Seán (1998) *The Death and Return of the Author. Criticism and Subjectivity in Barthes, Foucault and Derrida*. 2nd edition. Edinburgh: Edinburgh University Press.

Burr, Vivien (1995) *An Introduction to Social Constructionism*. London & New York: Routledge.

Buscombe, Edward (1981) [1973] "Ideas of Authorship". *Theories of Authorship. A Reader*. Ed. John Caughie. London: Routledge & Kegan Paul. Pp. 22–34.

Butler, Christopher (2002) *Postmodernism. A Very Short Introduction*. Oxford: Oxford University Press.

Butler, Jeremy G. (1998) "Hollywood and the Star System". *The Oxford Guide to Film Studies*. Eds. John Hill & Pamela Church Gibson. Oxford: Oxford University Press. Pp. 342–353.

Butler, Mark (2003) "Taking it Seriously: Intertextuality and Authenticity in Two Covers by the Pet Shop Boys". *Popular Music* 22/1, pp. 1–19.

205

Butt, John (2007) "Authenticity". *Grove Music Online*. Ed. L. Macy, http://www.grovemusic.com/shared/views/article.html?from=search&session_search_id=11588452&hitnum=1&section=music.46587 (29 May 2007).

Buxton, David (1990) "Music, the Star System, and the Rise of Consumerism". *On Record: Rock, Pop, and The Written Word*. Eds. Simon Frith & Andrew Goodwin. New York: Pantheon Books. Pp. 427–440.

Chan, Y.M. Sharon (2000) "Wired_Selves: From Artifact to Performance". *CyberPsychology & Behavior* 3/2, pp. 271 –285.

Chaney, David (1993) *Fictions of Collective Life. Public Drama in Late Modern Culture*. London & New York: Routledge.

Citron, Marcia J. (1993) *Gender and the Musical Canon*. Cambridge: Cambridge University Press.

Connell, John and Gibson, Chris (2003) *Sound Tracks. Popular Music, Identity and Place*. London & New York: Routledge.

Coombe, Rosemary J. (1994) "Author/izing the Celebrity: Publicity Rights, Postmodern Politics, and Unauthorized Genders". *The Construction of Authorship. Textual Appropriation in Law and Literature*. Eds. Martha Woodmansee & Peter Jaszi. Durham: Duke University Press. Pp. 101–131.

Crofts, Stephan (1998) "Authorship and Hollywood". *The Oxford Guide to Film Studies*. Eds. John Hill & Pamela Church Gibson. Oxford: Oxford University Press. Pp. 310–324.

Croteau, David and Hoynes, William (2003) *Media Society. Industries, Images and Audiences*. 3rd edition. Thousand Oaks, London & New Delhi: Pine Forge Press.

Cubitt, Sean (1991) *Timeshift. On Video Culture*. London & New York: Routledge.

Cubitt, Sean (2000) "'Maybellene': Meaning and the Listening Subject". *Reading Pop. Approaches to Textual Analysis in Popular Music*. Ed. Richard Middleton. Oxford: Oxford University Press. Pp. 141–159.

Danesi, Marcel (2002) *Understanding Media Semiotics*. London: Arnold.

DeNora, Tia (2002) *Music in Everyday Life*. Cambridge: Cambridge University Press.

Den Tandt, Christophe (2004) "From Craft to Corporate Interfacing: Rock Musicianship in the Age of Music Television and Computer-Programmed Music". *Popular Music and Society* 27/2, pp. 139–160.

Derrida, Jacque (1991) *A Derrida Reader. Between the Blinds*. Ed. Peggy Kamuf. New York & Oxford: Columbia University Press.

Diakopoulos, Nicholas (2005) "Remix Culture: Mixing Up Authorship", http://www-static.cc.gatech.edu/~nad/Remix%20culture%20mixing%20up%20authorship.doc (3 July 2007).

Dickinson, Kay (2003) "Pop Stars Who Can't Act. The Limits of Celebrity 'Multi-tasking'". *Mediative* 2/2003, pp. 74–85.

Dyer, Richard (1986) *Stars*. London: BFI Publishing.

Dyer, Richard (1991) "*A Star is Born* and the Construction of Authenticity". *Stardom. Industry of Desire*. Ed. Christine Gledhill. London & New York: Routledge. Pp. 132–140.

Eagleton, Terry (1983) *Literary Theory. An Introduction*. Oxford: Basil Blackwell.

Eisenstein, Sergei (1985) "The Cinematographic Principle and the Ideogram". *Film Theory and Criticism. Introductory Readings*. 3rd edition. Eds. Gerald Mast & Marshall Cohen. New York & Oxford: Oxford University Press. Pp. 90–123.

Ellis, John (1982) *Visible Fictions*. Revised edition. London & New York: Routledge.

Fabbri, Franco (1982) "A Theory of Musical Genres: Two Applications". *Popular Music Perspectives. Papers from The First International Conference On Popular Music Research, Amsterdam, June 1981*. Eds. David Horn & Philip Tagg. Göteborg & Exeter: IASPM. Pp. 52–81.

Fairclough, Norman (1992) *Discourse and Social Change*. Cambridge: Polity Press.

Fairclough, Norman (1997) [1995] *Miten media puhuu*. Trans. Virpi Blom & Kaarina Hazard. Tampere: Vastapaino.

Fikentscher, Kai (1998) "The DJ as Performer". *Music on Show: Issues of Performance*. Eds. Tarja Hautamäki & Helmi Järviluoma. University of Tampere: Tampere University Printing Service. Pp. 87–91.

Fisher, John Andrew (1998) Rock 'n' Recording: The Ontological Complexity of Rock Music. *Musical Worlds: New Directions in the Philosophy of Music*. Ed. Philip Alperson. Philadelphia, PA: Pennsylvania University Press. Pp. 109–123.

Fiske, John (1989) *Understanding Popular Culture*. London & New York: Routledge.

Fornäs, Johan (1995) "Listen to Your Voice! Authenticity and Reflexivity in Karaoke, Rock, Rap and Techno Music". *Popular Music – Style and Identity*. Eds. Will Straw, Stacey Johnson, Rebecca Sullivan & Paul Friedlander. Montreal: Dufferin Press. Pp. 99–110.

Foucault, Michel (1979) "What Is an Author?". *Textual Strategies. Perspectives in Post-structuralist Criticism*. Ed. Josué V. Harari. London: Menthuen. Pp. 141–160.

Frith, Simon (1983) *Sound Effects. Youth, leisure, and the politics of rock*. London: Constable.

Frith, Simon (1986) "Art versus Technology: the Strange Case of Popular Music". *Media, Culture, and Society* 8/3, pp. 263–279.

Frith, Simon (1987) "Towards an Aesthetic of Popular Music". *Music and Society: The Politics of Composition, Performance and Reception*. Eds. Richard Leppert & Susan McClary. Cambridge & New York: Cambridge University Press. Pp. 133–149.

Frith, Simon (1988) *Music for Pleasure. Essays in the Sociology of Pop*. Cambridge: Polity Press.

Frith, Simon (1993a) "Music and Morality". *Music and Copyright*. Ed. Simon Frith. Edinburgh: Edinburgh University Press. Pp. 1–21.

Frith, Simon (1993b) "Introduction". *Music and Copyright*. Ed. Simon Frith. Edinburgh: Edinburgh University Press. Pp. ix–xiv.

Frith, Simon (1996) *Performing Rites. On the Value of Popular Music*. Oxford: Oxford University Press.

Frith, Simon and Horne, Howard (1987) *Art into Pop*. London & New York: Menthuen & Co.

Frith, Simon (2001) "The Popular Music Industry". *The Cambridge Companion to Pop and Rock*. Eds. Simon Frith, Will Straw & John Street. Cambridge: Cambridge University Press. Pp. 26–52.

Frith, Simon; Straw, Will and Street, John (2001) "Star Profiles II". *The Cambridge Companion to Pop and Rock*. Eds. Simon Frith, Will Straw & John Street. Cambridge: Cambridge University Press. Pp. 193–210.

Fuchs, Cynthia (1999) "Images". *Key Terms in Popular Music and Culture*. Eds. Bruce Horner & Thomas Swiss. Malden & Oxford: Blackwell Publishers. Pp. 178–187.

Fulford-Jones, Will (2007a) "Remix". *Grove Music Online*. Ed. L. Macy, http://www.grovemusic.com/shared/views/article.html?from=search&session_search_id=893906764&hitnum=1&section=music.47227 (29 May 2007).

Fulford-Jones, Will (2007b) "Sampling". *Grove Music Online*. Ed. L. Macy, http://www.grovemusic.com/shared/views/article.html?from=search&session_search_id=1096436346&hitnum=1&section=music.47228 (29 May 2007).

Gilbert, Jeremy (2003) "Small Faces: The Tyranny of Celebrity in Post-Oedipal Culture". *Mediative* 2/2003, pp. 86–109.

Gledhill, Christine (1991) "Introduction". *Stardom. Industry of Desire*. Ed. Christine Gledhill. London & New York: Routledge. Pp. xiii–xx.

Gloag, Kenneth (2001) "Situating the 1960: Popular Music – Postmodernism – History". *Rethinking History* 5/3, pp. 397–410.

Goehr, Lydia (1992) *The Imaginary Museum of Musical Works. An Essay in the Philosophy of Music.* Oxford: Clarendon Press.

Goodwin, Andrew (1990) "Sample and Hold. Pop Music in the Digital Age of Reproduction". *On Record: Rock, Pop, and The Written Word.* Eds. Simon Frith & Andrew Goodwin. New York: Pantheon Books. Pp. 258–274.

Goodwin, Andrew (1992) *Dancing in the Distraction Factory. Music Television and Popular Culture.* Minneapolis: University of Minneapolis Press.

Goodwin, Andrew (1998) "Drumming and Memory. Scholarship, Technology, and Music-Making". *Mapping the Beat. Popular Music and Contemporary Theory.* Eds. Thomas Swiss, John Loop & Andrew Herman. Oxford: Blackwell Publishers. Pp. 121–136.

Gracyk, Theodore (1996) *Rhythm and Noise. An Aesthetics of Rock.* London: Duke University Press.

Gracyk, Theodore (2001) *I Wanna Be Me: Rock Music and the Politics of Identity.* Philadelphia: Temple University Press.

Grimshaw, Mark (1998) "Remix! Where's the Original?". *Music on Show: Issues of Performance.* Eds. Tarja Hautamäki & Helmi Järviluoma. University of Tampere: Tampere University Printing Service. Pp. 129–131.

Grossberg, Lawrence; Wartella, Ellen; Whitney, D. Charles (1998) *MediaMaking. Mass Media in a Popular Culture.* Thousand Oaks, London & New Delhi: Sage Publications.

Hall, Stuart (1980) "Encoding/decoding". *Culture, Media, Language. Working Papers in Cultural Studies, 1972–79.* Eds. Stuart Hall, Dorothy Hobson, Andrew Lowe & Paul Willis. London: Hutchinson & Co. Pp. 128–138.

Hall, Stuart (1996) "Signification, Representation, Ideology: Althusser and the Post-Structuralist Debates". *Cultural Studies and Communications.* Eds. James Curran, David Morley & Valerie Walkerdine. London: Arnold. Pp. 11–34.

Hall, Stuart (1997) "The Work of Representation". *Representation. Cultural Representations and Signifying Practices.* Ed. Stuart Hall. London & Thousand Oaks: Sage Publications. Pp. 13–64.

Harland, Richard (1999) *Literary Theory from Plato to Barthes. An Introductory History.* Basingstoke: Macmillan Press.

Hartley, John (2002) *Communication, Cultural and Media Studies. The Key Concepts.* 3rd edition. London & New York: Routledge.

Heath, Stephen (1981) [1973] "Comment on 'The Idea of Authorship". *Theories of Authorship. A Reader.* Ed. John Caughie. London: Routledge & Kegan Paul. Pp. 214–220.

Hennion, Antoine (1990) "The Production of Success. An Antimusicology of the Pop Song". *On Record: Rock, Pop, and The Written Word.* Eds. Simon Frith & Andrew Goodwin. New York: Pantheon Books. Pp. 185–206.

Herman, Bill D. (2006) "Scratching Out Authorship: Representations of the Electronic Music DJ at the Turn of the 21st Century". *Popular Communication* 4/1, pp. 21–38.

Hesmondhalgh, David (1996) "Rethinking Popular Music after Rock and Soul". *Cultural Studies and Communications.* Eds. James Curran, David Morley & Valerie Walkerdine. London: Arnold. Pp. 195–212.

Hesmondhalgh, David (2000) "International Times: Fusions, Exoticism, and Antiracism in Electronic Dance Music". *Western Music and Its Others. Difference, Representations, and Appropriation in Music.* Eds. Georgina Born & David Hesmondhalgh. Berkeley, Los Angeles & London: University of California Press. Pp. 280–304.

Hesmondhalgh, David (2006) "Digital Sampling and Cultural Inequality". *Social and Legal Studies* 15/1, pp. 53–75.

Hietala, Veijo (1992) *Kulttuuri vaihtoi viihteelle? Johdatusta postmodernismiin ja populaarikulttuuriin.* Helsinki: Kirjastopalvelu Oy.

Holmes, Su (2004) "Reality goes pop! Reality TV, Popular Music, and Narratives of Stardom in *Pop Idol*". *Television & New Media* 5/2, pp. 147–172.

Horner, Bruce (1999) "Discourse". *Key Terms in Popular Music and Culture*. Eds. Bruce Horner & Thomas Swiss. Malden & Oxford: Blackwell Publishers. Pp. 18–34.

Houni, Pia; Tiainen, Milla & Virtanen, Marjaana (2005) "Johdanto". *Musiikin ja teatterin tekijöitä*. Eds. Taina Riikonen, Milla Tiainen & Marjaana Virtanen. Helsinki: Suomen Musiikkitieteellinen Seura. Pp. 7–28.

Jaworski, Adam & Coupland, Nikolas (1999) "Introduction". *The Discourse Reader*. Eds. Adam Jaworski & Nikolas Coupland. London & New York: Routledge. Pp. 1–44.

Jensen, Klaus Bruhn (2002) "Contexts, Cultures and Computer: The Cultural Contexts of Mediated Communication". *A Handbook of Media and Communication Research. Qualitative and Quantitative Methodologies.* Ed. Klaus Bruhn Jensen. London & New York: Routledge. Pp. 171–190.

Jokinen, Arja; Juhila, Kirsi & Suominen Eero (1993) "Diskursiivinen maailma: teoreettiset lähtökohdat ja analyyttiset käsitteet". *Diskurssianalyysin aakkoset*. Eds. Arja Jokinen, Kirsi Juhila & Eero Suominen. Tampere: Vastapaino. Pp. 17–47.

Jokinen, Arja (1999) "Diskurssianalyysin suhde sukulaistraditioihin". *Diskurssianalyysi liikkeessä. Vuorovaikutus, toimijuus ja kulttuuri emipiirisen tutkimuksen haasteina*. Eds. Arja Jokinen, Kirsi Juhila & Eero Suominen. Tampere: Vastapaino. Pp. 37–53.

Jones, Steve (1993) "Music and Copyright in the USA". *Music and Copyright.* Ed. Simon Frith. Edinburgh: Edinburgh University Press. Pp. 67–85.

Joyce, Mark (1999) "The Soviet Montage Cinema of the 1920s". *An Introduction to Film Studies*. 2nd edition. Ed. Jill Nelmes. London & New York: Routledge. Pp. 417–450.

Järvinen, Hanna (2003) *The Myth of Genius in Movement. Historical Deconstruction of the Nijinsky Legend.* Turku: University of Turku.

Kallioniemi, Kari (1990) *Dandy, soul-mies ja rock-sankari. 60-luvun popmusiikki ja moderni kulttuuri.* Helsinki: Kansan Sivistystyön Liitto.

Kaplan, E. Ann (1987) *Rocking Around the Clock. Music Television, Postmodernism, and Consumer Society.* London & New York: Routledge.

Karvonen, Erkki (1999) *Elämää mielikuvayhteiskunnassa. Imago ja maine menestystekijöinä myöhäismodernissa maailmassa.* Tampere: Gaudeamus.

Kassabian, Anahid (2001) *Hearing Film. Tracking Identifications in Contemporary Hollywood Film Music.* London & New York: Routledge.

Keightley, Keir (2001) "Reconsidering Rock". *The Cambridge Companion to Pop and Rock.* Eds. Simon Frith, Will Straw & John Street. Cambridge: Cambridge University Press. Pp. 109–142.

Kellner, Douglas (1995) *Media Culture. Cultural Studies, Identity and Politics Between the Modern and the Postmodern.* London & New York: Routledge.

Kemp, Chris (2004) *Towards a Holistic Interpretation of Genre Classification.* Jyväskylä: University of Jyväskylä.

Killmeier, Matthew A. (2001) "Voices between the Tracks: Disk Jockeys, Radio, and Popular Music, 1955-60". *Journal of Communication Inquiry* 25/4, pp. 353–374.

Koivisto, Päivi (1997) "Muusa/muusikko. Tori Amos populaarimusiikin naamiaisissa." *Musiikin suunta* 3/1997, pp. 17–28.

Krasnow, Carolyn (1995) "Technologies of Authorship in Disco". *Popular Music Style and Identity.* Eds. Will Straw, Stacey Johnson, Rebecca Sullivan & Paul Friedlander. Montreal: Dufferin Press. Pp. 181–183.

Kress, Gunther & Leeuwen, van Theo (1999) "Representation and Interaction: Designing the Position of the Viewer". *The Discourse Reader*. Eds. Adam Jaworski & Nikolas Coupland. London & New York: Routledge. Pp. 377–404.

Kristeva, Julia (1986) *The Kristeva Reader*. Ed. Toril Moi. Oxford: Basil Blackwell.

Kärjä, Antti-Ville (2005) *"Varmuuden vuoksi omana sovituksena". Kansallisen identiteetin rakentuminen 1950-ja 1960-luvun taitteen suomalaisten elokuvien populaarimusiikillisissa esityksissä*. Turku: Turun yliopisto.

Lafrance, Mélisse (2002) "The Problems of Agency and Resistance in Tori Amos's 'Crucify'". *Disruptive Divas. Feminism, Identity & Popular Music*. Eds. Lori Burns & Mélisse Lafrance. New York & London: Routledge. Pp. 63–73.

Laing, David (1990) "Listen to Me". *On Record: Rock, Pop and the Written Word*. Eds. Simon Frith & Andrew Goodwin. New York: Pantheon. Pp. 326–340.

Laing, Dave (2007) "Folk-rock". *Grove Music Online*. Ed. L. Macy, http://www.grovemusic.com/shared/views/ article.html?from=search&session_search_id=398789285&hitnum=1&section=music.46853 (29 May 2007).

Laitinen, Katja (2003) "Keijukaiskuningatar ja hänen hovinsa. Laulaja Tori Amos ja Internet rockkultin keskiö-nä". *Kulttikirja. Tutkimuksia nykyajan kultti-ilmiöistä*. Eds. Urpo Kovala & Tuija Saresma. Helsinki: Suomalaisen Kirjallisuuden Seura. Pp. 38–54.

Lapsley, Robert & Westlake, Michael (1988) *Film Theory: An Introduction*. Manchester: Manchester University Press.

Lehtonen, Mikko (1994) *Kyklooppi ja kojootti. Subjekti 1600–1900 -lukujen kulttuuri- ja kirjallisuusteorioissa*. Tampere: Vastapaino.

Lehtonen, Mikko (1996) *Merkitysten maailma. Kulttuurisen tekstintutkimuksen lähtökohtia*. Tampere: Vastapaino.

Lenneberg, Hans (1980) "The Myth of the Unappreciated (Musical) Genius". *Musical Quarterly* 66:2, pp. 219–231.

Lepistö, Vappu (1991) *Kuvataiteilija taidemaailmassa. Tapaustutkimus kuvataiteellisen toiminnan sosiaalipsykologisista merkityksistä*. Helsinki: Tutkijaliitto.

Leppänen, Taru (1996) *Teos ja tekijyys. Säveltäjä ja muusikko musiikkiteoksen tuottajina*. Turun yliopisto. Taiteiden tutkimuksen laitos.

Leppänen, Taru & Moisala, Pirkko (2003) "Kulttuurinen musiikintutkimus". *Johdatus musiikintutkimukseen*. Eds. Tuomas Eerola, Jukka Louhivuori & Pirkko Moisala. Helsinki: Suomen musiikkitieteellinen seura. Pp. 71–86.

Livingston, Paisley (1997) "Cinematic Authorship". *Film Theory and Philosophy*. Eds. Richard Allen & Murray Smith. Oxford: Clarendon Press. Pp. 132–148.

Lyotard, Jean-Francois (1979) *The Postmodern Condition. A Report on Knowledge*. Trans. Geoff Bennington & Brian Massumi. Manchester: Manchester University Press.

Manovich, Lev (2001) *The Language of New Media*. Cambridge, Massachusetts: The MIT Press.

Manovitch, Lev (2004) "Who is the Author? Sampling / Remixing / Open Source", http://www.manovich.net/ DOCS/models_of_authorship.doc (3 July 2007).

Manovitch, Lev (2005) "Remixing and Remixability", http://www.manovich.net/DOCS/Remixability_2.doc (3 July 2007).

Marshall, P. David (1997) *Celebrity and Power. Fame in Contemporary Culture*. Minneapolis: University of Minnesota Press.

McClary, Susan (1991) *Feminine Endings. Music, Gender, and Sexuality*. Minnesota: University of Minnesota Press.

McGuigan, Jim (1992) *Cultural Populism*. London & New York: Routledge.

McLeod, Kembrew (2005) "Confessions on an Intellectual (Property): Danger Mouse, Mickey Mouse, Sonny Bono, and My Long and Winding Path as a Copyright Activist-Academic". *Popular Music and Society* 28/1, pp. 79–93.

McLeod, Ken (2003) "Space Oddities: Aliens, Futurism and Meaning in Popular Music". *Popular Music* 22/3, pp. 337–355.

Middleton, Richard (2000) "Introduction: Locating the Popular Music Text". *Reading Pop. Approaches to Textual Analysis in Popular Music*. Ed. Richard Middleton. Oxford: Oxford University Press. Pp. 1–19.

Middleton, Richard (2001) "Pop, rock and Interpretation". *The Cambridge Companion to Pop and Rock*. Eds. Simon Frith, Will Straw & John Street. Cambridge: Cambridge University Press. Pp. 213–225.

Middleton, Richard (2003) "Introduction". *The Cultural Study of Music. A Critical Introduction*. Eds. Martin Clayton, Trevor Herbert & Richard Middleton. New York & London: Routledge. Pp. 1–15.

Middleton, Richard (2006) *Voicing the Popular. On the Subjects of Popular Music*. London & New York: Routledge.

Middleton, Richard (2007a) "Rock". *Grove Music Online*. Ed. L. Macy, http://www.grovemusic.com/shared/views/article.html?from=search&session_search_id=316962353&hitnum=17&section=music.49135 (29 May 2007).

Middleton, Richard (2007b) "Pop. Introduction". *Grove Music Online*. Ed. L. Macy, http://www.grovemusic.com/shared/views/article.html?section=music.46845.1#music.46845.1 (29 May 2007).

Middleton, Richard (2007c) "Mass Media and the Cultural Economy of Popular Music. The Main Historical Shifts". *Grove Music Online*. Ed. L. Macy, http://www.grovemusic.com/shared/views/article.html?section=music.43179.1.2.1#music.43179.1.2.1 (29 May 2007).

Mills, Sara (1997) *Discourse*. London & New York: Routledge.

Modinos, Tuija (1994) *Nainen populaarikulttuurissa. Madonna ja "The Immaculate Collection"*. Jyväskylä: Jyväskylän yliopisto.

Moore, Allan F. (2001) *Rock: The Primary Text. Developing a musicology of rock*. 2nd edition. Aldershot & Burlington: Ashgate.

Moore, Allan F. (2002) "Authenticity as Authentication". *Popular Music* 21/2, pp. 209–223.

Muikku, Jari (1988) *Vinyylin viemää: äänilevyn tuottamisen karu todellisuus*. Helsinki: Työväenmusiikki-instituutin julkaisu.

Murray, Penelope (1989) "Introduction". *Genius. The History of an Idea*. Ed. Penelope Murray. Oxford & New York: Basil Blackwell. Pp. 1–8.

Mäkelä, Janne (2002) *Images in the Works. A Cultural History of John Lennon's Rock Stardom*. Cultural History. University of Turku.

Negus, Keith (1992) *Producing Pop. Culture and Conflict in the Popular Music Industry*. London, New York: Arnold.

Negus, Keith (1998) "Cultural Production and the Corporation: Musical Genres and the Strategic Management of Creativity in the US Recording Industry". *Media, Culture & Society* Vol. 20, pp. 359–379.

Negus, Keith (1999) *Music Genres and Corporate Cultures*. London & New York: Routledge.

Negus, Keith (2001) "Maintaining Cultural Order. Creativity, Genre Divisions and the Recording Industry. *The Aesthetics of Popular Art*. Ed. Jostein Grisprud. Kristiansand: Hoyskelforlaget AS – Norwegian Academic Press. Pp. 33–49.

Nimmo Dan & Savage, Robert L. (1976) *Candidates and Their Images. Concepts, Methods, and Findings.* Santa Monica: Goodyear Publishing Company.

Novitz, David (2001) "Postmodernism. Barthes and Derrida". *The Routledge Companion to Aesthetics.* Eds. Berys Gaut & Dominic McIver Lopes. London & New York: Routledge. Pp. 155–165.

O'Brien, Damien & Fitzgerald, Brian (2006) "Mashups, Remixes and Copyright Law". *Internet Law Bulletin*, http://eprints.qut.edu.au/archive/00004239/01/4239.pdf (3 July 2007).

Paasonen, Susanna (2002) *Figures of Fantasy: Women, Cyberdiscourse and the Popular Internet.* Turku: Turun yliopisto.

Phillips, Patrick (1999) "Genre, Star and Auteur". *An Introduction to Film Studies.* 2ⁿᵈ edition. Ed. Jill Nelmes. London & New York: Routledge. Pp. 161–207.

Porcello, Thomas (1991) "The Ethics of Digital Audio-sampling: Engineers' Discourse". *Popular Music* 10/1, pp. 69–84.

Poster, Mark (1995) *The Second Media Age.* Cambridge: Polity Press.

Potter, John (2007) "Singer-songwriter". *Grove Music Online.* Ed. L. Macy, http://www.grovemusic.com/shared/views/article.html?section=music.46855.1 (29 May 2007).

Pulkkinen, Tuija (1991) "Jälkistrukturalismi ja subjektius". *Taide modernissa maailmassa. Taiteensosiologiset teoriat Georg Lucáksista Fredric Jamesoniin.* Eds. Erkki Sevänen, Liisa Saariluoma & Risto Turunen. Pp. 124–140.

Reynolds, Simon & Joy Press (1995) *The Sex Revolts. Gender, Rebellion, and Rock'n'Roll.* Cambridge & Massachusetts: Harvard University Press.

Richardson, John (2005) "'The Digital Won't Let Me Go': Constructions of the Virtual and the Real in Gorillaz' 'Clint Eastwood'". *Journal of Popular Music Studies* 17/1, pp. 1–29.

Rojola, Sanna (2001) "Musiikin ja tutkimuksen tekijät". *Musiikki* 1/2001, pp. 92–96.

Rojola, Sanna (2004) "Luovaa mekaanisuutta ja mekaanista luovuutta". *Musiikki*, 1/2004. Pp. 54–76.

Sanjek, David (1994) "'Don't Have to DJ No More': Sampling and the 'Autonomous' Creator". *The Construction of Authorship. Textual Appropriation in Law and Literature.* Eds. Martha Woodmansee & Peter Jaszi. Durham: Duke University Press. Pp. 343–360.

Saukko, Paula (2003) *Doing Research in Cultural Studies. An Introduction to Classical and New Methodological Approaches.* London, Thousand Oaks & New Delhi: Sage Publications.

Schumacher, G. Thomas (1995) "This Is a Sampling Sport: Digital Sampling, Rap Music and the Law in Cultural Production". *Media, Culture & Society* Vol. 17, pp. 253–273.

Scott, Derek (1998) "Postmodernism and Music". *The Icon Critical Dictionary of Postmodern Thought.* Ed. Stuart Sim. Cambridge: Icon books. Pp. 134–146.

Seppä, Anita (2003) *The Aesthetic Subject: Exploring the Usefulness of Foucauldian tools in Feminism.* Helsinki: University of Helsinki.

Shuker, Roy (1994) *Understanding Popular Music.* London & New York: Routledge.

Sibilla, Gianni (2006) "'When New Media Was the Bid Idea': Internet and the Rethinking of Pop-music Languages". *Music, Meaning and Media.* Eds. Richard Littlefield, Erkki Pekkilä & David Neumeyer. Helsinki: Acta Semiotica Fennica. Pp. 148–162.

Silverman, Hugh J. (1994) *Textualities. Between Hermeneutics and Deconstruction.* London & New York: Routledge.

Sirppiniemi, Ano (2006) "Home Studio Aesthetics: Tracking Cultural Process of Popular Music Production. *Music, Meaning and Media*. Eds. Richard Littlefield, Erkki Pekkilä & David Neumeyer. Helsinki: Acta Semiotica Fennica. Pp. 174–191.

Spivey, Nancy Nelson (1997) *The Constructivist Metaphor: Reading, Writing, and the Making of Meaning*. San Diego & London: Academic Press.

Stam, Robert (2000) *Film Theory. An Introduction*. Oxford: Blackwell Publishers.

Storey, John (1996) "Cultural Studies: An Introduction". *What is Cultural Studies. A Reader*. Ed. John Storey. London, New York: Arnold. Pp. 1–13.

Straw, Will (1999) "Authorship". *Key Terms in Popular Music and Culture*. Eds. Bruce Horner & Thomas Swiss. Malden & Oxford: Blackwell Publishers. Pp. 199–208.

Straw, Will (2001a) "Dance Music". *The Cambridge Companion to Pop and Rock*. Eds. Simon Frith, Will Straw & John Street. Cambridge: Cambridge University Press. Pp. 158–73.

Straw, Will (2001b) "Consumption". *The Cambridge Companion to Pop and Rock*. Eds. Simon Frith, Will Straw & John Street. Cambridge: Cambridge University Press. Pp. 53–175.

Strinati, Dominic (1995) *An Introduction to Theories of Popular Culture*. London & New York: Routledge.

Swiss, Thomas (2002) "Jewel Case. Pop Stars, Poets, and the Press". *Pop Music and the Press*. Ed. Steve Jones. Philadelphia: Temple University Press. Pp. 171–182.

Tagg, Philip (1982) "Analysing Popular Music: Theory, Method and Practice". *Popular Music* 2/1982, pp. 37–69.

Tarvainen, Anne (2005) "Äänellisen minän muotoutuminen Björkin kappaleessa *Undo*". *Musiikki* 3/2005, pp. 66–91.

Taylor, Timothy D. (2001) *Strange Sounds. Music, Technology & Culture*. New York & London: Routledge.

Théberge, Paul (1997) *Any Sound You Can Imagine. Making Music/ Consuming Technology*. Hanover & London: Wesleyan University Press.

Théberge, Paul (1999) "Technology". *Key Terms in Popular Music and Culture*. Eds. Bruce Horner & Thomas Swiss. Massachusetts & Oxford: Blackwell Publishers. Pp. 209–224.

Théberge, Paul (2004) "Technology, Creative Practice and Copyright". *Music and Copyright*. 2nd edition. Eds. Simon Frith & Lee Marshall. Edinburgh: Edinburgh University Press. Pp. 139–156.

Thom, Paul (1993) *For an Audience: Philosophy of the Performing Arts*. Philadelphia: Temple University Press.

Thornton, Sarah (1995) *Club Cultures. Music, Media and Subcultural Capital*. Hanover & London: Wesleyan University Press.

Thwaites, Tony; Lloyd, Davis & Mules, Warwick (1994) *Tools for Cultural Studies. An Introduction*. South Melbourne: Macmillan Education Australia.

Tiainen, Milla (2005) *Säveltäjän sijainnit. Taiteilija, musiikki ja historiallinen kesto Paavo Heinisen ja Einojuhani Rautavaaran teksteissä*. Jyväskylä: Jyväskylän yliopisto.

Torvinen, Juha (2007) *Musiikki ahdistuksen taitona. Filosofinen tutkimus musiikin eksistentiaalis-ontologisesta merkityksestä*. Acta Musicologica Fennica 26. Helsinki: Suomen Musiikkitieteellinen Seura.

Toynbee, Jason (2000) *Making Popular Music. Musicians, Creativity and Institutions*. London: Arnold Publishers.

Toynbee, Jason (2003) "Music, Culture, and Creativity". *The Cultural Study of Music. A Critical Introduction*. Eds. Martin Clayton, Trevor Herbert and Richard Middleton. New York & London: Routledge. Pp. 102–112.

Toynbee, Jason (2006) "Making Up and Showing Off: What Musicians Do". *The Popular Music Studies Reader.* Eds. Andy Bennett, Barry Shank & Jason Toynbee. London & New York: Routledge. Pp. 71–77.

Turkle, Sherry (1995) *Life on the Screen. Identity in the Age of the Internet.* London & New York: Simon & Schuster.

Turner, Graeme (1992) *British Cultural Studies. An Introduction.* London & New York: Routledge.

Turner, Graeme (2004) *Understanding Celebrity.* London, Thousand Oaks: Sage Publications.

Välimäki, Susanna (2005) *Subject Strategies in Music. A Psychoanalytic Approach to Musical Signification.* Acta Semiotica Fennica 22, Approaches to Musical Semiotics 9. Helsinki & Imatra: Semiotic Society of Finland & International Semiotics Institute.

Wall, Tim (2003) *Studying Popular Music Culture.* London & New York: Arnold.

Walser, Robert (1993) *Running with the Devil: Power, Gender, and Madness in Heavy Metal Music.* Hanover: University Press of New England.

Warner, Timothy (2003) *Pop Music – Technology and Creativity. Trevor Horn and the Digital Revolution.* Burlington: Ashgate.

Weinstein, Deena (1998) "The History of Rock's Pasts through Rock Covers". *Mapping the Beat. Popular Music and Contemporary Theory.* Eds. Thomas Swiss, John Loop & Andrew Herman. Oxford: Blackwell Publishers. Pp. 137–151.

Weinstein, Deena (1999) "Art versus Commerce: Deconstructing a (Useful) Romantic Illusion". *Stars Don't Stand Still in the Sky. Music and Myth.* Eds. Karen Kelly & Evelyn Marcus. London: Routledge. Pp. 57–69.

Wicke, Peter (1990) *Rock Music. Culture, Aesthetics and Sociology.* Cambridge: Cambridge University Press.

Williams, Alastair (2001) *Constructing Musicology.* Aldershot, UK: Ashgate.

Worton, Michael & Still, Judith (1991) "Introduction". *Intertextuality: Theories and Practices.* Eds. Michael Worton & Judith Still. Pp. 1–44.

Woodmansee, Martha (1994a) *The Author, Art, and the Market: Rereading the History of Aesthetics.* New York: Columbia University Press.

Woodmansee, Martha (1994b) "On the Author Effect: Recovering Collectivity". *The Construction of Authorship. Textual Appropriation in Law and Literature.* Eds. Martha Woodmansee & Peter Jaszi. Durham: Duke University Press. Pp. 15–28.

Young, James O. (2001) "Authenticity in Performance". *The Routledge Companion to Aesthetics.* Eds. Berys Gaut & Dominic McIver Lopes. London & New York: Routledge. Pp. 383–394.

Zurbrugg, Nicholas (2000) *Critical Vices. The Myths of Postmodern Theory.* Amsterdam: G+B Arts International.

Miscellaneous literature on popular music (biographies, reviews etc.)

Amos, Tori & Powers, Ann (2005) *Tori Amos. Piece by Piece. A Portrait of the Artist. Her Thoughts. Her Conversations.* New York: Random House (Broadway Books).

Ankeny, Jason (2002a) "Kraftwerk. Biography". *All Music Guide to Rock. The Definitive Guide to Rock, Pop, and Soul.* Eds. Vladimir Bogdanov, Chris Woodstra & Stephan Thomas Erlewine. San Francisco: Backbeat Books. Pp. 632.

Ankeny, Jason (2002b) "Jewel. AMG Biography". *All Music Guide to Rock. The Definitive Guide to Rock, Pop, and Soul*. Eds. Vladimir Bogdanov, Chris Woodstra & Stephan Thomas Erlewine. San Francisco: Backbeat Books. Pp. 590.

Aston, Martin (1996) *Björkgraphy*. London: Simon & Schuster.

Barr, Tim (1998) *Kraftwerk. From Düsseldorf to the Future (with Love)*. London: Ebury Press.

Beadle, Jeremy J. (1993) *Will Pop Eat Itself? Pop Music in the Soundbite Era*. London: Faber and Faber.

Berk, Mike (2000) "Technology. Analog Fetishes and Digital Futures". *Modulations. A History of Electronic Music: Throbbing Words on Sound*. Ed. Peter Shapiro. New York: Caipirinha Productions. Pp. 188–209.

Bogdanov, Vladimir; Woodstra Chris; Erlewine, Stephan Thomas & Bush, John (2001; eds.) *All Music Guide to Electronica. The Definitive Guide to Electronic Music*. San Francisco: Backbeat Books.

Brewster, Bill & Broughton, Frank (1999) *Last Night a DJ Saved My Life. The History of the Disc Jockey*. London: Headline Book Publishing.

Bush, John (2002) "Old School Rap". *All Music Guide to Rock. The Definitive Guide to Rock, Pop, and Soul*. Eds. Vladimir Bogdanov, Chris Woodstra & Stephan Thomas Erlewine. San Francisco: Backbeat Books. Pp. 1100.

Carson, Mina; Lewis, Tisa & Shaw, Susan M. (2004) *Girls Rock! Fifty Years of Women Making Music*. Lexington, KY: University Press of Kentucky.

Cooper, Sean (2002) "Daft Punk. Biography". *All Music Guide to Rock. The Definitive Guide to Rock, Pop, and Soul*. Eds. Vladimir Bogdanov, Chris Woodstra & Stephan Thomas Erlewine. San Francisco: Backbeat Books. Pp. 278.

Crowe, Cameron (2004) "Standing in Joni Mitchell's Painting Room…". *Joni Mitchell. Dreamland* (liner notes). Warner Strategic Marketing, a Warner Music Group Company.

Des Pres, Josquin & Landsman, Mark (2000) *Creative Careers in Music*. New York: Allworth Press.

Erlewine, Stephen Thomas (2002a) "Björk. Biography". *All Music Guide to Rock. The Definitive Guide to Rock, Pop, and Soul*. Eds. Vladimir Bogdanov, Chris Woodstra & Stephan Thomas Erlewine. San Francisco: Backbeat Books. Pp. 101.

Erlewine, Stephen Thomas (2002b) "Prince. Biography". n *All Music Guide to Rock. The Definitive Guide to Rock, Pop, and Soul*. Eds. Vladimir Bogdanov, Chris Woodstra & Stephan Thomas Erlewine. San Francisco: Backbeat Books. Pp. 889.

Erlewine, Stephen Thomas (2002c) "Spirit. AMG Review". *All Music Guide to Rock. The Definitive Guide to Rock, Pop, and Soul*. Eds. Vladimir Bogdanov, Chris Woodstra & Stephan Thomas Erlewine. San Francisco: Backbeat Books. Pp. 590.

Hall, Christian (2005) "User's Guide to… Band on the Web". *Musician's Union Advice*, http://www.musiciansunion.org.uk/scripts/get.php?file=__Artists_websites.pdf (closed, last accessed 1 November 2006).

MacKenzie, Wilson (2002) "Coldplay. Biography". *All Music Guide to Rock. The Definitive Guide to Rock, Pop, and Soul*. Eds. Vladimir Bogdanov, Chris Woodstra & Stephan Thomas Erlewine. San Francisco: Backbeat Books. Pp. 234–235.

Nielsen, Per Reinholdt (2006) *Björkmusik*. Copenhagen: Tiderne Skrifter.

Nimmervoll, Ed (2002) "Kylie Minogue. Biography". *All Music Guide to Rock. The Definitive Guide to Rock, Pop, and Soul*. Eds. Vladimir Bogdanov, Chris Woodstra & Stephan Thomas Erlewine. San Francisco: Backbeat Books. Pp. 739–740.

O'Brien, Lucy (1995) *She Bop. The Definitive History of Women in Rock, Pop and Soul*. London: Penguin Books.

215

Phares, Heather (2002) "Selmasongs: Music From the Motion Picture Soundtrack Dancer in the Dark". *All Music Guide to Rock. The Definitive Guide to Rock, Pop, and Soul*. Eds. Vladimir Bogdanov, Chris Woodstra & Stephan Thomas Erlewine. San Francisco: Backbeat Books. Pp. 101–102.

Poschardt, Ulf (1995) *DJ-Culture*. Trans. Shaun Whiteside. Hamburg: Rogner & Beinhardt GmbH & Co. Verlags KG.

Reynolds, Simon (1998) *Energy Flash. A Journey through Rave Music and Dance Culture*. London: Picador.

Reynolds, Simon (2000) "Krautrock". *Modulations. A History of Electronic Music: Throbbing Words on Sound*. Ed. Peter Shapiro. New York: Caipirinha Productions. Pp. 24–34.

Rogers, Kalen (1994) *Tori Amos. All These Years. The Authorized Illustrated Biography*. London & New York: Omnibus Press.

Ruhlmann, William (2002) "Bruce Springsteen. Biography". *All Music Guide to Rock. The Definitive Guide to Rock, Pop, and Soul*. Eds. Vladimir Bogdanov, Chris Woodstra & Stephan Thomas Erlewine. San Francisco: Backbeat Books. Pp. 1062.

Sabin, Roger (1999) "Introduction". *Punk Rock: So What? The Cultural Legacy of Punk*. London & New York: Routledge.

Sicko, Dan (1999) *Techno Rebels. The Renegades of Electronic Funk*. New York: Billboard Books.

Souvignier, Todd (2003) *The World of DJs and the Turntable Culture*. Milwaukee: Hal Leonard Corporation.

Watts, Michael (1994) "Lone Star. Bruce Springsteen". *Melody Maker. Classic Rock Interviews*. Compiled by Alan Jones. London: Mandarin Paperbacks.

Newspaper, magazine and online articles

Adcock, Donna (1997) "Turns in Their Homework". *Yahoo! Music*, http://music.yahoo.com/read/interview/12052857 (3 July 2007).

Aine G. (2002) "Jori Hulkkonen Interview". *Deep House Network*, http://www.deephousenetwork.com/interviews.php?i_id=25 (3 July 2007).

Ankeny, Jason (2006) "The Residents. Biography". *All Music Guide*, http://www.allmusic.com/cg/amg.dll?p=amg&sql=11:bxfm964o3ep8~T1 (3 July 2007).

Ankeny, Jason & Torreano, Bradley (2006) "Eminem. Biography". *All Music Guide*, http://www.allmusic.com/cg/amg.dll?p=amg&sql=11:4n8j1vf1zzpa~T1 (3 July 2007).

Appel, Jen (1995) "Björk. Post". *Nude as the News. Rock Writing for the Musically Obsessed*, http://www.nudeasthenews.com/reviews/932 (3 July 2007).

Battaglia, Andy (2004) "Björk. Medulla". *Audio Video Revolution*, http://avclub.com/content/node/15492 (3 July 2007).

Beaumont, Michael (2004) "Björk. Medulla". *PopMatters Music Review*, http://www.popmatters.com/music/reviews/b/bjork-medulla.shtml (3 July 2007).

Beauvallet, Jean-Daniel (1999) "Björk et Michel Gondry. Michel Gondry – Bricorama Volumen, Compilation Video". *Les Inrocks*, http://www.lesinrocks.com/DetailArticle.cfm?iditem=81174 (3 July 2007).

Begrand, Adrien (2002) "Head Rush". *PopMatters Music Review*, http://www.popmatters.com/music/reviews/c/coldplay-rush.shtml (3 July 2007).

Berry, Colin (1998) "Sno-Koan". *Wired* 6.06/1998, http://www.wired.com/wired/archive/6.06/bjork.html (3 July 2007).

Birchmaier, Jason (2006) "The Neptunes. Biography". *All Music Guide*, http://www.allmusic.com/cg/amg.dll?p=amg&sql=11:bsevadoku8wo~T1 (3 July 2007).

Björk (1996) "Björk Meets Karlheinz Stockhausen. Compose Yourself". *Dazed and Confused*, http://home.westbrabant.net/~sinned/d23.htm (3 July 2007).

Björk (1997a) "Bjork redeems the remix". Björk's interview, http://home.westbrabant.net/~sinned/d93.htm (3 July 2007).

Björk (1997b) "SpinOnline Interview". *SpinOnline*, http://home.westbrabant.net/~sinned/d83.htm (3 July 2007).

Brown, G. (2001) "Amos Her Own Man. Singer-songwriter Probes Male Psyche in Reinterpretation of 12 Tunes". *Denver Post*, http://www.thedent.com/denverpost110201.html (3 July 2007).

Carew, Anthony (2001) "Björk. Vespertine". *Neumu = Art + Music + Words*, http://neumu.net/fortyfour/2001/2001-00199/2001-00199_fortyfour.shtml (3 July 2007).

Carmon, Irin (2001) "Tori's Got a Gun". *The Village Voice*, http://www.villagevoice.com/issues/0140/carmon.php (3 July 2007).

Coan, Caitlin (2001) "Amos' Strange New Album". *The Georgetown Voice*, http://www.georgetownvoice.com/2001-10-04/leisure/amos-i-strange-i-new-album (3 July 2007).

Collin, Matthew (1997) "Do You Think You Can Hide from Stardom?". *Mixmag*, http://www.techno.de/mixmag/97.08/DaftPunk.a.html (3 July 2007).

Collins, Troy (2004) "Björk. Medulla". *Junkmedia*, http://www.junkmedia.org/index.php?i=1204 (3 July 2007).

Cooper, Dan (2003) "Tori Amos. Strange Little Girls". *Stylus Magazine*, http://www.stylusmagazine.com/review.php?ID=65 (3 July 2007).

Corgan, Billy (2005) "Quotes". Official Brian Wilson homepage, http://www.brianwilson.com/brian/quotes.html (3 July 2007).

Crossing, Gary (2002) "Jewel – This Way". *Yahoo! Music*, http://uk.launch.yahoo.com/l_reviews_a/24121.html (3 July 2007).

Currie, Wendy (2000) "Coldplay. Parachutes". *The Reservoir. Music culture magazine*, http://www.the-reservoir.co.uk/albums/rock_coldplay_parachutes.html (closed, last accessed 8 June 2006).

Dax-DJ (2004) "Jori Hulkkonen". *Family House*, http://www.family-house.net/jori.html (3 July 2007).

DeCurtis, Anthony (1999) "The Artist Is Back – But Don't Call It a Comeback". *New York Times*, http://perso.wanadoo.fr/antoine.house/prince_interview_1999.html (3 July 2007).

DeCurtis, Anthony (2004) "Prince. Musicology". *Rolling Stone*, http://www.rollingstone.com/reviews/album/_/id/5238328?rnd=1113224409060&has-player=true (3 July 2007).

Détourn, Gal (2001) "Vespertine. Björk". *PlayLouder*, http://www.playlouder.com/review/+366bjork/

DeVito, Dominic J. (2001) "The Avalanches: Sampling Success with Australia's Newest Superstars". *Plan9music*, http://www.plan9music.com/avalanches.html (closed, last accessed 1 November 2006).

Diamond, Alex (2003) "Jewel-*0304*". *Pop Entertainment*, http://www.popentertainment.com/jewel2.htm (3 July 2007).

Dickison, Stephanie (2001) "You Don't Know Her At All". *PopMatters Music Review*, http://www.popmatters.com/music/reviews/j/jewel-thisway.shtml (3 July 2007).

Diehl, Matt (2003) "Matt Diehl Talks to the Rest of the Band – Coldplay Members Speak Out". An interview by Matt Diehl. *Interview* August/2003, http://www.findarticles.com/p/articles/mi_m1285/is_7_33/ai_105735865 (3 July 2007).

Dillard, Brian J. (2002) "Reviews. Björk". *Armchair-DJ*, http://www.armchair-dj.com/reviews/v/vespertine.asp (closed, last accessed 13 December 2005).

DiMartino, Dave (1998) "No Diamond in the Rough". *Yahoo! Music*, http://music.yahoo.com/read/interview/12048694 (3 July 2007).

DiMartino, Dave (2003) "Following Her Intuition". *Yahoo! Music*, http://music.yahoo.com/read/interview/12059227 (3 July 2007).

Dutta, Ronita (2003) "iVillage Talks to Jewel". *iVillage UK Ltd*, http://www.ivillage.co.uk/newspol/celeb/cint/articles/0,,528729_593730,00.html (3 July 2007).

Elliot, Paul (1997) "Who the Hell Does Björk Think She Is?". *Q* November/1997, http://home.westbrabant.net/~sinned/d64.htm (3 July 2007).

Erlewine, Stephen Thomas (2001) "Britney. Review". *All Music Guide*, http://www.allmusic.com/cg/amg.dll?p=amg&sql=10:0djgtq4zpu47 (3 July 2007).

Erlewine, Stephen Thomas (2003) "0304. AMG Review". *All Music Guide*, http://www.allmusic.com/cg/amg.dll?p=amg&uid=UIDSUB040406040511462445&sql=A0sq2g44ztv4z (3 July 2007).

Erlewine, Stephen Thomas (2004) "Musicology. Review". *All Music Guide*, http://www.allmusic.com/cg/amg.dll?p=amg&sql=10:a96wtrotklox (3 July 2007).

Erlewine, Stephen Thomas (2005) "Tori Amos. Biography". *All Music Guide*, http://www.allmusic.com/cg/amg.dll?p=amg&searchlink=TORI|AMOS&sql=11:um59kett7q7v~T1 (3 July 2007).

Fahnestock, Jesse (2001) "The Avalanches. *Since I Left You*". *Ink Blot Magazine*, http://www.inkblotmagazine.com/rev-archive/Avalanches_Since_I_Left_You.htm (3 July 2007).

Falik, Adam (2001) "Strange Little Tori". *Rolling Stone*, http://www.thedent.com/rscom100401.html (3 July 2007).

Foley, Jack (2003) "Jewel – 0304". *IndieLondon*, http://www.indielondon.co.uk/music/cd_jewel_0304.html (3 July 2007).

Fussman, Cal (2005) "Bruce Springsteen". *Esquire Magazine* August/2005, http://www.brucespringsteen.net/news (3 July 2007).

Gaffney, Diane (2002) "Coldplay's 'A Rush to the Head'". *Crazewire*, http://crazewire.com/features/2002102131.php (3 July 2007).

Gardner, Elysa (2006) "Jewel, *Goodbye Alice in Wonderland*". *USA Today*, http://www.usatoday.com/life/music/reviews/2006-05-01-listen-up_x.htm (3 July 2007).

Garrido, Mike (2002) "My Afternoon with the Avalanches". *Turntable2k*, http://www.turntable2k.com/avalanches.htm (closed, last accessed 1 June 2004).

Gill, Chris (2001) "Robopop". *Remix*, http://remixmag.com/mag/remix_robopop (3 July 2007).

Greenwood, Eric (2001a) "Bjork. Vespertine". *DrawerB*, http://old.drawerb.com/features/1002641279.htm (3 July 2007).

Greenwood, Eric (2001b) "Prince. The Rainbow Children". *DrawerB*, http://old.drawerb.com/features/1009815042.htm (3 July 2007).

Greenwood, Eric (2004) "Prince. Musicology". *DrawerB*, http://www.old.drawerb.com/reviews/1089391965.htm (3 July 2007).

Grönholm, Pertti (1997) "Jori Hulkkonen. Kemistä Keski-Euroopan bailuareenoille", *Rytmi* 5/97, pp. 31–33.

Hagen, Mark; Sutcliffe Phil & Jump, Steve (1999) "The Midnight Cowboy", *MOJO* 1/1999, pp. 70–89.

Hastings, Chris (2005) "Thank You for the Music! How Madonna's New Single Will Give Abba Their Greatest-ever Hit". *Telegraph*, http://news.telegraph.co.uk/news/main.jhtml?xml=/news/2005/10/16/nmad16.xml (3 July 2007).

Heumann, Michael (2004) "Björk. Medulla". *Stylus Magazine*, http://www.stylusmagazine.com/review.php?ID=2303 (3 July 2007).

Hornby, Nick (2005) "A Fan's Eye View". *Guardian* July/2005, http://www.brucespringsteen.net/news (3 July 2007).

Huey, Steve (2004) "Stevie Wonder. Biography". *All Music Guide*, http://www.allmusic.com/cg/amg.dll?p=amg&searchlink=STEWIE|WONDER&uid=SUB030412100830&sql=11:kpddylm8xpnb~T1 (3 July 2007).

Huey, Steve (2005) "Britney Spears. Biography". *All Music Guide*, http://www.allmusic.com/cg/amg.dll?p=amg&sql=11:teazqjkiojta~T1 (3 July 2007).

Huey, Steve (2006) "Max Martin. Biography". *All Music Guide*, http://www.allmusic.com/cg/amg.dll?p=amg&sql=11:8xotk6gxqkrj~T1 (3 July 2007).

Juhala, Jarmo (2000) "Jori Hulkkonen. Rytmin arkkitehti". *Rumba* 17/2000, pp. 28.

Keefe, Michael (2007) "Björk. Volta" *PopMatters Music Review*, http://www.popmatters.com/pm/music/reviews/33998/bjork-volta/ (3 July 2007).

Kellman, Andy (2001) "The Avalanches: Bio". *All Music Guide*, http://www.allmusic.com/cg/amg.dll?p=amg&sql=11:16bsa9cgl23g~T1 (3 July 2007).

Klemetti, Konsta (1999) "Harmonic hylsister. Jori Hulkkonen". *Rumba* 17/1999, pp. 13.

Klemola, Esa (1996) "Jori Hulkkonen: Perämeristä housebiittiä". *Rumba* 23/96, http://www.phinnweb.org/scrapbook/hulkkonen_rumba.html (3 July 2007).

Latimer, Lori (2001) "Björk. Vespertine". *Ink Blot Magazine*, http://www.inkblotmagazine.com/rev-archive/Bjork_Vespertine.htm (3 July 2007).

LeMay, Matt (2000) "The Avalanches. Since I Left You". *Pitchfork Media*, http://www.pitchforkmedia.com/article/record_review/15136-since-i-left-you (3 July 2007).

Lin, Marvin (1997) "Björk. Homogenic". *Nude as the News. Rock Writing for the Musically Obsessed*, http://www.nudeasthenews.com/reviews/318 (3 July 2007).

Lin, Marvin (2001) "Björk. Vespertine". *Nude as the News. Rock Writing for the Musically Obsessed*, http://www.nudeasthenews.com/reviews/352 (3 July 2007).

Lingas, Paul (2002) "Coldplay. A Rush of Blood to the Head". *Audio Video Revolution*, http://www.avrev.com/music/revs/coldplay.shtml (3 July 2007).

Lundy, Zeth (2004) "Don't U Miss the Music Gave Ya Back in the Day?" *PopMatters Music Review*, http://www.popmatters.com/music/reviews/p/prince-musicology.shtml (3 July 2007).

Maconie, Stuart (1995) "All Together Now". *Q* August/1995, http://home.westbrabant.net/~sinned/d63.htm (3 July 2007).

Mazur, Matt (2007). "Tori Amos. Americal Doll Posse". *PopMatters Music Review*, http://www.popmatters.com/pm/music/reviews/33738/tori-amos-american-doll-posse (3 July 2007).

McShane, Larry (2005) "Springsteen's Musical Education Continues". *Associated Press*, http://www.bruce-springsteen.net/news (3 July 2007).

Moayeri, Lily (2001) "Punk as They Wanna Be". *Yahoo! Music*, http://uk.music.yahoo.com/read/interview/12053561 (3 July 2007).

Nelson, Steffie (2001) "Tori Amos: Personality Crisis". *MTV.com*, http://www.mtv.com/bands/a/amos_tori/News_Feature100601/index.jhtml (3 July 2007).

219

Norment, Lynn (1997) "The Artist Formerly Known as Prince Has a New Wife, New Baby and a New Attitude". *Ebony* January/1997, http://www.findarticles.com/p/articles/mi_m1077/is_n3_v52/ai_18980644 (3 July 2007).

Odell, Michael (2002) "The Great Pretender", *Q* August/2002, pp.106–114.

Oliver, Lisa (2001) "Tori Amos – Strange Little Girls". *Yahoo! Music*, http://uk.launch.yahoo.com/l_reviews_a/21916.html (3 July 2007).

Osborne, Ben (2001) "We Are Not Control Freaks. We Are Freedom Freaks". *Guardian Unlimited*, http://www.guardian.co.uk/Archive/Article/0,4273,4150972,00.html (3 July 2007).

Paoletta, Michael (2001) "This Way". *Billboard*, http://www.billboard.com/bb/article_display.jsp?vnu_content_id=1099622 (closed, last accessed 8 July 2004).

Parker, Lyndsey (2004) "A Rush Of Words To The Mouth". *Yahoo! Music*, http://music.yahoo.com/read/interview/12027423 (3 July 2007).

Petridis, Alexis (2003) "Jewel: 0304". *Guardian Unlimited*, http://www.guardian.co.uk/arts/reviews/story/0,11712,1026985,00.html (3 July 2007).

Phares, Heather (2004) "Medúlla. Review". *All Music Guide*, http://www.allmusic.com/cg/amg.dll?p=amg&sql=10:keb1z88a5yv1 (3 July 2007).

Potts, Diana (2006) "Jori Hulkonen. Biography". *All Music Guide*, http://www.allmusic.com/cg/amg.dll?p=amg&sql=11:9me097lkkr0t~T1 (3 July 2007).

Prince (1997) "The Artist Formerly Known as Prince Enjoys Musical Freedom with Hit Album 'Emancipation'". *Jet* May/1997, http://www.findarticles.com/p/articles/mi_m1355/is_n26_v91/ai_19436608 (3 July 2007).

Rabin, Dustin (2005) "Everybody's Got a Voice". Björk, press interview, http://home.westbrabant.net/~sinned/d88.htm (3 July 2007).

Rabinovitch, Simona (2001) "Sampladelicatessen". *Remix*, http://remixmag.com/ar/remix_sampladelicatessen (3 July 2007).

Rauch, Stephen (2003) "Tori Amos. Little Earthquakes". *PopMatters Music Review*, http://www.popmatters.com/music/reviews/a/amostori-little.shtml (3 July 2007).

Richert, Willy (2001) "A Personal Voyage to Discovery". *RFI Musique*, http://www.rfimusique.com/musiqueen/articles/060/article_6541.asp (3 July 2007).

Robinson, Charlotte (2005) "Prince. Dirty Mind". *PopMatters Music Review*, http://www.popmatters.com/music/reviews/p/prince-dirty.shtml (3 July 2007).

Rutkoski, Rex (2001) "At a Crossroads", The Britney Spears Interview". *The Inside Connection – Today's #1 Source for the Music Industry*, http://www.insidecx.com/showinterview.asp?articleid=14 (3 July 2007).

Rutkoski, Rex (2002) "Coldplay Feels the Warmth. A Rush of Success". *The Inside Connection – Today's #1 Source for the Music Industry*, http://www.insidecx.com/showinterview.asp?articleid=22 (3 July 2007).

Rutkoski, Rex (2004) "Poetry in Motion. Getting Intimate with Jewel". *The Inside Connection – Today's #1 Source for the Music Industry*, http://www.insidecx.com/showinterview.asp?articleid=47 (3 July 2007).

Ryming, Peter Engels (1993) "The Siren from the Volcano-Island". *Agenda* September/1993, http://home.concepts.nl/~sinned/d4.htm (3 July 2007).

Silas, Petri (2002) "Jori Hulkkonen", *Soundi* 9/2002, pp. 22–23.

Silcott, Mireille (1997) "Personality Punks. French House Producers Daft Punk Hide Their Faces to Show Their Worth". *Montreal Mirror*, http://www.montrealmirror.com/ARCHIVES/1997/040397/cover.html (3 July 2007).

Sirén, Juha (2004) "Miehemme maailmalla. Koneisto tulee, tervetuloa dj Hulkkonen". *City-lehti* 15/2004, http://www.city.fi/artikkelit/artikkeli.php?seskey=&id=1253&area=pop (3 July 2007).

Smith, Brian A. (2003) "0304". *The Phantom Tollbooth*, http://www.tollbooth.org/2003/reviews/jewel1.html (3 July 2007).

Stefanos, Pierre (1995) "Björk. Post". *Ink Blot Magazine*, http://www.inkblotmagazine.com/rev-archive/Bjork_ Post.htm (3 July 2007).

Sterdan, Darryl (2003) "Save Her Soul". *The London Free Press*, http://www.fyilondon.com/perl-bin/niveau2. cgi?s=musique&p=75347.html&a=1 (closed, last accessed 8 June 2006).

Sullivan, Paul (2001) "Crazy as Coconuts. An Interview with the Avalanches". *Amazon*, http://www.amazon. co.uk/exec/obidos/tg/feature/-/241361/ref%3Ded%5Fart%5F426036%5Ftxt%5F1/202-7910227-1347832 (3 July 2007).

Sutcliffe, Phil (1998) "The Artist Formerly Known as Successful". *Q* September/1997, pp. 62–65.

Tangari, Joe (2002) "Coldplay. A Rush of Blood to the Head". *Pitchfork Media*, http://pitchforkmedia.com/ article/record_review/16250-a-rush-of-blood-to-the-head (3 July 2007).

Taylor, Chuck (2006) "Jewel. *Goodbye Alice in Wonderland*". *Billboard*, http://www.billboard.com/bbcom/re-views/album_review_display.jsp?vnu_content_id=1002424837 (3 July 2007).

Teilmann, Maurice S. (2001) "A Bizarre Interview with The Avalanches. Monkeys, Cults and Speaking in Tongues". *Synthesis*, http://www.synthesis.net/music/feature.php?bid=1313 (closed, last accessed 1 November 2006).

Thompson, Jason (2001) "Tori Amos. Strange Little Girls". *PopMatters Music Review*, http://www.popmatters. com/music/reviews/a/amostori-strange.shtml (3 July 2007).

Tranter, Nikki (2001) "Britney. Yeah, Britney". *PopMatters Music Review*, http://www.popmatters.com/music/ reviews/s/spearsbritney-britney.shtml (3 July 2007).

Udovitch, Mim (1994) "Björk". Interviewed by Mim Udovitch. *Rolling Stone* 17/11/94, http://ebweb.at/ortner/ tia/94/rolling941117/rolling941117.html (3 July 2007).

Wade, Ian (2001) "The Avalanches – 'Since I Left You'". *Yahoo! Music*, http://uk.launch.yahoo.com/l_ reviews_a/19201.html (3 July 2007).

Walters, Barry (2001) "Britney Spears. Britney". *Rolling Stone*, http://www.rollingstone.com/reviews/album/_/ id/225846/rid/5942550/ (3 July 2007).

Warner Music (2004) "News. Jewel". *Warner Music Australasia*, http://www.warnermusic.com.au/artist,w_ artist,101695 (the whole article was last accessed 13 December 2005).

Widder, Katy (2000) "Björk. Selmasongs (Companion Album to the Film *Dancer in the Dark*)". *PopMatters Music Review*, http://www.popmatters.com/music/reviews/b/bjork-selmasongs.shtml (3 July 2007).

Widder, Katy (2001) "Björk. Vespertine". *PopMatters Music Review*, http://www.popmatters.com/music/ reviews/b/bjork-vespertine.shtml (3 July 2007).

Wildy, Anna (2000) "The Avalanches DJ Show. Mixed Up Kids". *X-Press Magazine*, http://www.xpressmag. com.au/salt/coverstory/804avalanches.htm (3 July 2007).

Woholeski, Peter (2001) "Interview with Daft Punk". *DJ Times Magazine* May/2001, http://www.djtimes.com/ original/djmag/may01/daft.htm (3 July 2007).

Zugna, Daniel (2006) "Modular Rejects 'Half-Arsed' Avalanches Album". *Undercover*, http://www.undercover. com.au/news/2006/jun06/20060627_avalanches.html (3 July 2007).

Sound recordings and DVDs

Amos, Tori (2001) *Strange Little Girls*. Atlantic Recording Corporation. 7567-83486-2.

Björk (1999) *Björk: Volumen*. Björk Overseas Ltd/One Little Indian Records Ltd. 059328-9.

Daft Punk (1999) *D.A.F.T. A Story About Dogs, Androids, Firemen and Tomatoes*. Daft Life / Daft Trax. 7243 4 92276 9 9.

Eminem (1999) *The Slim Shady LP*. Aftermath Ent./Interscope Records. 490-287-2.

Coldplay (2000) *Parachutes*. EMI Records Ltd. 7243 527783 2 4. 527 7832.

Jewel (1995) *Pieces of You*. Atlantic Recording Corporation. 7567-807739-2.

Jewel (1998) *Spirit*. Atlantic Recording Corporation. 7567 80946-2.

Jewel (2001) *This Way*. Atlantic Recording Corporation. 7567 83519-2.

Jewel (2003) *0304*. Atlantic Recording Corporation. 7567 93209-2.

Prince (2004) *Musicology*. NPG Records. Sony Music Entertainment Inc. 51771652001.

Spears, Britney (2001) *Britney*. Zomba Recording Corporation. 82876 53637 2.

The Avalanches (2000) *Since I Left You*. XL Recordings Ltd. XLCD 138.

Appendix

List of analysed online media texts divided into seven categories

1) Music magazines (published also in print)

Billboard	(http://www.billboard.com)
DJ Times Magazine	(http://www.djtimes.com)
Remix	(http://www.remixmag.com)
Rolling Stone	(http://www.therollingstone.com)
The Inside Connection	(http://www.insidecx.com)
Wired	(http://www.wired.com) /
	(http://www.hotwired.com)
X-Press Magazine	(http://www.xpressmag.com)

2) Online magazines and dailies on popular music and culture

Armchair-DJ	(http://www.armchair-dj.com)
Deep House Network	(http://www.deephousenetwork.com)
Family House	(http://www.family-house.net)
Junkmedia	(http://www.junkmedia.org)
Neumu (= art + music + words)	(http://neumu.net)
PlayLouder	(http://www.playlouder.com)
Stylus Magazine	(http://www.stylusmagazine.com)
Synthesis	(http://www.synthesis.net)
The Phantom Tollbooth	(http://www.tollbooth.org)
The Reservoir	(http://www.the-reservoir.co.uk)
Undercover	(http://www.undercover.com.au)

3) Webportals on popular music and music technology

All Music Guide	(http://www.allmusic.com)
Audio Video Revolution	(http://www.avrev.com)
LesInrocks	(http://www.lesinrocks.com)
MTV.com	(http://www.mtv.com)
Plan 9 Music	(http://www.plan9music.com)
RFI Musique	(http://www.rfimusique.com)

Turntable2k	(http://www.turntable2k.com)
Yahoo! Music	(http://music.yahoo.com)

4) Review and feature websites

Crazewire	(http://www.crazewire.com)
Drawer B	(http://www.drawerb.com)
Ink Blot Magazine	(http://www.inkblotmagazine.com)
Nude as the News	(http://www.nudeasthenews.com)
Pitchfork	(http://www.pitchforkmedia.com)
Pop Entertainment	(http://www.popentertainment.com)
PopMatters Music Review	(http://www.popmatters.com)

5) Other magazines and newspapers (NB: some available online only)

City-lehti	(http://www.city.fi/lehti)
Guardian	(http://www.guardian.co.uk)
IndieLondon	(http://www.indielondon.co.uk)
iVillage UK Ltd	(http://www.ivillage.co.uk)
Montreal Mirror	(http://www.montrealmirror.com)
New York Times	(http://www.nytimes.com)
Telegraph	(http://www.telegraph.co.uk)
The Georgetown Voice	(http://www.georgetownvoice.com)
The London Free Press	(http://www.fyilondon.com)
The Village Voice	(http://www.villagevoice.com)
USA Today	(http://www.usatoday.com)

6) Miscellaneous websites

http://www.amazon.co.uk	
http://ebweb.at/ortner/tia	(quoting *Rolling Stone*)
http://www.findarticles.com	(quoting *Ebony, Jet, Interview*)
http://home.concepts.nl/~sinned/bjork.htm	(quoting *Agenda*)
http://home.westrabant.net	(quoting *Q, SpinOnline, Dazed and Confused*)
http://www.metacritic.com	
http://perso.wanadoo.fr/antoine.house	(quoting *New York Times*)
http://www.phinnweb.org	(quoting *Rumba*)
http://www.techno.de	(quoting *Mixmag*)

http://www.thedent.com   (quoting *Denver Post, Rolling Stone)*

http://www.warnermusic.com

7) Artist homepages

http://www.brianwilson.com

http://www.brucespringsteen.net   (quoting *Esquire Magazine, Associated Press, Guardian*)

http://www.daftpunk.com

http://www.jeweljk.com

http://www.jorihulkkonen.com

http://www.kraftwerk.com

http://www.kylie.com

http://www.theavalanches.com

http://www.toriamos.com

VDM

Verlag
Dr. Müller

Wissenschaftlicher Buchverlag bietet

kostenfreie

Publikation

von

wissenschaftlichen Arbeiten

Diplomarbeiten, Magisterarbeiten, Master und Bachelor Theses
sowie Dissertationen, Habilitationen und wissenschaftliche Monographien

Sie verfügen über eine wissenschaftliche Abschlußarbeit zu aktuellen oder zeitlosen
Fragestellungen, die hohen inhaltlichen und formalen Ansprüchen genügt,
und haben **Interesse an einer honorarvergüteten Publikation**?

Dann senden Sie bitte erste Informationen über Ihre Arbeit per Email
an info@vdm-verlag.de. Unser Außenlektorat meldet sich umgehend bei Ihnen.

VDM Verlag Dr. Müller Aktiengesellschaft & Co. KG
Dudweiler Landstraße 125a
D - 66123 Saarbrücken

www.vdm-verlag.de

Lightning Source UK Ltd.
Milton Keynes UK
UKOW05f1935160514

231836UK00005B/201/P